英译中国现代散文选

张培基 译注

Rendered into English by Zhang Peiji

（汉英对照）

(Annotated Bilingual Edition)

SELECTED
MODERN
CHINESE
PROSE
WRITINGS

外教社

上海外语教育出版社

图书在版编目(CIP)数据

英译中国现代散文选：汉、英对照 / 张培基译注.
—上海：上海外语教育出版社，1999.5
ISBN 7-81046-550-3

Ⅰ.英… Ⅱ.张… Ⅲ.散文－中国－对照读物－汉、英
Ⅳ.H319.4

中国版本图书馆CIP数据核字（1999）第18354号

出版发行：上海外语教育出版社
　　　　　　（上海外国语大学内）　邮编：200083
电　　话：021-65425300（总机）
电子邮箱：bookinfo@sflep.com.cn
网　　址：http://www.sflep.com.cn　　http://www.sflep.com
责任编辑：江雷红

印　　刷：昆山市亭林彩印厂
经　　销：新华书店上海发行所
开　　本：850×1168　1/32　印张15.5　字数319千字
版　　次：1999年5月第1版　2006年4月第9次印刷
印　　数：5 000册

书　　号：ISBN 7-81046-550-3 / I·093
定　　价：22.60元
　　　　本版图书如有印装质量问题，可向本社调换

内 容 提 要

　　本书精选中国现代散文名篇五十二篇，原著均出自五四以来一些名家之手。书中各篇均为汉英对照，并附详细注释及对原作者的一些必要的简介。对翻译过程中可能遇到的问题，如语言难点、翻译方法、历史背景等，编译者也作了一些分析讲解。

　　本书可供国内外汉英文学翻译研究者、大学翻译教师、大学高年级学生、文学翻译爱好者以及广大英语学习爱好者参考阅读。

目　录

ii

iv

前　言

　　什么是散文？广义地说，凡是不属韵文的文章都可称为散文。世界各国人对此有一致的看法。西方人甚至把小说也包括在散文内；我国有些现代叙事性文章名为散文，但称之为小说也无不可，不便硬加归类。不过，严格说来，我们说的散文应相当于西方的 Essay，与诗歌、小说、戏剧并起并坐，文字一般都比较短小精练，如随笔、小品文、杂感、游记、日记、书信、回忆录、通讯报道等等。

　　散文不受韵律、情节、分场分幕的约束，是一种灵活随便、轻松自如的文体。散文作者可无拘无束地直抒胸臆，独抒性灵，因而文如其人（The essay is whatever the author is.）。英语中 Prose（散文）这个词来源于拉丁文 Proversa o-ratio，其意思是"坦率的讲话"或"直话直说"（Straightfor-ward discourse），也正反映了上述特点。总之，散文最真实，最诚笃，不雕饰，不做作，因而是一种最易令人感到亲切的文体。

　　中国是一个散文传统非常深厚的国度，散文的成就不下于诗歌。但五四以来，由于人们对诗歌的形式仍在摸索探讨，诗歌的发展已落后于散文。正如鲁迅所说，"五四以来散文小品的成功，几乎在小说、戏剧和诗歌之上"（《南腔北调集·小品文的危机》)。

　　我自幼就和散文结下不解之缘。从小学开始,我在老师指导下零零散散读了不少古今中外的散文作品,并且不断写作文,包括中学和大学时代的英语作文,这实际上就是对散文写作的实践。以后,随着年龄的增长,逐渐觉得读散文是一种享受,认为它比诗歌易懂,比小说读来省时省劲。对我影响最大的是已故高中英语老师姚志英先生。他除了教我们精读、泛读、语法等正课外,还要我们另外背诵由他精选的英语短文。每星期都有一堂课是专为背诵而设的,由他在堂上临时点名几个人轮流上讲台,面对全班同学背诵一篇由他事先指定的短文。三年下来,我们一共背熟了九十六篇英语短文,其中除少数是诗歌外,绝大部分都是散文,诸如 Bacon、Addison、Gissing、Goldsmith、Lamb、Irving、Lincoln 等名家的精品,莫不在内。当时我们都觉得压力很大,但苦尽甘来,事后莫不感到受用不尽。这九十六篇短文装在头脑里,使我增加了对英语和散文的兴趣,增加了语感,慢慢悟出了写文章的路子。从那以后,在我从事翻译或写作时,过去熟读的点点滴滴会不知不觉地出现在脑子里面。每当我想起这位启蒙老师的敬业精神与科学的教学方法,内心总是充满感激之情。

　　近年来,在退休后的闲居生活中,我断断续续译了一些短文,一是为了消遣,二是出于对英文和散文的爱好,三是为了向国外介绍一些优秀的中国现代散文作品。新中国成立以来,中国文学译成外文后向国外介绍的大多数是诗歌、小说、戏剧,唯独散文被冷落了,不能不令人感到遗憾。当然其中有历史原因。在那"以阶级斗争为纲"的极左年代,处处缺乏宽松的气氛，散文因其本身"率真"的特点，很难流行，就更谈不上向国外推荐了。

本书的英译文有的曾在中国翻译工作者协会会刊《中国翻译》以及上海外国语大学学报《外国语》上发表。两刊编辑部都本着"文责自负"的原则，未对译文作任何删改。这次结集出版前，承蒙昔日上海圣约翰大学同窗、现北京外国语大学资深教授罗廷亮先生逐篇仔细过目，并提出不少宝贵意见，谨此致以深切的谢意。

鉴于所选散文仅五十二篇，还远远不足反映中国现代散文的丰富多彩，本书出版后我将继续从事这方面的选译，以便日后增订补充。

限于我的水平，本书欠妥之处在所难免，尚祈不吝赐教。

张 培 基
一九九八年四月
对外经济贸易大学

艰难的国运与雄健的国民

李大钊

历史的道路，不会是坦平的，有时走到艰难险阻的境界。这是全靠雄健的精神才能够冲过去的①。

一条浩浩荡荡的长江大河，有时流到很宽阔的境界②，平原无际，一泻万里③。有时流到很逼狭的境界，两岸丛山迭岭，绝壁断崖，江河流于其间，回环曲折，极其险峻④。民族生命的进展，其经历亦复如是。

人类在历史上的生活正如旅行一样。旅途上的征人⑤所经过的地方，有时是坦荡平原，有时是崎岖险路⑥。志于旅途的人，走到平坦的地方，因是高高兴兴地向前走，走到崎岖的境界，愈是奇趣横生⑦，觉得在此奇绝壮绝⑧的境界，愈能感到一种冒险的美趣⑨。

中华民族现在所逢的史路，是一段崎岖险阻的道路。在这一段道路上，实在亦有一种奇绝壮绝的境致，使我们经过此段道路的人，感得一种壮美的趣味。但这种壮美的趣味，是非有雄健的精神的，不能够感觉到的。

我们的扬子江、黄河，可以代表我们的民族精神，扬子江及黄河遇见沙漠、遇见山峡都是浩浩荡荡的往前流过去，

1

以成其浊流滚滚，一泻万里的魄势⑩。目前的艰难境界，那能阻抑我们民族生命的前进。我们应该拿出雄健的精神，高唱着进行的曲调，在这悲壮歌声中，走过这崎岖险阻的道路。要知⑪在艰难的国运中建造国家，亦是人生最有趣味的事……。

National Crisis vs Heroic Nation

Li Dazhao

The course of history is never smooth. It is sometimes beset with difficulties and obstacles and nothing
short of a heroic spirit can help surmount them.

A mighty long river sometimes flows through a broad
section with plains lying boundless on either side, its waters rolling on non-stop for thousands upon thousands of
miles. Sometimes it comes up against a narrow section
flanked by high mountains and steep cliffs, winding
through a course with many a perilous twist and turn. A
nation, in the course of its developlment, fares likewise.

The historical course of man's life is just like a journey. A traveller on a long journey passes through now a
broad, level plain, now a rugged, hazardous road. While
a determined traveller cheerfully continues his journey upon reaching a safe and smooth place, he finds it still more
fascinating to come to a rugged place, the enormously
magnificent spectacle of which, he feels, is better able to
generate in him a wonderful sensation of adventure.

The Chinese nation is now confronted with a rugged and dangerous section of its historical course. Nevertheless, there is also in this section a spectacle of enormous magnificence that inspires in us passers-by a delightful sensation of splendor. And this delightful sensation, however, can only be shared by those with a heroic spirit.

The Yangtse River and the Yellow River are both symbolic of our national spirit. The two mighty rivers negotiate deserts and gorges until their turbid torrents surge forward with irresistible force. The present national crisis can never obstruct the advance of our national life. Let us brace up our spirits and march through this rugged, dangerous road to the tune of our solemn, stirring songs. The greatest joy of life, mind you, is to build up our country during its most difficult days.

注　释

　　李大钊此文载于 1923 年 12 月 20
日《新民国》第 1 卷第 2 号上，短小隽
永，堪称一首诗意盎然的抒情散文诗。作
者用象征、比喻等手法，说明历史发展的
必然规律以及中国革命面临的艰难险
阻。译时除文字须符合英语规范外，应力
求传达原文的形象、诗一般的美感和雍
容警策的笔调。

　　① "这是全靠雄健的精神才能冲过去的" 译为 noth-
ing short of a heroic spirit can help surmount them，其中
nothing short of 相当于 nothing less than 或 only。

　　② "宽阔的境界" 须按上下文译为 a broad section。
"境界" 在这里不宜译为 realm、place、area 等。

　　③ "一泻万里" 译为 rolling on non-stop for thousands upon thousands of miles，但也可译为 rolling on
vigorously for tens of thousands of miles 或 rolling on for
thousands of miles at a stretch。

　　④ "回环曲折，极其险峻" 译为 winding through a

course with many a perilous twist and turn，其中 twist and turn 来自成语 twists and turns。此句亦可译为 following a dangerous tortuous course。

⑤ "征人"即"远行之人"，故译"旅途上的征人"为 a traveller on a long journey。

⑥ "有时……，有时……"译为 now...，now...（＝sometimes...and sometimes...）。

⑦ "奇趣横生"意即"极度吸引人"，故译为 fascinating。

⑧ "奇绝壮绝"意即"无限壮观"，故译为 the enormously magnificent spectacle。

⑨ "感到一种冒险的美趣"意即"一种敢于冒险的美妙感觉"，故译为 a wonderful sensation of adventure。

⑩ "遇见沙漠、遇见山峡都是浩浩荡荡的往前流过去，以成其浊流滚滚，一泻万里的魄势"译为 negotiate deserts and gorges until their turbid torrents surge forward with irresistible force，其中动词 to negotiate 的意思是"顺利通过"（to succeed in getting past something difficult）。又，注意 until 在这里的用法。它在此句不作"直到……为止"解，而是 so that finally（"以至于……"或"最后"）的意思。

⑪ "要知"译为 mind you，插入句中。成语 mind you 的意思是 mind what I say 或 however，相当于汉语的"请注意"或"说真的"。

螃　　蟹

鲁　　迅

老螃蟹觉得不安了，觉得全身太硬了①，自己知道要蜕壳②了。

他跑来跑去的寻。他想寻一个窟穴，躲了身子，将石子堵了穴口，隐隐的蜕壳。他知道外面蜕壳③是危险的。身子还软④，要被别的螃蟹吃去的。这并非空害怕，他实在亲眼见过。

他慌慌张张的走。

旁边的螃蟹⑤问他说："老兄，你何以这般慌？"

他说："我要蜕壳了。"

"就在这里蜕不很好么？我还要帮你呢。"

"那可太怕人了。"

"你不怕窟穴里的别的东西，却怕我们同种么？"

"我不是怕同种。"

"那还怕什么呢？"

"就怕你要吃掉我⑥。"

The Crab

Lu Xun

An old crab grew restless. Finding himself stiff all over, he knew it was time for him to moult his shell.

He dashed here and there in search of a cave to hide. He was going to block up the mouth of the cave so that he could moult in secret. He knew it would be very dangerous to shed his shell in the open because, with his new shell still being soft, he might be eaten up by other crabs. This fear was not groundless for he himself had really seen it happen to other moulting crabs.

The old crab kept moving about in a hurry.

A nearby crab asked, "Hey, brother, what's the rush?"

"I am going to moult," answered the old crab.

"Wouldn't it be all right to moult right here? I could help you out with it."

"How horrible that would be!"

"You mean while you're not scared of other things in the cave you're scared of your own kind?"

"No, I'm not scared of my own kind. "

"Then what are you scared of?"

"Nothing but being eaten up by you. "

注　释

　　《螃蟹》是近年发现的鲁迅佚文。文章发表于 1919 年 8 月间,时值五四运动方兴未艾,作者通过寓言故事,提醒人们新生事物往往有被旧事物消灭于萌芽状态的危险。

　　① "觉得全身太硬了" 译为 Finding himself stiff all over, 其中 all over 意即 "全身" 或 "浑身",作状语短语用。如逐字译为 Finding his whole body stiff 并无不可,但语言稍欠地道。

　　② "蜕壳" 译为 to moult his shell,其中 to moult 为专用语,意同 to cast off。

　　③ "外面蜕壳" 中的 "外面" 意即 "在露天",故译为 (to moult) in the open,以代替 to moult outside the cave。

　　④ "身子还软" 意即 "蜕去旧壳后新壳还软",故译为 with his new shell still being soft。如按字面直译为 with his body still being soft 则欠确切,因 "身子" 在此指 "新壳",不泛指 "躯体"。

　　⑤ "旁边的螃蟹" 译为 A nearby crab,比 A crab beside him 灵活。

⑥ "就怕你要吃掉我" 译为 Nothing but being eaten up by you，乃 I'm scared of nothing but being eaten up by you 之略。

落 花 生

我们屋后有半亩隙地。母亲说："让它荒芜着怪可惜，既然你们那么爱吃花生，就辟来做花生园罢①。"我们几姊弟②和几个小丫头都很喜欢——买种的买种，动土的动土，灌园的灌园；过不了几个月，居然收获了！

妈妈说："今晚我们可以做一个收获节③，也请你们爹爹来尝尝我们底新花生，如何？"我们都答应了。母亲把花生做成好几样的食品④，还吩咐这节期要在园里底茅亭举行。

那晚上底天色不大好⑤，可是爹爹也来到，实在很难得！爹爹说："你们爱吃花生么？"

我们都争着答应："爱！"

"谁能把花生底好处说出来？"

姊姊说："花生底气味很美。"

哥哥说："花生可以制油。"

我说："无论何等人都可以用贱价买它来吃；都喜欢吃它。这就是它的好处。"

爹爹说："花生底用处固然很多；但有一样是很可贵的。这小小的豆⑥不像那好看的苹果、桃子、石榴，把它们底果

12

实悬在枝上，鲜红嫩绿的颜色⑦，令人一望而发生羡慕的心。它只把果子埋在地底，等到成熟，才容人把它挖出来。你们偶然看见一棵花生瑟缩⑧地长在地上，不能立刻辨出它有没有果实，非得等到你接触它才能知道。"

我们都说："是的。"母亲也点点头。爹爹接下去说："所以你们要像花生⑨，因为它是有用的，不是伟大、好看的东西。"我说："那么，人要做有用的人，不要做伟大、体面的人了。"爹爹说："这是我对于你们的希望。"

我们谈到夜阑才散，所有花生食品虽然没有了，然而父亲底话现在还印在我心版上。

Peanuts

Xu Dishan

Behind our house there lay half a *mou* of vacant land. Mother said, "It's a pity to let it lie waste. Since you all like to eat peanuts so very much, why not plant some here?" That exhilarated us children and our servant girls as well, and soon we started buying seeds, ploughing the land and watering the plants. We gathered in a good harvest just after a couple of months!

Mother said, "How about giving a party this evening to celebrate the harvest and inviting your Daddy to have a taste of our newly-harvested peanuts?" We all agreed. Mother made quite a few varieties of goodies out of the peanuts, and told us that the party would be held in the thatched pavilion on the peanut plot.

It looked like rain that evening, yet, to our great joy, father came nevertheless. "Do you like peanuts?" asked father.

"Yes, we do!" we vied in giving the answer.

"Which of you could name the good things in

peanuts?"

"Peanuts taste good," said my elder sister.

"Peanuts produce edible oil," said my elder brother.

"Peanuts are so cheap," said I, "that anyone can afford to eat them. Peanuts are everyone's favourite. That's
why we call peanuts good."

"It's true that peanuts have many uses," said father,
"but they're most beloved in one respect. Unlike nice-
looking apples, peaches, and pomegranates, which hang
their fruit on branches and win people's admiration with
their brilliant colours, tiny little peanuts bury themselves
underground and remain unearthed until they're ripe.
When you come upon a peanut plant lying curled up on
the ground, you can never immediately tell whether or
not it bears any nuts until you touch them."

"That's true," we said in unison. Mother also
nodded. "So you must take after peanuts," father continued, "because they're useful though not great and nice-
looking."

"Then you mean one should be useful rather than
great and nice-looking," I said.

"That's what I expect of you," father concluded.

We kept chatting until the party broke up late at
night. Today, though nothing is left of the goodies made
of peanuts, father's words remain engraved in my mind.

15

注　释

本文是许地山（1892—1941）的一篇久为流传的散文。作者回忆自己童年时代的一个小小片断，以朴实无华、清新自然的笔调，从花生的平凡而有用，谈到做人的道理，富于哲理，反映他身处旧社会的污泥浊流而洁身自好、不慕虚名的思想境界。

英译时以保持原作娓娓讲故事的朴素风格为要，译文除符合英语习惯和规范外，遣词宜力求通俗，造句宜力求简洁。

① 原句也可译为 why not have them planted here 或 why not make a peanut plot of it，但现译更直截了当，且避免在同一句中重复 peanuts 一词。

② "几姊弟"在下文将涉及，为防累赘，译 children。

③ "做一个收获节"不宜直译为 hold a harvest festival，现取意译。

④ "食品"也可译为 food，但不如 goodies 贴切；goodies 指"好吃的东西"，常用于口语。

⑤"那晚上底天色不大好"译为 It looked like rain that evening，符合原意和英语习惯。

⑥"这小小的豆"译为 tiny little peanuts。英语中常把 tiny 和 little 用在一起，有"小得可怜（爱）"等含意。

⑦"鲜红嫩绿"不宜直译，译 brilliant colours 即可。

⑧"瑟缩"意即"蜷曲而不舒展"，故有现译。

⑨"你们要像花生"译为 you must take after peanuts，其中 take after 是成语，意即 take ... as an example（学习……的榜样）。

差不多先生传

胡　　适

你知道中国最有名的人是谁？

提起此人，人人皆晓，处处闻名。他姓差，名不多①，是各省各县各村人氏。你一定见过他，一定听过别人谈起他。差不多先生的名字天天挂在大家的口头，因为他是中国全国人的代表。

差不多先生的相貌和你和我都差不多。他有一双眼睛，但看的不很清楚；有两只耳朵，但听的不很分明；有鼻子和嘴，但他对于气味和口味都不很讲究。他的脑子也不小，但他的记性却不很精明，他的思想也不很细密②。

他常常说："凡事只要差不多，就好了。何必太精明呢？"

他小的时候，他妈叫他去买红糖，他买了白糖回来。他妈骂他，他摇摇头说："红糖白糖不是差不多吗？"

他在学堂的时候，先生问他："直隶省③的西边是哪一省？"他说是陕西。先生说："错了。是山西，不是陕西。"他说："陕西同山西，不是差不多吗？"

后来他在一个钱铺④里作伙计；他也会写，也会算，只是总不会精细。十字常常写成千字，千字常常写成十字。掌柜的生气了,常常骂他。他只是笑嘻嘻地赔小心道:"千字比十字只多一小撇,不是差不多吗?"

有一天,他为了一件要紧的事,要搭火车到上海去。他从从容容地走到火车站,迟了两分钟,火车已经开走了。他白瞪着眼,望着远远的火车上的煤烟,摇摇头道:"只好明天再走了,今天走同明天走,也差不多。可是火车公司未免太认真了。8 点 30 分开,同 8 点 32 分开,不是差不多吗?"他一面说,一面慢慢地走回家,心里总不明白为什么火车不肯等他两分钟。

有一天,他忽然得了急病,赶快叫家人去请东街的汪医生。那家人急急忙忙地跑去,一时寻不着东街的汪大夫,却把西街牛医王大夫请来了。差不多先生病在床上,知道寻错了人;但病急了,身上痛苦,心里焦急,等不得了,心里想道:"好在王大夫同汪大夫也差不多,让他试试看罢。"于是这位牛医王大夫走近床前,用医牛的法子给差不多先生治病。不上一点钟,差不多先生就一命呜呼了。

差不多先生差不多要死的时候,一口气断断续续地说道 :"活人同死人也……差……差不多,……凡事只要……差……差……不多……就……好了,……何……何……必……太……太认真呢?"他说完了这句格言⑤,方才绝气了。

他死后,大家都很称赞差不多先生样样事情看得破,想得通⑥;大家都说他一生不肯认真,不肯算帐,不肯计较,真是一位有德行的人。于是大家给他取个死后的法号,叫他做圆通大师。

他的名誉越传越远,越久越大。无数无数的人都学他的榜样。于是人人都成了一个差不多先生。——然而中国从此就成为一个懒人国了。

Mr. About-the-Same

Hu Shih

Do you know who is the most well-known person in China?

The name of this person is a household word all over the country. His surname is Cha and his given name, Buduo, which altogether mean "About the Same". He is a native of every province, every county and every village in this country. You must have seen or heard about this person. His name is always on the lips of everybody because he is representative of the whole Chinese nation.

Mr. Cha Buduo has the same physiognomy as you and I. He has a pair of eyes, but doesn't see clearly. He has a pair of ears, but doesn't hear well. He has a nose and a mouth, but lacks a keen sense of smell and taste. His brain is none too small, but he is weak in memory and sloppy in thinking.

He often says, "Whatever we do, it's OK to be just about right. What's the use of being precise and accurate?"

21

One day, when he was a child, his mother sent him out to buy her some brown sugar, but he returned with some white sugar instead. As his mother scolded him about it, he shook his head and said, "Brown sugar or white sugar, aren't they about the same?"

One day in school, the teacher asked him, "Which province borders Hebei on the west?" He answered, "Shaanxi." The teacher corrected him, "You are wrong. It's Shanxi, not Shaanxi." He retorted, "Shaanxi or Shanxi, aren't they about the same?"

Later Mr. Cha Buduo served as an assistant at a money shop. He could write and calculate all right, but his mathematics were often faulty. He would mistake the Chinese character 十 (meaning 10) for 千 (meaning 1000) or vice versa. The shop owner was infuriated and often took him to task. But he would only explain apologetically with a grin, "The Character 千 differs from 十 in merely having one additional short stroke. Aren't they about the same?"

One day, he wanted to go to Shanghai by train on urgent business. But he arrived at the railway station unhurriedly only to find the train already gone, because he was two minutes late. He stood staring helplessly at the smoke belching from the diminishing train, and shook his head, "Well, all I can do is leave tomorrow. After all, today and tomorrow are about the same. But isn't the railway company taking it too seriously? What's the difference between departing at 8:30 and 8:32?" He walked home slowly while talking to himself and kept puzzling over why the train hadn't waited for him for two minutes more.

One day he suddenly fell ill and immediately told one of his family to fetch Dr. Wāng of East Street. The latter went in a hurry, but could't find the physician on East Street. So he fetched instead Veterinarian Wáng of West Street. Mr. Cha Buduo, lying on his sickbed, knew that a wrong person had been brought home. But, what with pain and worry, he could ill afford to wait any longer. So he said to himself, "Luckily, Vet Wáng is about the same as Dr. Wāng. Why not let Vet Wáng have a try?" Thereupon, the veterinarian walked up to his bed to work on him as if he were a cow. Consequently, Mr. Cha Buduo kicked the bucket before an hour was out.

When Mr. Cha Buduo was about to breathe his last, he uttered intermittently in one breath, "Live or die, it's about ... about ... the same .... Whatever we do ... it's OK ... to be ... just ... just about right .... Why ... why ... take it ... so seriously?" As soon as he finished this pet phrase of his, he stopped breathing.

After Mr. Cha Buduo's death, people all praised him for his way of seeing through things and his philosophical approach to life. They say that he refused to take things

23

seriously all his life and that he was never calculating or particular about personal gains or losses. So they called him a virtuous man and honored him with the posthumous reverent title Master of Easy-Going.

His name has spread far and wide and become more and more celebrated with the passing of time. Innumerable people have come to follow his example, so that everybody has become a Mr. Cha Buduo. But lo, China will hence be a nation of lazybones!

注　释

胡适(1891—1962)的《差不多先生传》是一篇针砭社会陋习的讽刺小品，1924年6月28日发表在《申报·平民周刊》的创刊号上，曾不胫而走，传诵一时。此文至今读来，犹感有极深刻的现实意义。

①"他姓差，名不多"如仅仅译为 His surname is Cha and his given name, Buduo，外国读者只知其音，不知其意，故在后面加补充说明 which altogether mean "About-the-Same"。

②"他的思想也不很细密"译为 He is ... sloppy in thinking，其中 sloppy 作"无条理"、"凌乱"解。

③"直隶"为旧省名，即今之"河北"，故译为 Hebei。

④"钱铺"又称"钱庄"，大多仅从事兑换业务，后为银行所代替。"钱铺"可译为 private bank 或 banking house，但均不如 money (exchange) shop 确切。

⑤"格言"在这里意同"口头语"，现参照上下文译为 pet phrase。

⑥"想得通"意即"达观"或"随遇而安"，故译为
philosophical approach to life。

不要抛弃学问①

胡　　适

诸位毕业同学：你们现在要离开母校了，我没有什么礼物送你们，只好送你们一句话罢。

这一句话是："不要抛弃学问。"以前的功课也许有一大部分是为了这张毕业文凭，不得已而做的，从今以后，你们可以依自己的心愿去自由研究了②。趁现在年富力强的时候，努力做一种专门学问。少年是一去不复返的，等到精力衰时，要做学问③也来不及了。即为吃饭计，学问决不会辜负人的④。吃饭而不求学问，三年五年之后，你们都要被后来少年淘汰掉的。到那时再想做点学问来补救，恐怕已太晚了。

有人说："出去做事之后，生活问题急需解决，哪有工夫去读书？即使要做学问，既没有图书馆，又没有实验室，哪能做学问？"

我要对你们说：凡是要等到有了图书馆方才读书的，有了图书馆也不肯读书。凡是要等到有了实验室方才做研究的，有了实验室也不肯做研究。你有了决心要研究一个问题，自然会撙衣节食⑤去买书，自然会想出法子来设置仪器。

至于时间，更不成问题⑥。达尔文一生多病，不能多作工，每天只能做一点钟的工作。你们看他的成绩！每天花一点钟看 10 页有用的书，每年可看 3 600 多页书，30 年可读 11 万页书。

　　诸位，11 万页书可以使你成一个学者了。可是，每天看三种小报也得费你一点钟的工夫，四圈麻将也得费你一点半钟的光阴。看小报呢？还是打麻将呢？还是努力做一个学者呢？全靠你们自己的选择⑦！

　　易卜生说："你的最大责任是把你这块材料铸造成器。"

　　学问便是铸器的工具。抛弃了学问便是毁了你们自己。

　　再会了！你们的母校眼睁睁地要看⑧你们十年之后成什么器。

Never Give up the Pursuit of Learning

Hu Shih

Dear Students of the Graduating Class,

As you are leaving your alma mater, I have nothing to offer you as a gift except a word of advice.

My advice is, "Never give up the pursuit of learning." You have perhaps finished your college courses mostly for obtaining the diploma, or, in other words, out of sheer necessity. However, from now on you are free to follow your own bent in the choice of studies. While you are in the prime of life, why not devote yourselves to a special field of study? Youth will soon be gone never to return. And it will be too late for you to go into scholarship when in your declining years. Knowledge will do you a good turn even as a means of subsistence. If you give up studies while holding a job, you will in a couple of years have had yourselves replaced by younger people. It will then be too late to remedy the situation by picking up studies again.

Some people say, "Once you have a job, you'll come

up against the urgent problem of making a living. How can you manage to find time to study? Even if you want to, will it be possible with no library or laboratory available?"

Now let me tell you this. Those who refuse to study for lack of a library will most probably continue to do so even though there is a library. And those who refuse to do research for lack of a laboratory will most probably continue to do so even though a laboratory is available. As long as you set your mind on studies, you will naturally cut down on food and clothing to buy books or do everything possible to acquire necessary instruments.

Time is no object. Charles Darwin could only work one hour a day due to ill health. Yet what a remarkable man he was ! If you spend one hour a day reading 10 pages of a book, you can finish more than 3 600 pages a year, and 110 000 pages in 30 years.

Dear students, 110 000 pages will be quite enough to make a learned man of you. It will take you one hour to read three tabloids a day, and one and half hours to finish four rounds of mah-jong a day. Reading tabloids, playing mah-jong or striving to be a learned man, the choice lies with you.

Henrik Ibsen says, "It is your supreme duty to cast yourself into a useful implement."

Learning is the casting mould. Forsake learning, and

you will ruin yourself.

Farewell ! Your alma mater is watching eagerly to see what will become of you ten years from now.

注　释

胡适是中国现代史上一个颇有影响
而又相当复杂的学者。除学术著作外，
他写过很多富于洞察力和启发性的文
章。《不要抛弃学问》是他 1928—1930
年在上海任中国公学校长时为毕业生所
作赠言，至今仍有参考价值。

①"不要抛弃学问"在这里的意思是"不要放弃对学
问的追求"，因此不能直译为 Never Give up Learning，必
须加字：Never Give up the Pursuit of Learning。

②"你们可以依自己的心愿去自由研究了"译为 you
are free to follow your personal bent in the choice of stud-
ies，其中 to follow one's bent 是成语，和 to follow one's
inclination 同义，作"做自己感兴趣或爱做的事"解。

③"做学问"译为 to go into scholarship，等于 to engage in learning。

④"学问决不会辜负人的"译为 Knowlede will do
you a good turn，其中 to do one a good turn 是成语，作
"做对某人有益的事"解。

⑤ "摒衣节食"即"省吃省穿"，现译为 cut down on food and clothing，其中 to cut down on 是成语，与 to economize on 同义，作"节约"解。又，上语也可译为 to live frugally。

⑥ "至于时间，更不成问题"译为 Time is no object，其中 no object 是成语，等于 no problem，作"不成问题"或"不在话下"解。

⑦ "全靠你们自己的选择"译为 the choice lies with you 或 it is up to you to make the choice。

⑧ "你们的母校眼睁睁地要看……"中的"眼睁睁地"通常的意思是"无可奈何地"，现在这里作"热切地"解，故译为 eagerly。

我 之 于 书[①]

夏丏尊

二十年来，我生活费中至少十分之一二是消耗在书上的[②]。我的房子里[③]比较贵重的东西就是书。

我一向没有对于任何问题作高深研究的野心，因之所买的书范围较广，宗教、艺术、文学、社会、哲学、历史、生物，各方面差不多都有一点。最多的是各国文学名著的译本，与本国古来的诗文集，别的门类只是些概论等类的入门书而已。

我不喜欢向别人或图书馆借书。借来的书，在我好像过不来瘾似的[④]，必要是自己买的才满足。这也可谓是一种占有的欲望。买到了几册新书，一册一册地加盖藏书印[⑤]记，我最感到快悦的是这时候。

书籍到了我的手里，我的习惯是先看序文，次看目录。页数不多的往往立刻通读[⑥]，篇幅大的，只把正文任择一二章节略加翻阅，就插在书架上。除小说外，我少有全体读完的大部的书，只凭了购入当时的记忆，知道某册书是何种性质，其中大概有些什么可取的材料而已。什么书在什么时候再去读再去翻，连我自己也无把握，完全要看一个时期一个时期的兴趣。关于这事,我常自比为古时的皇帝,而把插在架上的书譬诸列屋而居的宫女⑦。

我虽爱买书,而对于书却不甚爱惜。读书的时候,常在书上把我所认为要紧的处所标出。线装书大概用笔加圈,洋装书竟用红铅笔划粗粗的线。经我看过的书,统体干净的很少。

据说,任何爱吃糖果的人,只要叫他到糖果铺中去做事,见了糖果就会生厌。自我入书店以后,对于书的贪念也已消除了不少了,可不免要故态复萌⑧,想买这种,想买那种。这大概因为糖果要用嘴去吃,摆存毫无意义,而书则可以买了不看,任其只管插在架上的缘故吧。

Books and I

Xia Mianzun

For twenty years past, books have eaten into at least 10-20 percent of my pocket. Now the only things of some value under my roof, if any, are my books.

Since I have never entertained ambition for making a profound study of any subject, the books I have acquired cover almost everything — religion, art, literature, sociology, philosophy, history, biology, etc. Most of them are Chinese translations of literary works by famous foreign writers and anthologies of Chinese poetry and prose through the ages. The rest, often called an outline or introduction, are merely on rudiments of various subjects.

I never care to borrow books from other people or a library. It seems that books bought can better satisfy my bibliomania than books borrowed. You may also attribute this to some sort of desire for personal possessions. Whenever I have some new acquisitions, it always gives me great pleasure and satisfaction to stamp my ex-libris on them one by one.

As soon as a new book comes to hand, I always read the preface first and then the table of contents. If it happens to be a thin one, I often finish reading it at one sitting. Otherwise, I often browse through one or two chapters or sections before putting it onto my bookshelf. I seldom read a thick book from cover to cover unless it is a novel. By dint of the first impression it made on me at the time of buying, I have a rough idea of what a book is about and what useful materials in it are available to me. But I have little idea which book is to be read or looked over again at what time. It is completely subject to the whims of the moment. This often prompts me to liken myself and the books on my shelves respectively to an ancient emperor and his concubines housed separately in a row of adjoining rooms.

Much as I love books, I take little care of them. In doing my reading, I often mark out what I regard as important in a book. If it is a thread-bound Chinese book, I use a writing brush to draw small circles as markings. Otherwise, I use a red pencil to draw heavy underlines. Consequently, the books I have read are rarely clean.

It is said that those who have a great liking for candies will sicken to see them when later they happen to work in a candy store. Likewise, ever since I began to work in a bookstore, my obsession with books has been very much on the decline. Nevertheless, I still cannot help slipping back into the same old rut, eager to buy this and that book. This is probably because candies are to be eaten with the mouth and not worth keeping as knick-knacks while books can be bought without being read and just left on a shelf.

注　释

夏丏尊(1886—1946)浙江上虞人，是我国著名文学家、教育家、出版家。他的文学创作以散文为主，多为随笔、杂感，内容积极、健康，风格平淡朴素。此文于1933年11月发表在《中学生》杂志上。

①"我之于书"译为 Books and I，比 I and Books 符合英语习惯，读音也较顺口。

②"我的生活费中至少十分之一二是消耗在书上的"译为 books have eaten into at least 10-20 percent of my pocket，其中成语 to eat into 作"耗尽"或"花费"解，意同 to use up 或 to spend gradually；pocket 作"腰包"解。

③"我的房子里"译为 under my roof，意同 in my house。

④"好像过不来瘾似的"中的"瘾"指"藏书癖"，故译为 bibliomania，意即 desire or passion for collecting books。

⑤"藏书印"译为 ex-libris，为专用语。

⑥"往往立刻通读"译为 I often finish reading it at

one sitting，其中 at one sitting（亦作 at a sitting）为成语，作"坐着一口气"或"一下子"解。

　　⑦ "宫女"本可译为 court ladies 或 palace maids，但原文实际上指的是"妃子"，故译为 concubines。

　　⑧ "故态复萌"译为 slipping back into the same old rut，或 relapsing into my old habit。

中年人的寂寞

夏 丏 尊

我已是一个中年的人。一到中年，就有许多不愉快的现象，眼睛昏花了，记忆力减退了，头发开始秃脱①而且变白了，意兴，体力，什么都不如年青的时候，常不禁会感觉到难以名言的②寂寞的情味。尤其觉得难堪的是知友的逐渐减少③和疏远，缺乏交际上的温暖的慰藉。

不消说，相识的人数是随了年龄增加的，一个人年龄越大，走过的地方当过的职务越多，相识的人理该越增加了。可是相识的人并不就是朋友。我们和许多人相识，或是因了事务关系，或是因了偶然的机缘④——如在别人请客的时候同席吃过饭之类。见面时点头或握手，有事时走访或通信，口头上彼此也称"朋友"，笔头上有时或称"仁兄"，诸如此类，其实只是一种社交上的客套，和"顿首""百拜"同是仪式的虚伪⑤。这种交际可以说是社交，和真正的友谊相差似乎很远。

真正的朋友，恐怕要算"总角之交"或"竹马之交"了⑥。在小学和中学的时代容易结成真实的友谊，那时彼此尚不感到生活的压迫，入世未深，打算计较的念头也少，朋友的结成全由于志趣相近或性情适合,差不多可以说是"无所为"的⑦,性质比较地纯粹。二十岁以后结成的友谊,大概已不免搀有各种各样的颜色分子在内;至于三十岁四十岁以后的朋友中间,颜色分子愈多,友谊的真实成分也就不免因而愈少了。这并不一定是"人心不古"⑧,实可以说是人生的悲剧。人到了成年以后,彼此都有生活的重担须负,入世既深,顾忌的方面也自然加多起来,在交际上不许你不计较,不许你不打算,结果彼此都"钩心斗角"⑨,像七巧板似地只选定了某一方面和对方去接合⑩。这样的接合当然是很不坚固的,尤其是现代这样什么都到了尖锐化的时代。

在我自己的交游中,最值得系念的老是一些少年时代以来的朋友。这些朋友本来数目就不多,有些住在远地,连相会的机会也不可多得。他们有的年龄大过了我,有的小我几岁,都是中年以上的人了,平日各人所走的方向不同。思想趣味境遇也都不免互异,大家晤谈起来,也常会遇到说不出的隔膜的情形。如大家话旧,旧事是彼此共喻的,而且大半都是少年时代的事,"旧游如梦",把梦也似的过去的少年时代重提,因谈话的进行,同时会联想起许多当时的事情,许多当时的人的面影,这时好像自己仍回归到少年时代去了⑪。我常在这种时候感到一种快乐,同时也感到一种伤感,那情形好比老妇人突然在抽屉里或箱子里发见了她盛年时的影片。

逢到和旧友谈话,就不知不觉地把话题转到旧事上去,这是我的习惯。我在这上面无意识地会感到一种温暖的慰藉。可是这些旧友一年比一年减少了,本来只是屈指可数的几个,少去一个是无法弥补的。我每当听到一个旧友死去的消息,总要惆怅多时。

　　学校教育给我们的好处不但只是灌输知识,最大的好处恐怕还在给与我们求友的机会上。这好处我到了离学校以后才知道,这几年来更确切地体会到,深悔当时毫不自觉,马马虎虎地过去了。近来每日早晚在路上见到两两三三的携着书包、携了手或挽了肩膀走着的青年学生,我总艳羡他们有朋友之乐,暗暗地要在心中替他们祝福。

Mid-life Loneliness

Xia Mianzun

I am already a middle-aged man. At middle age, I feel sad to find my eyesight and memory failing, my hair thinning and graying, and myself no longer mentally and physically as fit as when I was young. I often suffer from a nameless loneliness. The most intolerable of all is the lack of friendly warmth and comfort due to the gradual passing away and estrangement of more and more old pals.

Needless to say, the number of acquaintances increases with one's age. The older one gets, the more widely travelled one is and the more work experience one has, the more acquaitances one is supposed to have. But not all acquaintances are friends. We come to know many people either in the way of business or by mere chance — say, having been at the same table at a dinner party. We may be on nodding or hand-shaking terms, call each other "friend", sometimes write to each other with the salutation of "Dear So-and-So", etc. , etc. All these are, in fact, nothing but civilities of social life, as hypocritical as the polite formula *dunshou* (kowtow) or *baibai* (a hundred greetings) used after the signature in old-fashioned Chinese letter-writing. We may call them social intercourse, but they seem to have very little in common with genuine friendship.

Real friendship between two persons originates perhaps from the time of life when they were children playing innocently together. Real friendship is easily formed in primary or middle school days when, being socially inexperienced and free from the burden of life, you give little thought to personal gains or losses, and make friends entirely as a result of similar tastes and interests or congenial disposition. It is sort of "friendship for friendship's sake" and is relatively pure in nature. Friendship among people in their 20's, however, is more or less coloured by personal motives. And friendship among those aged over 30 becomes correspondingly still less pure as it gets even more coloured. Though this is not necessarily due to "degeneration of public morality", I do have good reasons to call it the tragedy of life. People at middle age, with the heavy burden of life and much experience in the ways of the world, have more scruples about this and that, and cannot choose but become more calculating in social dealings till they start scheming against each other. They always keep a wary eye, as it were, on each other in their association. Such association is of course fragile, especially in this modern age of prevailing sharp conflicts.

Of all my friends, those I have known since childhood are most worthy of remembrance. They are few in number. Some of them live far away and we seldom have an opportunity to see each other. Some of them are older than I am, and some a few years younger. But all of us are in late mid-life. Since we have each followed a different course in life, our ways of thinking, interests and circumstances are bound to differ, and often we lack mutual understanding somehow or other in our conversation. Nevertheless, when, we talk over old times, we will always agree on things in the past — mostly about things in our childhood days. While we retell the dream-like childhood days in the course of our conversation, numerous scenes and persons of bygone days will unfold again before our eyes, and we will feel like reliving the old days. Often at this moment, I'll feel at once happy and sad — like an old lady suddenly fishing out from her drawer or chest a photo of her taken in the bloom of her youth.

When chatting away with my old friends, I am in the habit of unwittingly channeling the topic of conversation toward things of former days. From that I unknowingly derive some sort of warm solace. But old friends are dwindling away year by year. They are originally few in number, so the disappearance of any of them is an irreparable loss to me. The news of any old pal's death will invariably make me sad in my heart for a long, long time.

The imparting of knowledge is not the sole advantage of school education. Its greatest advantage is perhaps the opportunity it affords us for making friends. It was not until I had already left school that I began to realize this advantage. And in recent years I have come to understand it even more deeply. I much regret having carelessly frittered away my school days without making many friends. Recently, every morning or evening, whenever I see school kids with satchels walking in twos and threes, hand in hand or shoulder to shoulder, I always envy them for enjoying happy friendship, and inwardly offer them my best wishes.

注　释

　　这篇杂感是我国著名文学家、教育家夏丏尊于1934年11月发表在由他主编的《中学生》杂志上。文章用平淡朴素的语言诉说了中年人的苦恼，感叹"真实的友谊"不可多得，字里行间流泄出对当时社会现状的不满。

　　①"头发开始秃脱"指头发变稀，也可译为 my head balding。今译 my hair thinning，以 hair 取代 head，是为了照顾下面的 graying 一字。

　　②"难以名言的"译为 nameless，意同 indescribable，但 nameless 常用来指不好的事物，如：a nameless fear、nameless atrocities。

　　③"逐渐减少"在原文指逐渐作古，如直译为 the gradual dwindling away 则未能明确表达"死去"的意思，故译为 gradual passing away。

　　④"我们和许多人相识，或是因了事务关系，或是因了偶然的机缘……"译为 We come to know many people either in the way of business or by mere chance..., 其中 in the way of 是成语，作"为了"解。成语 in the way of 可有若干不同的意思，如"关于"、"以……方法"、"为了"等，须由上下文来决定。

⑤ "和'顿首'、'百拜'同是仪式的虚伪"译为 as hypocritical as the polite formula *dunshou* (kowtow) or *baibai* (a hundred greetings) used after the signature in old fashioned Chinese letter-writing。其中 kowtow、a hundred greetings 以及 used after the signature in old fashioned Chinese letter-writing 均为译者的补充说明，属一种释义译法。

⑥ "真正的朋友，恐怕要算'总角之交'或'竹马之交'了"译为 Real friendship between two persons originates perhaps from the time of life when they were children playing innocently together，其中"总角之交"和"竹马之交"合而为一，用意译法处理。

⑦ "差不多可以说是'无所为'的"译为 It is sort of "friendship for friendship's sake"，其中 sort of（有几分）用来表达"差不多可以说"。又"无所为"意即"无其他目的"或"无条件的"，故译为 friendship for friendship's sake（为友谊而友谊）。

⑧ "这并不一定是'人心不古'"译为 Though this is not necessarily due to "degeneration of public morality"。也可考虑采用另一译法：Though this should not be ascribed exclusively to "degeneration of public morality"。

⑨ "结果彼此都'钩心斗角'"译为 till they start scheming against each other。注意其中 till 的一种特殊用

法。它在这里指"结果"，意即 so that finally 或 and at last，不作"直到……为止"解。

⑩ "像七巧板似地只选定了某一方面和对方接合"不宜直译。现按"人们在交往中互相提防，互存戒心"的内涵，用意译法处理：They always keep a wary eye, as it were, on each other in their association，其中插入语 as it were 作"似乎"、"可以说"等解。

⑪ "这时好像自己仍回归到少年时代去了"译为 and we feel like reliving the old days，其中 to relive 作"（凭想像）重新过……的生活"(to experience... again, especially in imagination) 解。

我坐了木船

叶圣陶

从重庆到汉口,我坐了木船。

木船危险,当然知道。一路上数不尽的滩,礁石随处都是,要出事,随时可以出。还有盗匪①——实在是最可怜的同胞,他们种地没得吃,有力气没处出卖,当了兵经常饿肚皮,无奈何只好出此下策②。——假如遇见了,把铺盖或者身上衣服带下去,也是异常难处的事儿③。

但是,回转来想,从前没有轮船,没有飞机,历来走川江④的人都坐木船。就是如今,上上下下的还有许多人在那里坐木船,如果统计起来,人数该比坐轮船坐飞机的多。人家可以坐,我就不能坐吗?我又不比人家高贵。至于危险,不考虑也罢。轮船飞机就不危险吗?安步当车似乎最稳妥了,可是人家屋檐边也可以掉下一张瓦片来。要绝对避免危险就莫要做人⑤。

要坐轮船坐飞机,自然也有办法⑥。只要往各方去请托,找关系,或者干脆买张黑票。先说黑票,且不谈付出超过定额的钱,力有不及,心有不甘⑦,单单一个"黑"字,就叫你不愿领教。"黑"字表示作弊,表示越出常轨。你买黑票,无异同作弊,赞助越出常轨⑧。一个人既不能独立转移风气,也该在消极方面有所自守,邦同作弊,赞助越出常轨的事儿,总可以免了吧。——这自然是书生之见⑨,不免通达的人一笑。

再说请托找关系,听人家说他们的经验,简直与谋差使一样的麻烦。在传达室恭候,在会客室恭候⑩,幸而见了那要见的人,他听说你要设法买船票,或是飞机票,爱理不理的答复你说,"困难呢……下个星期再来打听吧……"于是你觉着好像有一线希望,又好像毫无把握,只得挨到下星期再去。跑了不知多少趟,总算有眉目了⑪,又得往这一处签字,那一处盖章,看种种的脸色,候种种的传唤,为的是得一份充分的证据,可以去换张票子。票子到手,身分可以改变了,什么机关的部属,什么长的秘书,什么人的本人或是父亲,或者姓名仍旧,或者必须改名换姓,总之要与你自己暂时脱离关系。最有味的是冒充什么部的士兵⑫,非但改名换姓,还得穿上灰布棉军服,腰间束条皮带。我听了这些,就死了请托找关系的念头。即使饿得要死,也不定要去奉承颜色谋差使,为了一张票子去求教人家,不说我自己犯不着,人家也太费心了。重庆的路又那么难走,公共汽车站排队往往等上一个半个钟头,天天为了票子去跑,实在吃不消。再说与自己暂时脱离关系,换上他人的身分,虽然人家不大爱惜名气,我可不愿滥用那些名气。我不是部属,不是秘书,不是某人,不是某人的父亲,我是我。我毫无成就,样样不长进,我可不愿与任何人易地而处,无论长期的或是暂时的。为了走一趟路,必须易地而处,在我总觉着像被剥夺了什么似的。至于穿灰布棉军服更为难了,为了走一趟路才穿上那套衣服,岂不亵渎了那套衣服⑬?亵渎的人固然不少,我可总不忍——这一套又是书生之见。

抱着书生之见,我决定坐木船。木船比不上轮船,更比不上飞机,千真万确。可是绝对不用请托,绝对不用找关系,也无所谓黑票。你要船,找运输行,或者自己到码头上去找,找着了,言明价钱,多少钱坐到汉口,每块钱花得明明白白⑭。在这一点上,我觉得木船好极了⑮,我可以不说一句讨情的话,不看一副难看的嘴脸,堂堂正正的凭我的身分东西归。这是大多数坐轮船坐飞机的朋友办不到的,我可有这种骄傲。

决定了之后,有两位朋友特来劝阻,一位从李家沱,一位从柏滨,不怕水程跋涉,为的是关爱我,瞧得起我。他们说了种种理由,预想了种种可能的障害,结末说,还是再考虑一下的好。我真感谢他们,当然不敢说不必再行考虑,只好带玩笑的说,"吉人天相,"安慰他们激动的心情。现在,他们接到我平安到达的消息了,他们也真的安慰了。

I Took a Wooden Boat

Ye Shengtao

I took a wooden boat from Chongqing to Hankou.

Of course I know it is risky to travel by wooden boat. With countless shoals and reefs to negotiate, accidents may happen any time. To complicate matters, there are bandits lurking around — those pitiful fellow countrymen who, unable to ward off starvation by farming or soldiering or whatnot, have been reduced to the disreputable business as a last resort. I'll be in a real fix if they should rob me of, say, my bedding or clothes.

Now, on reflection, I realize that in the days before steamers and aircraft came into use, people used to travel by wooden boat up and down the Sichuan section of the Yangtse River. Even today, many continue to do so, and statistics will invariably show a higher percentage of people travelling by wooden boat than by steamer or aircraft. Why shouldn't I do the same? Why should I think it beneath myself to travel by wooden boat? As for safety, is it less dangerous to travel by steamer or aircraft? Going on foot seems to be the best choice, but a tile falling off the eaves of somebody's house might prove equally disastrous to foot passengers. Enjoying absolute safety is humanly impossible.

It stands to reason that I can go by steamer or aircraft if I care to. I can simply go around fishing for help or personal connections, or just buy a "black" ticket. But I'll have to pay more than the regular price for a "black" ticket, which I can ill afford and which I disdain to do. And the very word "black" generates in me a feeling of repulsion. "Black" signifies fraud or illegal practice. Buying a "black" ticket is as good as getting involved in a fraud or an illegal practice. If it is beyond one's capacity to single-handedly stem the prevailing social evils, one should at least be self-disciplined so as not to make matters worse. All this is undoubtedly the pedantic view of a bookish person — a view which must sound ridiculous to all sensible gentlemen.

Some people have told me from their own experience that soliciting help or seeking personal connections is something as difficult as hunting for a job. You may be kept cooling your heels in a janitor's office or a reception room before an interview is granted. Hearing that you are trying to get a steamer or air ticket, the much sought-after interviewer may reply in a cold and indifferent manner, "Ah, that's difficult... Come see me next week

. . . . " Thereupon you seem to see a ray of hope, and you may also feel totally uncertain of success. All you can do is wait until then. After making you don't know how many visits, there eventually appear signs of a positive outcome. Then you have to go here and there to get a signature or a seal, meet with all sorts of cold reception and wait for all sorts of summonses — all for the purpose of obtaining a useful certificate to buy a ticket with. Once with a ticket in hand, your status automatically changes. You can now call yourself the employee of a certain government office or a certain official's secretary. You can call yourself so-and-so or so-and-so's father. You can either keep your original name or have it changed. In short, you must temporarily break off relations with your old self. The funniest thing is when you try to pass for a soldier of a certain army unit, you must not only have your name changed, but also wear a grey-cloth cotton-padded army uniform with a leather belt around your waist. All that kills my idea of soliciting help or seeking personal connections. I disdain to go humbly begging for a job even when I am starving, let alone to go asking for other people's help in getting me a mere ticket. Neither is it necessary for me to go to all that trouble, nor should I bother other people for that matter. Going around is hard in the city of Chongqing. You have to queue up for at least 30 minutes or more to get on a bus. It would really be too much for me to go about for the ticket every day. As to the temporary divorce from my old self and the concealing of my identity, I hate to usurp all those designations though other people may think otherwise. I'm neither a government employee, nor a secretary, nor so-and-so, nor so-and-so's father. I am myself. I am just an ordinary man with no urge to do better, so I hate to change places with anybody else, whether for a while or for good. To change places just for the sake of a trip would make me feel like being deprived. Wouldn't it be sinful for me to wear the grey-cloth cotton-padded army uniform for nothing more than making a single trip? Though many other people violate the taboo, I for my part cannot bear to do the same. This again is the impractical view of a bookish person.

It was with this impractical view that I decided to take a wooden boat. It is absolutely true that a wooden boat cannot compare with a steamer, much less an airplane. But there is no need for soliciting help or seeking personal connections, nor the need for the so-called "black" ticket. All you need to do is contact the transport company, or go direct to the wharf to look for a wooden boat. Once you have located it, you will know what the fare is from Chongqing to Hankou, and every dollar will be paid for what it is worth, no more, no less. I find the wooden boat super in this respect. I am saved the humiliation of begging for help or the need of confronting the nasty look on somebody's face. I can travel with my true identity. This is something quite beyond the majority of those travelling by steamer or aircraft. I am proud of it.

After I had made up my mind, two friends of mine, in spite of the difficult boat journey all the way from Li Jia Tuo and Bai Bin respectively, came to dissuade me from taking the wooden boat out of concern and respect for me. They enumerated various reasons against my decision as well as various possible mishaps, advising me in the end to re-consider the matter. I felt very grateful to them, and of course refrained from showing any reluctance to re-consider the matter. By way of allaying their anxiety, I said jokingly, "A good guy always enjoys Heaven's protection." Now, the subsequent news of my safe arrival in Hankou must have set their minds at rest.

注　释

叶圣陶(1894—1988)原名叶绍钧，
江苏苏州人，为现代文学家、教育家。
《我坐了木船》一文以平淡的口吻叙述
他在抗战胜利后乘木船从重庆到汉口的
一番经历，对当时的黑暗社会作了无情
的鞭挞。

①"还有盗匪"译为 To complicate matters，there are
bandits lurking around，其中 To complicate matters 是为
承上启下而添加的成分。又，lurking around 作"潜伏"解，
也是添加成分，原文虽无其字，而有其意。

②"无奈何只好出此下策"译为 have been reduced to
the disreputable business as a last resort，其中 disreputable business（不体面的行当）指"下策"。又，reduced to
意即"被逼从事……"；as a last resort 意即"作为最后
一着"。

③"异常难处的事儿"译为 I'll be in a real fix，其中
in a fix 是成语，作"陷入困境"或"尴尬"解。

④"川江"即"四川段的长江"，故译 the Sichuan section of the Yangtse River。

⑤“要绝对避免危险就莫要做人”译为 Enjoying absolute safety is humanly impossible，其中 humanly 意即“从做人的角度看”。

⑥“要坐轮船坐飞机，自然也有办法”译为 It stands to reason that I can go by steamer or aircraft if I care to，其中 It stands to reason 是成语，意即“当然”。

⑦“付出超过定额的钱，力有不及，心有不甘”译为 to pay more than the regular price for a "black" ticket，which I can ill afford and which I disdain to do。“心有不甘”意即“不屑一干”，故译 disdain to do。

⑧“你买黑票，无异同作弊，赞助越出常轨”译为 Buying a "black" ticket is as good as getting involved in a fraud or an illegal practice，其中 as good as 是成语，作“实际上等于”或“与……几乎一样”解。

⑨“书生之见”译为 the pedantic view of a bookish person，其中 pedantic view 意同 impractical view，作“不现实的观点”解。

⑩“在传达室恭候，在会客室恭候”译为 You may be kept cooling your heels in a janitor's office or a reception room before an interview is granted，其中 cooling your heels 是成语，作“长等”、“空等”解。

⑪“跑了不知多少趟，总算有眉目了”译为 After making you don't know how many visits，there eventually appear signs of a positive outcome，其中 you don't know how 是插入语，修饰 many。

⑫ "最有味的是冒充什么部的士兵"译为 The funniest thing is when you try to pass for a soldier of a certain army unit，其中 to pass for 作"冒充"解。

⑬ "为了走一趟路才穿上那套衣服,岂不亵渎了那套衣服?"译为 Wouldn't it be sinful for me to wear the grey-cloth cotton-padded army uniform for nothing more than making a single trip?"亵渎"原作"轻慢"、"冒失"解，用在此处略带讽刺口气，意为"做了不该做的事"，故译为 sinful。

⑭ "每块钱花得明明白白"意即"该花多少就花多少"或"每块钱都花得值得"，故译 every dollar is paid for what it is worth。

⑮ "我觉得木船好极了"译为 I find the wooden boat super in this respect，其中 super 相当于 fantastic 或 wonderful。

背　影

朱　自　清

　　我与父亲不相见已二年余了,我最不能忘记的是他的背影。那年冬天,祖母死了,父亲的差使也交卸了,正是祸不单行的日子,我从北京到徐州,打算跟着父亲奔丧回家。到徐州见着父亲,看见满院狼藉的东西,又想起祖母,不禁簌簌地流下眼泪。父亲说:"事已如此,不必难过,好在天无绝人之路!"

　　回家①变卖典质,父亲还了亏空;又借钱办了丧事。这些日子,家中光景很是惨淡,一半为了丧事,一半为了父亲的赋闲②。丧事完毕,父亲要到南京谋事,我也要回北京念书,我们便同行。

　　到南京时,有朋友约去游逛,勾留了一日;第二日上午便须渡江到浦口,下午上车北去。父亲因为事忙,本已说定不送我,叫旅馆里一个熟识的茶房③陪我同去。他再三嘱咐茶房,甚是仔细。但他终于不放心,怕茶房不妥帖,颇踌躇了一会。其实那年我已二十岁,北京来往过两三次,是没有甚么要紧的了。他踌躇了一会,终于决定还是自己送我去。我两三回劝他不必去④;他只说,"不要紧,他们去不好⑤!"

我们过了江，进了车站。我买票，他忙着照看行李。行李太多了，得向脚夫行些小费⑥，才可过去。他便又忙着和他们讲价钱。我那时真是聪明过分⑦，总觉他说话不大漂亮⑧，非自己插嘴不可。但他终于讲定了价钱；就送我上车。他给我拣定了靠车门的一张椅子；我将他给我做的紫毛大衣铺好坐位。他嘱我路上小心，夜里要警醒些，不要受凉。又嘱托茶房好好照应我。我心里暗笑他的迂⑨；他们只认得钱，托他们直是白托！而且我这样大年纪的人，难道还不能料理自己么？唉，我现在想想，那时真是太聪明了⑩！

　　我说道，"爸爸，你走吧。"他望车外看了看，说，"我买几个橘子去。你就在此地，不要走动。"我看那边月台的栅栏外有几个卖东西的等着顾客。走到那边月台，须穿过铁道，须跳下去又爬上去。父亲是一个胖子，走过去自然要费些事。我本来要去的，他不肯，只好让他去。我看见他戴着黑布小帽，穿着黑布大马褂⑪，深青布棉袍，蹒跚地走到铁道边，慢慢探身下去，尚不大难。可是他穿过铁道，要爬上那边月台，就不容易了。他用两手攀着上面，两脚再向上缩；他肥胖的身子向左微倾，显出努力的样子。这时我看见他的背影，我的眼泪很快地流下来了。我赶紧拭干了泪，怕他看见，也怕别人看见。我再向外看时，他已抱了朱红的橘子往回走了。过铁道时，他先将橘子散放在地上，自己慢慢爬下，再抱起橘子走。到这边时，我赶紧去搀他。他和我走到车上，将橘子一股脑儿放在我的皮大衣上。于是扑扑衣上的泥土，心里很轻松似的，过一会说，"我走了；到那边来信！"我望着他走出去。他走了几步，回过头看见我，说，"进去吧，里边没人⑫。"等他的背影混入来来往往的人里，再找不着了，我便进来坐下，我的眼泪又来了。

　　近几年来，父亲和我都是东奔西走⑬，家中光景是一日不如一日。他少年出外谋生，独力支持，做了许多大事。那知老境却如此颓唐！他触目伤怀，自然情不能自己⑭。情郁于中，自然要发之于外；家庭琐屑便往往触他之怒。他待我渐渐不同往日⑮。但最近两年的不见，他终于忘却我的不好，只是惦记着我，惦记着我的儿子。我北来后，他写了一信给我，信中说道，"我身体平安，惟膀子疼痛利害，举箸提笔，诸多不便，大约大去⑯之期不远矣。"我读到此处，在晶莹的泪光中，又看见那肥胖的，青布棉袍，黑布马褂的背影。唉！我不知何时再能与他相见！

The Sight of Father's Back

Zhu Ziqing

It is more than two years since I last saw father, and what I can never forget is the sight of his back. Misfortunes never come singly. In the winter of more than two years ago, grandma died and father lost his job. I left Beijing for Xuzhou to join father in hastening home to attend grandma's funeral. When I met father in Xuzhou, the sight of the disorderly mess in his courtyard and the thought of grandma started tears trickling down my cheeks. Father said, "Now that things've come to such a pass, it's no use crying. Fortunately, Heaven always leaves one a way out. "

After arriving home in Yangzhou, father paid off debts by selling or pawning things. He also borrowed money to meet the funeral expenses. Between grandma's funeral and father's unemployment, our family was then in reduced circumstances. After the funeral was over, father was to go to Nanjing to look for a job and I was to return to Beijing to study, so we started out together.

I spent the first day in Nanjing strolling about with some friends at their invitation, and was ferrying across the Yangtse River to Pukou the next morning and thence taking a train for Beijing on the afternoon of the same day. Father said he was too busy to go and see me off at the railway station, but would ask a hotel waiter that he knew to accompany me there instead. He urged the waiter again and again to take good care of me, but still did not quite trust him. He hesitated for quite a while about what to do. As a matter of fact, nothing would matter at all because I was then twenty and had already travelled on the Beijing-Pukou Railway a couple of times. After some wavering, he finally decided that he himself would accompany me to the station. I repeatedly tried to talk him out of it, but he only said, "Never mind! It won't do to trust guys like those hotel boys!"

We entered the railway station after crossing the River. While I was at the booking office buying a ticket, father saw to my luggage. There was quite a bit of luggage and he had to bargain with the porter over the fee. I was then such a smark aleck that I frowned upon the way father was haggling and was on the verge of chipping in a few words when the bargain was finally clinched. Getting on the train with me, he picked me a seat close to the carriage door. I spread on the seat the brownish furlined overcoat he had got tailor made for me. He told me to be watchful on the way and be careful not to catch cold at night. He also asked the train attendants to take good care of me. I sniggered at father for being so impractical, for it was utterly useless to entrust me to those attendants, who cared for nothing but money. Besides, it was certainly no problem for a person of my age to look after himself. Oh, when I come to think of it, I can see how smarty I was in those days!

I said, "Dad, you might leave now." But he looked out of the window and said, "I'm going to buy you some tangerines. You just stay here. Don't move around." I caught sight of several vendors waiting for customers outside the railings beyond a platform. But to reach that platform would require crossing the railway track and doing some climbing up and down. That would be a strenuous job for father, who was fat. I wanted to do all that myself, but he stopped me, so I could do nothing but let him go. I watched him hobble towards the railway track in his black skullcap, black cloth mandarin jacket and dark blue cotton-padded cloth long gown. He had little trouble climbing down the railway track, but it was a lot more difficult for him to climb up that platform after crossing the railway track. His hands held onto the upper part of the platform, his legs huddled up and his corpulent body tipped slightly towards the left, obviously making an enormous exertion. While I was watching him from behind, tears gushed from my eyes. I quickly wiped them away lest he or others should catch me crying. The next moment when I looked out of the window again , father was already on the way back, holding bright red tangerines in both hands. In crossing the railway track, he first put the tangerines on the ground, climbed down slowly and then picked them up again. When he came near the train, I hurried out to help him by the hand. After boarding the train with me, he laid all the tangerines on my overcoat, and patting the dirt off his clothes, he looked somewhat relieved and said after a while, "I must be going now. Don't forget to write me from Beijing!" I gazed after his back retreating out of the carriage. After a few steps, he looked back at me and said, "Go back to your seat. Don't leave your things alone." I, however, did not go back to my seat until his figure was lost among crowds of people hurrying to and fro and no longer visible. My eyes were again wet with tears.

In recent years, both father and I have been living an unsettled life, and the circumstances of our family going from bad to worse. Father left home to seek a livelihood when young and did achieve quite a few things all on his own. To think that he should now be so downcast in old age! The discouraging state of affairs filled him with an uncontrollable feeling of deep sorrow, and his pent-up emotion had to find a vent. That is why even mere domestic trivialities would often make him angry, and meanwhile he became less and less nice with me. However, the separation of the last two years has made him more forgiving towards me. He keeps thinking about me and my son. After I arrived in Beijing, he wrote me a letter, in which he says, "I'm all right except for a severe pain in my arm. I even have trouble using chopsticks or writing brushes. Perhaps it won't be long now before I depart this life. " Through the glistening tears which these words had brought to my eyes I again saw the back of father's corpulent form in the dark blue cotton-padded cloth long gown and the black cloth mandarin jacket. Oh, how I long to see him again!

注　释

《背影》是朱自清(1898—1948)影响最大的抒情名篇之一，写于1925年10月。作者用的是提炼的口语，文笔秀丽，细腻缜密，读来有一种亲切婉转、娓娓动听的感觉。但《背影》的巨大艺术魅力主要来自它饱含的真挚感情。

① "回家"指作者和父亲一起从徐州回扬州奔丧。英译时有必要交代清楚扬州是他们的老家，所以采用加字法：After arriving home in Yangzhou。

② "一半为了丧事，一半为了父亲的赋闲"译为 Between Grandma's funeral and father's unemployment，其中 Between... and... 等于 What with... and (what with)...，作"半因……，半因……"或"由于……的共同影响"解。

③ "茶房"旧时指旅馆、餐馆、轮船等内的服务员，可译为 waiter、attendant、boy 等。

④ "我两三回劝他不必去"译为 I repeatedly tried to talk him out of it，比 I repeatedly tried to dissuade him from accompanying me to the station 通俗简洁。

⑤ "他们去不好"中的"他们"指"茶房"，全句意译为 It won't do to trust guys like those hotel boys。如直译为 It won't do to let one of the hotel boys go with you，也无不可，但未能把"对茶房缺乏信任感"的意思表达出来。

⑥ "小费"在这里不指按规定价格付费之外另给的"赏金"，不能用 tip 表达，现译为 fee。

⑦ "我那时真是聪明过分"中的"聪明"是反话，现全句译为 I was then such a smart aleck，其中 smart aleck 意即"自以为是的人"或"自以为样样懂的人"。

⑧ "总觉得他说话不大漂亮"意即嫌父亲不会讲价钱，现全句译为 I frowned upon the way father was haggling，其中 frowned upon 作"表示不赞同"解。

⑨ "迂"在这里作"不切实际"或"没有见识"解，现结合上下文译为 impractical。

⑩ "那时真是太聪明了"也是反语，现译为 how smarty I was in those days，其中 smarty 和 smart aleck 同义。

⑪ "马褂"为旧时男子穿在长袍外的对襟短褂，通常译为 mandarin jacket。

⑫ "里边没人"不宜按字面直译，现译为 Don't leave your things alone。

⑬ "父亲和我都是东奔西走"不宜按字面直译，现意译为 both father and I have been living an unsettled life。

⑭ "他触目伤怀，自然情不能自己"意即"他看到家庭

71

败落,情不自禁地为之悲伤",现译为 The discouraging state of affairs filled him with an uncontrollable feeling of deep sorrow。

⑮ "他待我渐渐不同往日"意即"他待我渐渐不如过去那么好",故译为 he became less and less nice with me。

⑯ "大去"为旧时用语,意即"与世长辞",现译为 depart this life。

匆　匆

朱　自　清

　　燕子去了,有再来的时候;杨柳枯了,有再青的时候;桃花谢了,有再开的时候①。但是,聪明的,你告诉我,我们的日子为什么一去不复返呢?——是有人偷了他们罢:那是谁?又藏在何处呢?是他们自己逃走了罢:现在又到了那里呢②?

　　我不知道他们给了我多少日子③;但我的手确乎是渐渐空虚了④。在默默里算着,八千多日子已经从我手中溜去⑤;像针尖上一滴水滴在大海里,我的日子滴在时间的流里,没有声音,也没有影子。我不禁头涔涔而泪潸潸了⑥。

　　去的尽管去了,来的尽管来着;去来的中间,又怎样地匆匆呢?早上我起来的时候,小屋里射进两三方⑦斜斜的太阳。太阳他有脚啊,轻轻悄悄地挪移⑧了;我也茫茫然跟着旋转。于是——洗手的时候,日子从水盆里过去;吃饭的时候,日子从饭碗里过去;默默时,便从凝然的双眼前过去。我觉察他去的匆匆了,伸出手遮挽时,他又从遮挽着的手边过去,天黑时,我躺在床上,他便伶伶俐俐地从我身上跨过,从我脚边飞去了。等我睁开眼和太阳再见,这算又溜走了一日。我掩着面叹息。但是新来的日子的影儿又开始在叹息里闪过了。

　　在逃去如飞的日子里，在千门万户的世界里的我能做些什么呢？只有徘徊罢了，只有匆匆罢了；在八千多日的匆匆里，除徘徊外，又剩些什么呢？过去的日子如轻烟，被微风吹散了，如薄雾，被初阳蒸融了；我留着些什么痕迹呢？我何曾留着像游丝样的痕迹呢？我赤裸裸来到这世界，转眼间也将赤裸裸的回去罢？但不能平的⑨，为什么偏要白白走这一遭啊？

　　你聪明的，告诉我，我们的日子为什么一去不复返呢？

Transient Days

Zhu Ziqing

If swallows go away, they will come back again. If willows wither, they will turn green again. If peach blossoms fade, they will flower again. But, tell me, you the wise, why should our days go by never to return? Perhaps they have been stolen by someone. But who could it be and where could he hide them? Perhaps they have just run away by themselves. But where could they be at the present moment?

I don't know how many days I am entitled to altogether, but my quota of them is undoubtedly wearing away. Counting up silently, I find that more than 8,000 days have already slipped away through my fingers. Like a drop of water falling off a needle point into the ocean, my days are quietly dripping into the stream of time without leaving a trace. At the thought of this, sweat oozes from my forehead and tears trickle down my cheeks.

What is gone is gone, what is to come keeps coming. How swift is the transition in between! When I get up in the morning, the slanting sun casts two or three squarish patches of light into my small room. The sun has feet too, edging away softly and stealthily. And, without knowing it, I am already caught in its revolution. Thus the day flows away through the sink when I wash my hands; vanishes in the rice bowl when I have my meal; passes away quietly before the fixed gaze of my eyes when I am lost in reverie. Aware of its fleeting presence, I reach out for it only to find it brushing past my outstretched hands. In the evening, when I lie on my bed, it nimbly strides over my body and flits past my feet. By the time when I open my eyes to meet the sun again, another day is already gone. I heave a sigh, my head buried in my hands. But, in the midst of my sighs, a new day is flashing past.

Living in this world with its fleeting days and teeming millions, what can I do but waver and wander and live a transient life? What have I been doing during the 8,000 fleeting days except wavering and wandering? The bygone days, like wisps of smoke, have been dispersed by gentle winds, and, like thin mists, have been evaporated by the rising sun. What traces have I left behind? No, nothing, not even gossamer-like traces. I have come to this world stark naked, and in the twinkling of an eye, I am to go back as stark naked as ever. However, I am taking it very much to heart: why should I be made to pass through this world for nothing at all?

O you the wise, would you tell me please: why should our days go by never to return?

注　释

　　《匆匆》是朱自清的早期散文,写于
1922 年 7 月 28 日。文章充满诗意,对时
光的消失深表感叹和无奈,流露出当时
青年知识分子的苦闷和忧伤情绪。

　　① 原文开头三个句子结构类似,译文采用三个相应
的句式,力求形似。同时,每句均以 if 从句为首,使人想起
英国诗人雪莱（Shelley）的名句 If Winter comes, can
Spring be far away,有助于烘托原文的韵味。

　　② "现在又到了那里呢" 译为 But where could they
be at the present moment,其中 at the present moment 等
于 now,也可用 at the moment 或 at this moment in time
等表达。

　　③ "我不知道他们给了我多少日子" 译为 I don't
know how many days I am entitled to altogether,其中
entitled to 相当于 qualified for,作 "能有……" 或 "有权
得到……" 解。此句也可译为 I don't know how many
days I have been given to live。

　　④ "但我的手确乎是渐渐空虚了" 不宜逐字直译,现

78

以意译法处理：but my quota of them is undoubtedly wearing away，其中 quota of them 的意思是"一定数额的日子"，也即"寿命的预期数额"。也可用 my alloted span 代替 my quota of them。

⑤ "八千多日子已经从我手中溜去"译为 more than 8,000 days have already slipped away through my fingers，其中 to slip away through one's fingers 是英语习语。

⑥ "我不禁头涔涔而泪潸潸了"的译文中添加了 At the thought of this（一想到这儿），承上启下，原文虽无其字而有其意。

⑦ "两三方"译为 two or three squarish patches，其中 squarish 的意思是"似方形的"，比 square 模糊些，似较可取。

⑧ "挪移"在此有"慢慢离开"的含义，现以英语短语动词（phrasal verb）to edge away 表达。注意原文第三段中若干表示动作的词语在译文中均挑选恰当的英语短语动词表达，效果较好。如："从……（双眼前）过去"译为 to pass away before ...；"伸出手遮挽……"译为 to reach out for ...；"从……（手边）过去"译为 to brush past ...；"从……（身上）跨过"译为 to stride over ...；"从……（脚边）飞去了"译为 to flit past ...；"闪过去了"译为 to flash past。

⑨ "不能平的"意即"为之耿耿于怀"或"为之想不开"，现译为 I am taking it very much to heart，其中 to take... to heart 是英语成语，作"为……烦恼"或"为……想不开"解。

木匠老陈[①]

巴　金

生活的经验固然会叫人忘记许多事情[②]。但是有些记忆经过了多少时间的磨洗[③]也不会消灭。

故乡里那些房屋，那些街道至今还印在我的脑子里。我还记得我每天到学堂去总要走过的木匠老陈的铺子。

木匠老陈那时不过四十岁光景，脸长得像驴子脸，左眼下面有块伤疤，嘴唇上略有几根胡须。大家都说他的相貌丑，但是同时人人称赞他的脾气好。

他平日在店里。但是他也常常到相熟的公馆里去做活[④]，或者做包工，或者做零工[⑤]。我们家里需要木匠的时候，总是去找他。我就在这时候认识他。他在我们家里做活，我只要有空，就跑去看他工作。

我那时注意的，并不是他本人，倒是他的那些工具：什么有轮齿的锯子啦，有两个耳朵的刨子啦，会旋转的钻子啦，象图画里板斧一般的斧子啦。这些奇怪的东西我以前全没有看见过。一块粗糙的木头经过了斧子劈，锯子锯，刨子刨，就变成了一方或者一条光滑整齐的木板，再经过钻子、凿子等等工具以后，又变成了各种各样的东西[⑥]；像美丽的窗格,镂花的壁板等等细致的物件,都是这样制成的。

老陈和他的徒弟的工作使我的眼界宽了不少⑦。那时我还在家里读书,祖父聘请了一位前清的老秀才来管教我们。老秀才不知道教授的方法,他只教我们认一些字,呆板地读一些书。此外他就把我们关在书房里,端端正正地坐⑧在凳子上,让时间白白地过去。过惯了这种单调的生活以后,无怪乎我特别喜欢老陈了。

老陈常常弯着腰,拿了尺子和墨线盒在木板上面画什么东西。我便安静地站在旁边专心地望着,连眼珠也不转一下。他画好了墨线,便拿起锯子或者凿子来。我有时候觉得有些地方很奇怪,不明白,就问他,他很和气地对我一一说明。他的态度比那个老秀才的好得多⑨。

家里的人看见我对老陈的工作感到这么大的兴趣,并不来干涉我,却嘲笑地唤我做老陈的徒弟,父亲甚至开玩笑地说要把我送到老陈那里学做木匠。但这些嘲笑都是好意的,父亲的确喜欢我。因此有一个时候我居然相信父亲真有这样的想法,而且我对老陈说过要跟他学做木匠的话。

"你要学做木匠?真笑话!有钱的少爷应该读书,将来好做官!穷人的小孩才学做木匠,"老陈听见我的话,马上就笑起来。

"为什么不该学做木匠?做官有什么好?修房子,做家具,才有趣啊!我做木匠,我要给自己修房子,爬到上面去,爬得高高的,"我看见他不相信我的话,把它只当做小孩子的胡说⑩,我有些生气,就起劲地争论道。

"爬得高,会跌下来,"老陈随口说了这一句,他的笑容渐渐地收起来了。

"跌下来，你骗我！我就没有见过木匠跌下来。"

老陈看我一眼，依旧温和地说："做木匠修房子，常常拿自己性命来拚。一个不当心在上面滑了脚，跌下来，不跌成肉酱，也会得一辈子的残疾。"他说到这里就埋下头，用力在木板上推他的刨子，木板查查地响着，一卷一卷的刨花接连落在地上。他过了半晌又加了一句："我爹就是这样子跌死的。"

我不相信他的话。一个人会活活地跌死！我没有看见过，也没有听见人说过。既然他父亲做木匠跌死了，为什么他现在还做木匠呢？我简直想不通。

"你骗我，我不信！那么你为什么还要做木匠？难道你就不怕死！"

"做木匠的人这样多，不见得个个都遭横死。我学的是这行手艺，不靠它吃饭又靠什么？"他苦恼地说。然后他抬起头来看我，他的眼角上嵌得有泪珠。他哭了！

我看见他流眼泪，不知道要怎么办才好，就跑开了。

不久祖父生病死了，我也进了学堂，不再受那个老秀才的管束了。祖父死后木匠老陈不曾到我们家里来过。但是我每天到学堂去都要经过他那个小小的铺子。

有时候他在店里招呼我；有时候他不在，只有一两个徒弟在那里钉凳子或者制造别的物件。他的店起初还能够维持下去，但是不久省城里发生了巷战，一连打了三天，然后那两位军阀因为别人的调解又握手言欢了。老陈的店在这个时期遭到"丘八"的光顾，他的一点点积蓄都给抢光了，只剩下一个空铺子⑪。这以后他虽然勉强开店，生意却很萧条。我常常看见他哭丧着脸在店里做工。他的精神颓丧，但是他仍然不停手地做活。我听说他晚上时常到小酒馆里喝酒。

又过了几个月他的店终于关了门。我也就看不见他的踪迹了。有人说他去吃粮当了兵⑫，有人说他到外县谋生去了。然而有一天我在街上碰见了他。他手里提着一个篮子，里面装了几件木匠用的工具。

"老陈，你还在省城！人家说你吃粮去了⑬！"我快活地大声叫起来。

"我只会做木匠，我就只会做木匠！一个人应该安分守己，"他摇摇头微微笑道，他的笑容里带了一点悲哀。他没有什么大改变，只是人瘦了些，脸黑了些，衣服脏了些。

"少爷，你好好读书。你将来做了官，我来给你修房子，"他继续含笑说。

我抓住他的袖子，再也说不出一句话来。他告辞走了。他还告诉我他在他从前一个徒弟的店里帮忙。这个徒弟如今发达了，他却在那里做一个匠人。

以后我就没有再看见老陈。我虽然喜欢他，但是过了不几天我又把他忘记了。等到公馆里的轿夫告诉我一个消息的时候，我才记起他来。

那个轿夫报告的是什么消息呢？

他告诉我：老陈同别的木匠一起在南门一家大公馆里修楼房⑭，工程快要完了，但是不晓得怎样，老陈竟然从楼上跌下来，跌死了。

在那么多的木匠里面，偏偏是他跟着他父亲落进了横死的命运圈里。这似乎是偶然，似乎又不是偶然。总之，一个安分守己的人就这样地消灭了⑮。

Carpenter Lao Chen

Ba Jin

Lots of things are apt to fade from memory as one's life experiences accumulate. But some memories will withstand the wear and tear of time.

Those houses and streets in my home town still remain engraved on my mind. I still can recall how every day on my way to school I would invariably walk past Carpenter Lao Chen's shop.

Carpenter Lao Chen was then only about forty years old, with a longish face like that of a donkey, a scar under his left eye, and a wispy moustache on his upper lip. People said he looked ugly, yet they praised him for his good temper.

He usually worked in his own shop. But from time to time he was employed by some rich people he knew well to work at their residences, either as a hired hand on contract or as an oddjobber. Whenever my family needed a carpenter, he was always the man we wanted. That was how I got to know him. While he was in our home, I would come out to watch him work in my spare time.

What attracted my attention, however, was not the man himself, but the tools he used, such as the saw with toothed blade, the plane with two ear-like handles, the revolving drill, the hatchet that looked like the broad axe in drawings — things entirely strange to me. A piece of coarse wood, after being processed with the hatchet, saw and plane, would become pieces of smooth and tidy wood, square or rectangular in shape. After further treatment with the chisel, drill, etc. , they would end up as various kinds of exquisite articles, such as beautiful window lattices, ornamental engravings on wooden partitions.

The work which Lao Chen and his apprentices did was a real eye-opener to me. I was then studying at home under the tutorship of an old scholar of the Qing Dynasty whom my grandfather had engaged. The old scholar knew nothing about teaching methods. All he did was make me learn some Chinese characters and do some dull reading. Apart from that, he had me cooped up in my study and sit bolt upright doing nothing while time was slipping through my fingers. Because of this monotonous life, it was no wonder that I developed a particular liking for Carpenter Lao Chen.

He was often bent over drawing something on a plank with a ruler and an ink marker. And I would stand by and watch quietly and intently, my eyes riveted on him. After making the line with the ink marker, he would pick up the saw or the chisel. Sometimes, when something puzzled me, I would ask him questions out of curiosity, and he would explain patiently everything in detail. He was much more agreeable than the old scholar.

My folks, however, showed no sign of disapproval when they found me so much interested in Lao Chen's work, but only teasingly called me an apprentice of his. Father even said jokingly that he was going to apprentice me to Lao Chen. All that was the well-meaning remarks of an affectionate father. Once I even believed that father had meant what he said, and I even told Lao Chen that that was exactly what I had in mind.

"You want to learn carpentry?" said Lao Chen immediately with a smile. "No kidding! A wealthy young master like you should study and grow up to be a government official! Only poor people's kids learn carpentry."

Somewhat annoyed by the way he shrugged off my words as childish nonsense, I argued heatedly, "Why not become a carpenter? What's the good of being a government official? It's great fun to build houses and make furniture. If I'm a carpenter, I'll climb high up, very high up, to build a house for myself."

"You may fall down if you climb high," said he casually, the smile on his face fading away.

"Fall down? You're fooling me! I've never seen a carpenter fall down. "

Shooting a glance at me, he continued with undiminished patience.

"A carpenter often has to risk his own life in building a house. One careless slip, and you fall down. You'll be disabled for life, if not reduced to a pulp. "

Thereupon, he bent his head and forcefully pushed his plane over a plank, the shavings of which fell continuously onto the ground amidst the screeching sound. Then he added after a moment's silence,

"That's how my father died. "

I just could not bring myself to believe it. How could a man die like that? I had never seen it happen, nor had I ever heard of it. If his father had died of an accident as a carpenter, why should Lao Chen himself still be a carpenter now? I just couldn't figure it out.

"You're fooling me. I don't believe you! How come you're still a carpenter? Can you be unafraid of death?"

"Lots of guys are in this trade," he went on gloomily. "It doesn't follow that everybody meets with such a violent death. Carpentry is my trade. What else could I rely on to make a living?"

He looked up at me, some teardrops visible from the corners of his eyes. He was crying!

I was at a loss when I saw him in tears, so I went away quietly.

Not long afterwards, my grandpa fell ill and died, and I was enrolled in a school, no longer under the control of the old scholar. Lao Chen never came again to work in our household after grandpa's death. But every day on my way to school, I would pass by his small shop.

Sometimes he beckoned me from his shop. Sometimes he was absent, leaving a couple of his apprentices there hammering nails into a stool or making some other articles. At first, he could somehow scrape along. Soon street fighting broke out in the provincial capital, lasting three days until the dispute between two warlords was settled through the mediation of a third party. In the course of the fighting, soldiers looted Lao Chen's shop until it was empty of everything. After that, nevertheless, he still managed to keep his shop open though business was bad. I often saw him working in his shop with a saddened look on his face. Dejected as he was, he worked on as usual. I heard that he often went drinking at a small wine shop in the evening.

Several months later, his shop closed down for good and I lost all trace of him. Some said he had gone soldiering, others said he had gone to another county to seek a livelihood. One day, however, I ran into him in the street. He was carrying a basket filled with some carpenter's tools.

"Lao Chen," I yelled out in joy, "you're still here in

the provincial capital! People say you've joined up!"

"I'm good at nothing else but carpentry, I'm good at nothing else but carpentry! One should be content with one's lot." He shook his head, wearing a faint smile with a touch of sorrow. There was not much change in him except that he was thinner, his face darker and his clothes more dirty.

"Young master," he continued smilingly, "you should study hard. Let me build a house for you some day when you're a government official."

I took hold of his sleeve, unable to utter a word. He said goodbye to me and went away. He had told me that he was now working at the shop of a former apprentice of his. The apprentice was doing quite well while Lao Chen was now his hired hand.

Thenceforth I never saw Lao Chen again. Much as I liked him, I soon forgot him. It was not until the sedan-chair bearer of a rich household passed on to me the news that I remembered him again.

What news did the sedan-chair bearer tell me?

He told me: Lao Chen, together with other carpenters, was building a mansion for a rich household at the southern city gate. When it was nearing completion, it suddenly came to pass that he fell off the building and died.

Why did Lao Chen, of all carpenters, die such a vio-

lent death like his father? All that seems accidental, and
also seems predestined. In short, an honest man has thus
passed out of existence.

注　释

　　巴金(1903—　　)的《木匠老陈》
写于 1934 年,后编入他的散文集《生之
忏悔》。这是一篇传记体的回忆性文章,
热情洋溢,充满浓郁的抒情色彩,对旧时
淳朴的劳动大众的苦难深表同情。

　　① "木匠老陈"译为 Carpenter Lao Chen,其中 Carpenter 为称号化名词,故在前面不加任何冠词。这是现代
英语中的常见用法。

　　② "生活的经验……叫人忘记许多事情"意即"随着
生活经历的积累,许多往事,难免给忘了",故译为 Lots of
things are apt to fade from memory as one's life experiences accumulate。

　　③ "时间的磨洗"意即"岁月的腐蚀",现译为 the
wear and tear of time,其中 wear and tear 是英语成语,作
"磨损"(loss and damage resulting from use)解。

　　④ "他……到相熟的公馆里去做活"中的"公馆"指"大
户"、"有钱人家",故全句译为 he was employed by some
rich people he knew well to work at their residences。

91

⑤ "包工"指"按合同操作"，"零工"指"不按合同操作"，故两者按上下文分别译为 a hired hand on contract 和 an odd-jobber。

⑥ "又变成各种各样（细致）的东西"译为 would end up as various kinds of exquisite articles，其中 end up 是成语，作"最终成为"解。这里使用它是为了避免重复前句中的 become 一词。

⑦ "……使我的眼界宽了不少"译为 ... was a real eye-opener to me，其中 eye-opener 作"令人大开眼界的事物"（something very surprising, from which one learns something unknown before）解，通常和 revelation 意相近。

⑧ "端端正正地坐……"译为 sit bolt upright ...，其中 bolt upright 是常用搭配，bolt 可与 to sit 或 to stand 等连用，作"笔直"解。此句也可译为 sit very straight ...。

⑨ "他的态度比那个老秀才的好多了"中的"好"的意思是"令人愉快"或"易于相处"，故全句译为 He was much more agreeable than the old scholar，其中 agreeable 意即"易于相处"（pleasant 或 likable）。

⑩ "……不相信我的话，把它当做小孩子的胡说"译为 ... shrugged off my words as childish nonsense，其中 shrugged off 是英语成语，本作"耸肩对……表示不屑理睬"解，现指"不当一回事"，与 to ignore 意同。

⑪ "老陈的店……遭到'丘八'的光顾，他的一点点积蓄都给抢光了，只剩下一个空铺子"中的"丘八"为旧时对士兵的轻蔑称呼，现全句译为 soldiers looted Lao Chen's shop until it was empty of everything，其中 until 一词的意思不是"直到……为止"，而是"以至于"（to the point that / so that finally / and at last）。

⑫"有人说他去吃粮当了兵"中的"吃粮"旧时和"当兵"同义，现全句译为 Some said he had gone soldiering 即可。

⑬"人家说你吃粮去了！"译为 People say you've joined up，其中 to join up 为成语，意同 to join the army。

⑭"在……一家大公馆修楼房"译为 was building a mansion for a rich household，其中 mansion 的意思是"大楼"（a large house，usually belonging to a wealthy person）。如按字面把"楼房"译为 a large multi-storied house 未尝不可，但欠简练。

⑮"总之，一个安分守己的人就这样地消灭了"一句带有"惋惜"、"同情"的口气，故译为 In short，an honest man has thus passed out of existence，其中 has thus passed out of existence 似比 has thus perished 确切。

朋　友

这一次的旅行使我更了解一个名词的意义,这个名词就是:朋友。

七八天以前我曾对一个初次见面的朋友说:"在朋友们面前我只感到惭愧①。你们待我太好了,我简直没法报答你们。"这并不是谦虚的客气话,这是真的事实。说过这些话,我第二天就离开了那个朋友,并不知道以后还有没有机会再看见他。但是他给我的那一点点温暖至今还使我的心颤动②。

我的生命大概不会很长久罢。然而在短促的过去的回顾中却有一盏明灯,照彻了我的灵魂的黑暗,使我的生存有一点光彩。这盏灯就是友情。我应该感谢它,因为靠了它我才能够活到现在;而且把旧家庭给我留下的阴影扫除了的也正是它。

世间有不少的人为了家庭抛弃朋友,至少也会在家庭和朋友之间划一个界限,把家庭看得比朋友重过若干倍。这似乎是很自然的事情。我也曾亲眼看见一些人结婚以后就离开朋友,离开事业。……

94

朋友是暂时的，家庭是永久的。在好些人的行为里我发见了这个信条。这个信条在我实在是不可理解的。对于我，要是没有朋友，我现在会变成怎样可怜的东西，我自己也不知道③。

然而朋友们把我救了。他们给了我家庭所不能给的东西。他们的友爱，他们的帮助，他们的鼓励，几次把我从深渊的边沿救回来。他们对我表示了无限的慷慨④。

我的生活曾经是悲苦的，黑暗的。然而朋友们把多量的同情，多量的爱，多量的欢乐，多量的眼泪分了给我，这些东西都是生存所必需的。这些不要报答的慷慨的施舍，使我的生活里也有了温暖，有了幸福⑤。我默默地接受了它们。我并不曾说过一句感激的话，我也没有做过一件报答的行为。但是朋友们却不把自私的形容词加到我的身上。对于我，他们太慷慨了⑥。

这一次我走了许多新地方，看见了许多新朋友。我的生活是忙碌的：忙着看，忙着听，忙着说，忙着走。但是我不曾遇到一点困难，朋友们给我准备好了一切，使我不会缺少什么。我每走到一个新地方，我就像回到我那个在上海被日本兵毁掉的旧居一样。

每一个朋友，不管他自己的生活是怎样苦，怎样简单，也要慷慨地分一些东西给我，虽然明知道我不能够报答他。有些朋友，连他们的名字我以前也不知道，他们却关心我的健康，处处打听我的"病况"，直到他们看见了我那被日光晒黑了的脸和膀子，他们才放心地微笑了。这种情形的确值得人掉眼泪。

有人相信我不写文章就不能够生活。两个月以前，一个同情我的上海朋友寄稿到《广州民国日报》的副刊,说了许多关于我的生活的话。他也说我一天不写文章第二天就没有饭吃⑦。这是不确实的。这次旅行就给我证明:即使我不再写一个字,朋友们也不肯让我冻馁。世间还有许多慷慨的人,他们并不把自己个人和家庭看得异常重要,超过一切。靠了他们我才能够活到现在,而且靠了他们我还要活下去。

朋友们给我的东西是太多、太多了⑧。我将怎样报答他们呢? 但是我知道他们是不需要报答的。

最近我在一个法国哲学家的书里读到了这样的话:"生命的一个条件就是消费……世间有一种不能跟生存分开的慷慨,要是没有了它,我们就会死,就会从内部干枯。我们必须开花。道德,无私心就是人生的花。"

在我的眼前开放着这么多的人生的花朵了。我的生命要到什么时候才会开花? 难道我已经是"内部干枯"了么?

一个朋友说过:"我若是灯,我就要用我的光明来照彻黑暗。"

我不配做一盏明灯。那么就让我做一块木柴罢。我愿意把我从太阳那里受到的热放散出来,我愿意把自己烧得粉身碎骨给人间添一点点温暖。

Friends

Ba Jin

On my recent travels, I came to realize still more fully the significance of the word "friend".

Seven or eight days ago, I said to a friend whom I had just come to know, "I can't help feeling embarrassed before my friends. You're all so nice to me. I simply don't know how to repay your kindness." I did not make this remark out of mere modesty and courtesy. I truly meant what I said. The next day, I said goodbye to this friend, not knowing if I could ever see him again. But the little warmth that he gave me has been keeping my heart throbbing with gratitude.

The length of my days will not be unlimited. However, whenever I look back on my brief past life, I find a beacon illuminating my soul and thereby lending a little brightness to my being. That beacon is friendship. I should be grateful to it because it has helped me keep alive up to now and clear away the shadow left on me by my old family.

Many people forsake their friends in favour of their own families, or at least draw a line of demarcation between families and friends, considering the former to be many times more important than the latter. That seems to be a matter of course. I have also seen with my own eyes how some people abandon their friends as well as their own careers soon after they get married.... .

Friends are transient whereas families are lasting — that is the tenet, as I know, guiding the behaviour of many people. To me, that is utterly inconceivable. Without friends, I would have been reduced to I don't know what a miserable creature.

Friends are my saviours. They give me things which it is beyond my family to give me. Thanks to their fraternal love, assistance and encouragement, I have time and again been saved from falling into an abyss while on its verge. They have been enormously generous towards me.

There was a time when my life was miserable and gloomy. My friends then gave me in large quantities sympathy, love, joy and tears — things essential for existence. It is due to their bountiful free gifts that I also have my share of warmth and happiness in my life. I accepted their kindnesses quietly without ever saying a word of thanks and without ever doing anything in return. In spite of that, my friends never used the epithet "self-centered" when referring to me. They are only too generous towards me.

I visited many new places and met many new friends on my recent trip. My time was mostly taken up by looking around, listening, talking and walking. But I never ran into any trouble because my friends had done their utmost to make sure that I would be short of nothing. Whatever new places I called at, I always felt at home as if I were back in my old residence in Shanghai which had already been raged to the ground by Japanese troops.

No matter how hard up and frugal my friends themselves were, they would unstintingly share with me whatever they had, although they knew I would not be able to repay them for their kindness. Some, whom I did not even know by name, showed concern over my health and went about inquiring after me. It was not until they saw my suntanned face and arms that they began to smile a smile of relief. All that was enough to move one to tears.

Some people believe that, without writing, I would lose my livelihood. One of my sympathizers, in an article published two months ago in the *Guangzhou Republic Daily* supplement, gives a full account of the conditions of my life. He also says that I would have nothing to live on once I should lay down my pen. That is not true at all. It has already been proved by my recent travels that my friends would never let me suffer from cold and hunger even if I should go without writing a single word. There are a great many kind-hearted people in the world who never attach undue importance to themselves and their own families and who never place themselves and their families above anything else. It is owing to them that I still survive and shall continue to survive for a long time to come.

I owe my friends many, many kindnesses. How can I repay them? But, I understand, they don't need me to do that.

Recently I came across the following words in a book by a French philosopher:

> *One condition of life is consumption .... Survival in this world is inseparable from generosity, without which we would perish and become dried-up from within. We must put forth flowers. Moral integrity and unselfishness are the flowers of life.*

Now so many flowers of life are in full bloom before my eyes. When can my life put forth flowers? Am I already dried-up from within?

A friend of mine says, "If I were a lamp, I would illuminate darkness with my light."

I, however, don't qualify for a bright lamp. Let me

100

be a piece of firewood instead. I'll radiate the heat that I have absorbed from the sun. I'll burn myself to ashes to provide this human world with a little warmth.

注　释

　　《朋友》是巴金1933年6月写于广州的一篇旅途随笔。作者通过自己的经历,用朴素流畅的语言赞颂人间友情之可贵,字里行间处处洋溢着他的真挚、热情。

　　① "在朋友面前我只感到惭愧"中的"惭愧"的意思是"不好意思",不作"羞愧"解,因此不宜按字面译为 ashamed 等。可译为 embarrassed 或 ill at ease 等。

　　② "使我的心颤动"译为 Keeping my heart throbbing with gratitude,其中 with gratitude 是添加的成分,原文虽无其字而有其意。

　　③ "我现在会变成怎样可怜的东西,我自己也不知道"译为 I would have been reduced to I don't know what a miserable creature,其中 I don't know 作插入语用。

　　④ "无限的慷慨"译为 enormously generous,其中 enormously 作 extremely 或 exceedingly 解,属强化修饰词 (intensifying adjective)。

　　⑤ "这些不要报答的慷慨施舍,使我的生活里也有了

温暖，有了幸福"译为 It is due to their bountiful free gifts that I also have my share of warmth and happiness in my life，其中 bountiful 的意思是"慷慨"或"大量"；my share of 作"我(应有)的一份"解，用以表达原文中"也"的内涵。

⑥"太慷慨"译为 only too generous，其中 only too 是成语，作 very 或 all too 解。

⑦"一天不写文章第二天就没有饭吃"中的"一天……第二天就……"在译文中用连接词 once 即可表达。又"没有饭吃"不宜按字面直译，现意译为 have nothing to live on。

⑧"朋友给我的东西是太多、太多了"中的"东西"主要指"帮助"，侧重在精神方面，虽然也可译为 things，但在此不如 kindnesses（= kind acts）更为贴切。

梦

巴　金

据说"至人①无梦"。幸而我只是一个平庸的人。

我有我的梦中世界，在那里我常常见到你。

昨夜又见到你那慈祥的笑颜了。

还是在我们那个老家，在你的房间里，在我的房间里②，你亲切地对我讲话。你笑，我也笑。

还是成都的那些旧街道，我跟着你一步一步地走过平坦的石板路，我望着你的背影，心里安慰地想：父亲还很康健呢。一种幸福的感觉使我的全身发热了。

我那时不会知道我是在梦中，也忘记了二十五年来的艰苦日子。

在戏园里，我坐在你旁边，看台上的武戏③，你还详细地给我解释剧中情节。

我变成二十几年前的孩子了。我高兴，我没有挂虑地微笑④，我不加思索地随口讲话。我想不到我在很短的时间以后就会失掉你，失掉这一切。

然而睁开眼睛，我只是一个人，四周就只有滴滴的雨声。房里是一片黑暗。

没有笑,没有话语。只有雨声:滴——滴——滴。

我用力把眼睛睁大,我撩开蚊帐,我在漆黑的空间中找寻你的影子。

但是从两扇开着的小窗,慢慢地透进来灰白色的亮光,使我的眼睛看见了这个空阔的房间。

没有你,没有你的微笑。有的是寂寞、单调。雨一直滴——滴地下着。

我唤你,没有回应。我侧耳倾听,没有脚声。我静下来,我的心怦怦地跳动。我听得见自己的心的声音。

我的心在走路,它慢慢地走过了二十五年,一直到这个夜晚。

我于是闭了嘴,我知道你不会再站到我的面前。二十五年前我失掉了你。我从无父的孩子已经长成一个中年人了。

雨声继续着。长夜在滴滴声中进行⑤。我的心感到无比的寂寞。怎么,是屋漏么?我的脸颊湿了。

小时候我有一个愿望:我愿在你的庇荫下⑥做一世的孩子。现在只有让梦来满足这个愿望了。

至少在梦里,我可以见到你,我高兴,我没有挂虑地微笑,我不加思索地随口讲话。

为了这个,我应该感谢梦。

Dreams

Ba Jin

It is said that "a virtuous man seldom dreams". Fortunately, I am but an ordinary man.

I dream my own dreams, in which I often meet you.

Last night I again saw your kindly smiling face.

It was the same old home of ours. You talked to me cordially now in your room, now in my room. You smiled and I also smiled.

It was the same old streets of Chengdu. I followed you step by step on the smooth flagstones. Looking at you from behind, I inwardly consoled myself with the thought that father was still hale and hearty. A sensation of blissfulness warmed me up all over.

I was unaware that I was in a dream. I also forgot the hardships I had gone through during the past 25 years.

While I sat beside you inside a theater watching the fighting scenes of a Peking opera, you explained its story to me in great detail.

I was again the small kid of 25 years before. I was joyful, I smiled naive smiles, I chattered away freely. I did not have the slightest inkling that you together with everything else would in a moment vanish out of sight.

When I opened my eyes, I found that I was all by myself and nothing was heard except the pit-a-pat of rain drops.

No more smile, no more chitchat. Only the drip drip drip of rain.

Forcing my eyes to open wider and drawing aside the mosquito net, I began to search for you in the pitch darkness.

A greyish light, nevertheless, edged in through two small windows to enable me to see the spacious room.

You and your smile were no more. Only loneliness and monotony remained. The rain kept pitter-pattering.

I called to you, but no response. I listened attentively, but heard no footsteps. I quieted down, my heart beating hard. I could hear its thumping.

My heart had been tramping along all the time. Up to now, it had been on its slow journey for 25 years.

Thereupon I kept my mouth shut. I knew you would never appear standing before me. I had lost you 25 years before. Since then, I had grown from a fatherless child into a middle-aged man.

The rain continued to fall. The long night wore on

amidst its dripping sound. I was seized with acute loneliness. Well, was the roof leaking? Or was it my tears that had wetted my cheeks?

When I was young, I wished I could remain a kid forever under your wing. Now I can fulfil this wish only in my dreams.

There in a dream, I can at least come face to face with you. I can be happy, I can smile naive smiles, I can chatter away freely.

For all this, I should be thankful to my dreams.

注　释

　　《梦》是巴金写于 1941 年 8 月 3 日
的一篇优美散文，后编入他的散文集
《龙·虎·狗》中。

　　①"至人"在古代指思想道德达到最高境界的人，现
译为 a virtuous man。也可译为 a man of the highest
virtue 或 a man of moral integrity 等。

　　②"在你的房间里，在我的房间里"意即"一回儿在你
的房间里，一回儿在我的房间里"，故译为 You talked to
me now in your room，now in my room。

　　③"武戏"指京剧中的武打场面，英译时应在 the
fighting scents 后面加上 of a Peking opera。

　　④"没有挂虑地微笑"意即"天真的微笑"，故译为
smiled naive smiles。

　　⑤"长夜在滴滴声中进行"有时间过得很慢、很沉闷
的含义。现全句译为 The long night wore on amidst its
dripping sound，其中 to wear on 是英语成语，用来指时间
"缓缓消逝"或"慢慢地挨过"。

　　⑥"在你的庇荫下"译为 under your wing，是英语成
语，意同 under your protection and care。

《激流》总序①

巴　金

　　几年前我流了眼泪读完托尔斯泰小说《复活》,曾经在扉页上写了一句话:"生活本身就是一个悲剧。"

　　事实并不是这样。生活并不是一个悲剧。它是一个"搏斗"。我们生活来做什么?或者说我们为什么要有这生命?罗曼·罗兰的回答是"为的是来征服它"②。我认为他说得不错。

　　我有了生命以来,在这个世界上虽然仅仅经历了二十几个寒暑,但是这短短的时期也并不是白白度过的。这其间我也曾看见了不少的东西,知道了不少的事情。我的周围是无边的黑暗③,但是我并不孤独,并不绝望。我无论在什么地方总看见那一股生活的激流在动荡,在创造它自己的道路,通过乱山碎石中间。

　　这激流永远动荡着,并不曾有一个时候停止过,而且它也不能够停止;没有什么东西可以阻止它。在它的途中,它也曾发射出种种的水花,这里面有爱,有恨,有欢乐,也有痛苦。这一切造成了奔腾的一股激流,具着排山之势④,向着唯一的海流去。这唯一的海是什么,而且什么时候它才可以流到这海里，就没有人能够确定地知道了。

　　我跟所有其余的人一样，生活在这世界上，是为着来征服生活。我也曾参加在这个"搏斗"里面。我有我的爱，有我的恨，我的欢乐，也有我的痛苦。但是我并没有失去我的信仰：对于生活的信仰。我的生活还不会结束，我也不知道在前面还有什么东西等着我⑤。然而我对于将来却也有一点概念。因为过去并不是一个沉默的哑子，它会告诉我们一些事情。

　　在这里我所要展开给读者看的乃是过去十多年生活的一幅图画。自然这里只有生活的一小部分，但已经可以看见那一股由爱与恨、欢乐与受苦所组织成的生活的激流是如何地在动荡了。我不是一个说教者，所以我不能够明确地指出一条路来，但是读者自己可以在里面去找它。

　　有人说过，路本没有，因为走的人多了，便成了一条路。又有人说路是有的，正因为有了路才有许多人走。谁是谁非，我不想判断。我还年轻，我还要活下去，我还要征服生活。我知道生活的激流是不会停止的，且看它把我载到什么地方去！

Preface to the *Torrent* Trilogy

Ba Jin

Several years ago, after I finished reading Leo Tolstoy's *Resurrection* with tears in my eyes, I wrote on its title page, "Life itself is a tragedy".

However, that is not how things are, for life is not a tragedy, but a "struggle". What do we live for? Or why do we live this life at all? The answer given by Romain Rolland is "to conquer life". I think he is right.

Ever since I was born, I have passed no more than twenty odd summers in this world, but this short period of time has not been spent for nothing at all. I have since seen a lot of things and come to know a lot of things. Though it is all darkness around me, I have never felt lonely, nor have I ever given up hope. Everywhere I go, I always see the torrent of life tumbling along to open up its way through a confused mass of mountains and rocks.

This torrent is always surging ahead; it has never stopped for a single moment and will never stop. Nothing whatever can hold it up. While on its way, it sometimes throws clouds of spray into the air embodying love and hate, and happiness and sorrow. All that makes up the tumultuous torrent rushing with terrific force towards the only sea. No one knows for sure what that only sea is and when the torrent is going to empty into it.

Like everybody else, I live in this world for the purpose of conquering life. I have also taken part in the "struggle". I have my own love and hate, and happiness and sorrow. But I have never lost my faith — a faith in life. There is still some way to go before my life runs out, and I do not know what the future has in store for me. Nevertheless, I am not without some idea of what the future is like because the past, being no silent mute, will give me some hint.

What I unfold here in the Trilogy before my readers is a picture of life of the past ten odd years. Of course it reflects only a small section of life, but enough, however, to afford a glimpse of the turbulent torrent of life with its love and hate, happiness and sorrow. I am no religious preacher, so I cannot point out a definite way out. Readers may here find a way out for themselves.

Some say that there is at first no road at all and that a road is created simply by the treading of passers-by. Others say that there is at first already a road available before more and more people come to walk on it. I do not want to judge who are right or who are wrong. I am still young, I want to live on, I want to conquer life. I know the torrent of life will never stop. Let's see where it is going to carry me !

注　释

这篇散文是作者为自己创作的小说
《激流三部曲》(《家》、《春》、《秋》)所写
的序。

① 标题译为 Preface to the *Torrent* Trilogy，其中
Trilogy 是译者增添的词，用来说明文章是"三部曲"的
"总"序。

② "为的是来征服它"引自罗曼·罗兰关于法国大革
命的剧本《爱与死的搏斗》。

③ "无边的黑暗"译为 all darkness，其中 all 作 complete 解，是常见的搭配。

④ "具着排山之势"不宜直译。现意译为 with terrific
force，其中 terrific 作 very great 解。

⑤ "我也不知道在前面还有什么东西等着我"译为
and I do not know what the future has in store for me，其
中短语 in store for 作 waiting 或 about to happen 解。

做 一 个 战 士

巴　　金

一个年轻的朋友写信问我："应该做一个什么样的人？"我回答他："做一个战士。"

另一个朋友问我："怎样对付生活①？"我仍旧答道："做一个战士。"

《战士颂》的作者曾经写过这样的话：

"我激荡在这绵绵不息、滂沱四方的生命洪流中，我就应该追逐这洪流，而且追过它，自己去造更广、更深的洪流。"

"我如果是一盏灯，这灯的用处便是照彻那多量的黑暗。我如果是海潮，便要鼓起波涛②去洗涤海边一切陈腐的积物。"

这一段话很恰当地写出了战士的心情③。

在这个时代，战士是最需要的。但是这样的战士并不一定要持枪上战场。他的武器也不一定是枪弹。他的武器还可以是知识、信仰和坚强的意志。他并不一定要流仇敌的

116

血,却能更有把握地致敌人的死命④。

战士是永远追求光明的。他并不躺在晴空下享受阳光⑤,却在暗夜里燃起火炬,给人们照亮道路,使他们走向黎明⑥。驱散黑暗,这是战士的任务。他不躲避黑暗,却要面对黑暗,跟躲藏在阴影里的魑魅、魍魉搏斗。他要消灭它们而取得光明。战士是不知道妥协的。他得不到光明便不会停止战斗。

战士是永远年轻的。他不犹豫,不休息。他深入人丛中,找寻苍蝇、毒蚊等等危害人类的东西⑦。他不断地攻击它们,不肯与它们共同生存在一个天空下面。对于战士,生活就是不停的战斗。他不是取得光明而生存,便是带着满身伤痕而死去。在战斗中力量只有增长,信仰只有加强。在战斗中给战士指路的是"未来","未来"给人以希望和鼓舞。战士永远不会失去青春的活力。

战士是不知道灰心与绝望的。他甚至在失败的废墟上,还要堆起破碎的砖石重建九级宝塔。任何打击都不能击破战士的意志。只有在死的时候他才闭上眼睛。

战士是不知道畏缩的。他的脚步很坚定。他看定目标,便一直向前走去。他不怕被绊脚石摔倒,没有一种障碍能使他改变心思。假象绝不能迷住战士的眼睛,支配战士的行动的是信仰。他能够忍受一切艰难、痛苦,而达到他所选定的目标。除非他死,人不能使他放弃工作。

这便是我们现在需要的战士。这样的战士并不一定具有超人的能力⑧。他是一个平凡的人。每个人都可以做战士,只要他有决心。所以我用"做一个战士"的话来激励那些在徬徨、苦闷中的年轻朋友。

Be a Fighter

Ba Jin

A young friend of mine asked me in a letter, "What kind of man should I be?" My answer was, "Be a fighter."

Another friend of mine inquired, "How should I live my life?" Again my answer was, "Be a fighter."

The author of *In Praise of the Fighter* says:

Riding on the ceaseless rushing torrent of life, I should pursue and overtake it so as to create an even greater and deeper torrent of my own.

If I were a lamp, it would be my duty to light up thick darkness. If I were the sea tide, I would marshal rolling waves to cleanse the beach of all accumulated filth.

This quotation reflects aptly the state of mind of a fighter.

Fighters are badly needed in our time. But such fighters do not necessarily go to the battlefield gun in

118

hand. Their weapons are not necessarily bullets. Their weapons may be knowledge, faith and strong will. They can bring the enemy sure death without drawing his blood.

A fighter is always in pursuit of light. Instead of basking in the sunshine under a clear sky, he holds a burning torch in the darkness of night to illuminate people's way so that they can continue their journey till they see the dawn of a new day. It is the task of a fighter to dispel darkness. Instead of shirking darkness, he braves it and fights the hidden demons and monsters therein. He is determined to wipe them out and win light. He knows no compromise. He will keep on fighting until he wins light.

A fighter is perennially young. He is never irresolute or inactive. He plunges deep into teeming crowds in search of such vermin as flies and venomous mosquitoes. He will fight them relentlessly and refuse to coexist with them under the same sky. To him, life means nothing but continuous fighting. He either survives by winning light, or perishes with his body covered all over with cuts and bruises. Fighting just serves to increase his stamina and strengthen his faith. In the course of the struggle, it is the "future" that serves as the beacon light to him; the "future" gives people hope and inspiration. He will never lose his youthful vigour.

A fighter will never lose heart or despair. He will pile up broken pieces of brick and stone to rebuilt a nine-story pagoda on the ruins of failure. No blows will ever break his will. He will never close his eyes until he has breathed his last.

A fighter is always fearless. His steps are firm. Once he has settled on an objective, he will press right ahead. He is never afraid of being tripped by a stumbling block. No obstacles will ever make him change his mind. His eyes will never be hoodwinked by false appearances. His actions are guided by faith. He can endure any hardships or sufferings while striving to attain his chosen objective. He will never abandon work as long as he is alive.

This is the kind of fighter we now need. He is not necessarily possessed of superhuman capability. He is just an ordinary person. Anyone can be a fighter so long as he has the determination. Hence a few words of mine about "being a fighter" to encourage those young people who wander about in a depressed state, not knowing which way to go.

注　释

《做一个战士》是现代著名作家巴
金写于 1938 年的一篇杂文。时值抗战
初期，文章表达了作者自己的高昂思想
情怀和对青年们的殷切期望。

①"怎样对付生活？"意即"怎样生活？"，故译为 How
should I live my life?

②"鼓起波涛"中的"鼓起"意即"集结"或"动员"，
因此"鼓起波涛"译为 marshal rolling waves。

③"战士的心情"译为 the state of mind of a fighter
或 the frame of mind of a fighter 均可。

④"并不一定要流仇敌的血，却能更有把握地致敌人
的死命"译为 can bring the enemy sure death without
drawing his blood，其中 the enemy 在指"敌军"、"敌国"、
"敌对势力"时是集合名词（collective noun），动词用复数
或单数均可。"仇敌的血"可译为 his blood、their blood 或
its blood。

⑤"躺在晴空下享受阳光"译为 basking in the sunshine under a clear sky，其中 basking 除作"取暖"解外，

并有"舒适"、"享受"的含义。

⑥"走向黎明"译为 continue their journey till they see the dawn of a new day，其中 see 和 of a new day 均为添加成份，用以烘托原意。

⑦"危害人类的东西"译为 vermin，为复数，本指老鼠、虱子等害虫，意同 pests。

⑧"具有超人的能力"译为 is … possessed of super-human capability，其中 possessed of 为惯用配搭，与 in possession of 或 having 同义。

笑

雨声渐渐的住了,窗帘后隐隐的透进清光来。推开窗户一看,呀!凉云散了,树叶上的残滴,映著月儿,好似萤光千点①,闪闪烁烁的动着。——真没想到苦雨孤灯之后,会有这么一幅清美的图画②!

凭窗站了一会儿,微微的觉得凉意侵人。转过身来,忽然眼花缭乱,屋子里的别的东西,都隐在光云里;一片幽辉,只浸着墙上画中的安琪儿③。——这白衣的安琪儿,抱着花儿,扬著翅儿,向着我微微的笑。

"这笑容仿佛在那儿看见过似的,什么时候,我曾……"我不知不觉的便坐在窗口下想,——默默的想。

严闭的心幕,慢慢的拉开了,涌出五年前的一个印象。——一条很长的古道。驴脚下的泥,兀自滑滑的。田沟里的水,潺潺的流着。近村的绿树,都笼在湿烟里。弓儿似的新月,挂在树梢④。一边走着,似乎道旁有一个孩子,抱着一堆灿白的东西。驴儿过去了,无意中回头一看。——他抱着花儿,赤着脚儿,向着我微微的笑。

"这笑容又仿佛是那儿看过似的!"我仍是想——默默

123

的想⑤。

又现出一重心幕来，也慢慢的拉开了，涌出十年前的一个印象。——茅檐下的雨水，一滴一滴的落到衣上来；土阶边的水泡儿⑥，泛来泛去的乱转。门前的麦垅和葡萄架子，都濯得新黄嫩绿的非常鲜丽。——一会儿好容易雨晴了，连忙走下坡儿去。迎头看见月儿从海面上来了，猛然记得有件东西忘下了，站住了，回过头来。这茅屋里的老妇人——她倚着门儿，抱着花儿，向着我微微的笑。

这同样微妙的神情，好似游丝一般，飘飘漾漾的合了拢来，绾在一起。

这时心下光明澄静，如登仙界⑦，如归故乡。眼前浮现的三个笑容，一时融化在爱的调和里看不分明了。

Smile

Bing Xin

As the rain gradually ceased to patter, a glimmer of light began to filter into the room through the window curtain. I opened the window and looked out. Ah, the rain clouds had vanished and the remaining raindrops on the tree leaves glistened tremulously under the moonlight like myriads of fireflies. To think that there should appear before my eyes such a beautiful sight after the miserable rain on a lonely evening!

Standing at the window for a while, I felt a bit chilly. As I turned round, my eyes suddenly dazzled before the bright light and could not see things distinctly. Everything in the room was blurred by a haze of light except the angel in a picture on the wall. The angel in white was smiling on me with a bunch of flowers in his arms, his wings flapping.

"I seem to have seen the same smile before. When was that?..." Before I knew, I had sunk into a chair under the window, lost in meditation.

A scene of five years ago slowly unveiled before my mind's eye. It was a long ancient country road. The ground under my donkey's feet was slippery with mud. The water in the field ditches was murmuring. The green trees in the neighbouring village were shrouded in a mist. The crescent new moon looked as if hanging on the tips of the trees. As I passed along, I somewhat sensed the presence of a child by the roadside carrying something snow white in his arms. After the donkey had gone by, I happened to look back and saw the child, who was barefoot, looking at me smilingly with a bunch of flowers in his arms.

"I seem to have seen the same smile somewhere before ! " I was still thinking to myself.

Another scene, a scene of ten years ago, slowly unfolded before my mind's eye. Rainwater was falling drop by drop onto my clothes from the eaves of a thatched cottage. Beside the earthern doorstep, bubbles in puddles of rainwater were whirling about like mad. Washed by the rain, the wheat fields and grape trellises in front of the cottage door presented a picturesque scene of vivid yellow and tender green. After a while, it cleared up at long last and I hurried down the slope. Up ahead I saw the moon rising high above the sea. Suddenly it occurred to me that I had left something behind. When I stopped and turned round, my eyes fell on an old woman at her cottage door

126

smiling at me, a bunch of flowers in her arms.

The three subtle smiles, drifting in the air towards each other like gossamer, became interwoven.

At this moment all was bright, clear and calm in my heart. I felt as if I were ascending to heaven or on the way back to my hometown. In my mind's eye, the three smiling faces now merged into a harmonious whole of love and became indistinguishable.

注　释

这篇散文是我国著名女作家冰心
(1900—1999)的早期成名之作,于 1921
年 1 月发表在《小说月报》第一期上。冰
心的散文以秀丽典雅、纯真无邪著称。
她早期信奉"爱的哲学",泛爱宇宙中的
一切,尤其是对母亲、儿童和自然美的
爱。《笑》正体现了她的这种思想。她讴
歌超现实的"爱",也就是对当时社会的
黑暗和污浊的不满和失望。

①"萤光千点"译为 myriads of fireflies,比 thousands of fireflies 更切近美文 (belles lettres)。

②"真没想到……!"译为 To think that... ! 是英
语惯用句型,以感叹的语气表达某种想不到的事。

③"安琪儿"即"天使",是 angel 一词的音译。天使
为西方教堂所崇奉,其形象常为带翅膀的男性小孩。

④"弓儿似的新月,挂在树梢"译为 The crescent new
moon looked as if hanging on the tips of the trees,其中
looked as if 是增加的成分,变隐喻为明喻。

⑤"我仍是想——默默的想"译为 I was still thinking to myself。To think to oneself 是英语习惯用语，作"一个人暗自在想"解。

⑥"水泡儿"指雨水坑中的水泡儿，故译为 bubbles in puddles of rainwater，其中 in puddles of rainwater 原文中虽无其词，但却有其意。

⑦"仙界"指"极乐世界"，也可译为 the land of the divine。现译为 heaven，较简洁。

雨雪时候的星辰①

冰　心

　　寒暑表降到冰点下十八度的时候,我们也是在廊下睡觉。每夜最熟识的就是天上的星辰了。也不过只是点点闪烁的光明,而相看惯了,偶然不见,也有些想望与无聊②。

　　连夜雨雪,一点星光都看不见③。荷和我④拥衾对坐,在廊子的两角,遥遥谈话。

　　荷指着说⑤:"你看维纳斯(Venus)升起来了!"我抬头望时⑥,却是山路转折处⑦的路灯。我怡然一笑,也指着对山的一星灯火说:"那边是丘比特(Jupiter)呢!"

　　愈指愈多。松林中射来零乱的风灯,都成了满天星宿。真的,雪花隙里,看不出天空和森林的界限,将繁灯当作繁星,简直是抵得过⑧。

　　一念至诚的将假作真,灯光似乎都从地上飘起。这幻成的星光,都不移动,不必半夜梦醒时,再去追寻它们的位置。

　　于是雨雪寂寞之夜,也有了慰安了!

Stars on a Snowy Night

Bing Xin

The thermometer had dropped to 18 degrees below zero, but we still chose to sleep in the porch as usual. In the evening, the most familiar sight to me would be stars in the sky. Though they were a mere sprinkle of twinkling dots, yet I had become so accustomed to them that their occasional absence would bring me loneliness and ennui.

It had been snowing all night, not a single star in sight. My roommate and I, each wrapped in a quilt, were seated far apart in a different corner of the porch, facing each other and chatting away.

She exclaimed pointing to something afar, "Look, Venus is rising!" I looked up and saw nothing but a lamp round the bend in a mountain path. I beamed and said pointing to a tiny lamplight on the opposite mountain, "It's Jupiter over there!"

More and more lights came into sight as we kept pointing here and there. Lights from hurricane lamps flickering about in the pine forest created the scene of a star-studded sky. With the distinction between sky and forest obscured by snowflakes, the numerous lamp-lights now easily passed for as many stars.

Completely lost in a make-believe world, I seemed to see all the lamplights drifting from the ground. With the illusory stars hanging still overhead, I was spared the effort of tracing their positions when I woke up from my dreams in the dead of night.

Thus I found consolation even on a lonely snowy night!

注　释

《雨雪时候的星辰》是冰心的早期
抒情散文。文章赞美自然，想象精细，文
笔清新，充满诗情画意。

①　题目《雨雪时候的星辰》译为 Stars on a Snowy
Night。"雨雪"作"下雪"解，"雨"在此是动词，读音为 yù。

②　"无聊"译为 ennui，是英语常用文学语言，意即 a
feeling of boredom caused by a lack of excitement or activ-
ity。

③　"一点星光都看不见"译为 not a single star in
sight，是句中独立主格，和 not a single star being in sight
同。又译文用 s 押头韵，night 和 sight 押韵脚，有音韵美。

④　"荷和我……"译为 My roommate and I...，其中
用 My roommate（同寝之友）代替专门名词 He（荷），以免
外国读者把 He 读解为男性第三人称的代词。

⑤　"荷指着说……"不宜死译为 She said pointing her
finger at ...，因英语 to point one's finger at 有"指责"
的含义。

⑥　"我抬头望时"不宜逐字死译为 I raised my head to

take a look。译为 I looked up 即可。

⑦ "山路转折处"译为 round the bend in a mountain path。注意 bend 后面跟介词 in，属习惯用法。

⑧ "将繁灯当作繁星，简直是抵得过"译为 the numerous lamplights now easily passed for as many stars，其中短语 to pass for 的意思是"被看作"、"被当作"等。

我的父母之乡

冰　心

清晓的江头①，
　白雾茫茫；
是江南天气②，
　雨儿来了——
　　我只知道有蔚蓝的海，
　　却原来还有碧绿的江，
　　　这是我父母之乡！

繁星 156③

　　福建福州永远是我的故乡，虽然我不在那里生长，但它是我的父母之乡！

　　到今日为止，我这一生中只回去过两次。第一次是一九一一年，是在冬季。从严冷枯黄的北方归来④，看到展现在我眼前的青山碧水⑤，红花绿叶，使我惊讶而欢喜！我觉得我的生命的风帆，已从蔚蓝的海，驶进了碧绿的江。这天我们在闽江口从大船下到小船，驶到大桥头，来接我们的伯父堂兄们把我们包围了起来，他们用乡音和我的父母热烈地交谈。我的五岁的大弟弟悄悄地用山东话问我说："他们怎么都会说福州话？"因为从来在我们姐弟心里，福州话是最难懂难说的！

这以后的一年多的时间里，我们就过起了福州城市的生活。新年、元宵、端午、中秋……岁时节日，吃的玩的都是十分丰富而有趣。特别是灯节，那时我们家住在南后街，那里是灯市的街，元宵前后，"花市灯如昼"，灯影下人流潮涌，那光明绚丽的情景就说不尽了⑥。

第二次回去，是在一九五六年，也是在冬季。那时还没有鹰厦铁路，我们人大代表团是从江西坐汽车进去的。一路上红土公路，道滑如拭⑦，我还没有看见过土铺的公路，维修得这样平整的！这次我不但到了福州，还到了漳州、泉州、厦门、鼓浪屿……那是祖国的南疆了。在厦门前线，⑧我还从望远镜里看见了金门岛上的行人和牛，看得很清楚……

回忆中的情景很多，在此就不一一描写了。总之，我很喜欢我的父母之乡。那边是南国风光，山是青的，水是绿的，小溪流更是清可见底！院里四季都有花开。水果是从枇杷、荔枝、龙眼，一直吃到福桔！对一个孩子来说，还有什么比这个更惬意的呢？

我在故乡走的地方不多，但古迹、侨乡，到处可见，福建华侨，遍于天下⑨。我所到过的亚、非、欧、美各国都见到辛苦创业⑩的福建侨民，握手之余，情溢言表。在他们家里、店里，吃着福州菜，喝着茉莉花茶，使我觉得作为一个福建人是四海都有家的。

我的父母之乡是可爱的。有人从故乡来⑪，或是有朋友新近到福建去过，我都向他们问起福建的近况。他们说：福建比起二十多年前来，进步得不可辨认了。最近呢，农业科学化了，又在植树造林⑫，山岭田地更加郁郁葱葱了。他们都动员我回去看看，我何尝不想呢⑬？不但我想，在全世界的天涯海角，更不知有多少人在想！我愿和故乡的人，以及普天下的福建侨民，一同在精神和物质文明方面，把故乡建设得更美好⑭！

The Land of My Ancestors

Bing Xin

> *The River mouth at dawn,*
> *Behind a white haze of mist.*
> *'Tis southern climes,*
> *Behold, the rain is coming.*
> *I've seen the blue sea all along,*
> *Little aware of this green River.*
> *O the land of my ancestors!*

> —*Sparkling Stars*, 156

Fuzhou of Fujian Province will always be my old home. Though I was brought up elsewhere, Fuzhou is nonetheless the land of my ancestors!

As yet, I have been back to Fuzhou no more than twice in my lifetime. I made the first trip in the winter of 1911. Returned from the bitter cold North with its drab and dried up vegetation, I was amazed and delighted when greeted by the charming scenery of sapphire mountains

138

and emerald rivers as well as red flowers and green leaves. I felt the sailing boat of my life steering its way into the green River after leaving the blue sea behind. At the Minjiang River, we changed from the big ship to a small boat, which took us to Daqiaotou (Big Bridge), where we were met by Uncle and cousins. They gathered round us and talked warmly with my parents in the local dialect. Thereupon, my 5-year-old younger brother whispered in my ear with a Shandong accent, "How come they can all speak the Fuzhou dialect?" We had both thought that the Fuzhou dialect was indeed most difficult for anyone to learn.

From then on, we lived an urban life for more than a year in Fuzhou. During such festivals as Lunar New Year, Lantern, Dragon Boat and Mid-Autumn, we all celebrated the festivities with plenty of food and fun. Particular mention, however, should be made of the Lantern Festival when Nanhoujie, the street known for its lantern fair and also the street where we lived, became as bright as broad daylight at night with myriads of lanterns and streams of spectators. The splendor and magnificence of the scene is beyond all description.

I made the second visit in 1956, also in winter. As the Yingtan-Xiamen Railway had not yet been built, the NPC delegation, with myself as a member, had to go from Jiangxi Province by car. The highway from Jiangxi to

Fuzhou, paved with red soil, was as smooth as a mirror. It was the most level soil-paved highway I had ever seen. This time I visited not only Fuzhou, but also Zhangzhou, Quanzhou, Xiamen and Gulangyu—the southern frontiers of our country. At the Xiamen seaside, I could see clearly through a telescope pedestrians and cows on the Quemoy Islands.

My experiences of this trip, however, are too numerous to be recounted one by one here. Anyway, I deeply love Fuzhou, my ancestral home. Over there we have the typical southern scenery with blue mountains, green waters, limpid brooks... ! There in the courtyard we can always see some kind of flower in full bloom throughout the year. Fruits ranging from loquats, lichees, longans to tangerines are in plenty. Is there anything more palatable to a little child than these fruits?

I did not visit all the local attractions in Fuzhou. Everywhere we could find historical relics as well as villages and towns inhabited by relatives of overseas Chinese and returned overseas Chinese. Fujianese expatriates are found all over the world. They have mostly started from scratch by the sweat of their brow. When I met some of them on my visits to Asian, African, European and American countries, they all expressed warm feeling towards me while shaking my hand. As I ate Fuzhou food and sipped jasmine tea in their homes or shops, I felt that

140

being a Fujianese, I could make myself at home wherever I travelled in the world.

My ancestral home is so endearing. Whenever I meet somebody hailing from Fuzhou or a friend who has recently been there, I always inquire of them about the present conditions in Fujian. They all tell me that compared with two decades ago, Fujian has made so much progress that it is now almost beyond recognition. Recently I have learned that people there have gone in for scientific farming and afforestation so that green and luxuriant vegetation has appeared on all mountains and fields. People have been advising me to pay another visit to my old home. Yes, I am more than eager to do so. And so are my numerous fellow townsmen in all corners of the world. I hope that together with all the people in my home town as well as all overseas Chinese from Fujian, I can do my bit to make a still better place of my ancestral home, both materially and culturally.

注　释

冰心出生后不久就远离故乡福州，
以后只回去过两次。她这篇短文写于
1982 年 3 月 29 日，以轻倩的笔调，抒写
有关故乡和童年的回忆，并对当前故乡
的建设表达了深切的关怀。

①“江头”指闽江入海处，故译 the River mouth。

②“江南天气”译为 southern climes，其中 climes 是
英语诗歌用语，常用复数，意同 climate。

③《繁星》是冰心 1923 年出版的第一部诗集，收小诗
凡 164 首。现将《繁星》译为 Sparkling Stars。

④“从严冷枯黄的北方归来”译为 Returned from the
bitter cold North with its drab and dried up vegetation，其
中 Returned 是不及物动词 return 的过去分词，在此作形
容词。又 vegetation 是译文中的添加成分，作“草木”、“植
被”解。

⑤“青山碧水”译为 sapphire mountains and emerald
rivers，其中 sapphire 和 emerald 均为实物颜色词，原意分
别为“蓝宝石”和“绿宝石”。译文用这两个实物颜色词是

142

为了增加修辞效果。

⑥ "就说不尽了"意即"就难以形容了"，故译 beyond description，为英语成语。

⑦ "道滑如拭"意即"道路平坦"，译为 The highway...was as smooth as a mirror，其中 mirror 为英语常用有关比喻。

⑧ "在厦门前线"译为 At the Xiamen seaside，其中用 seaside 代替 frontline，是为便于国外读者理解。

⑨ "福建华侨，遍于天下"译为 Fujianese expatriates are found all over the world，其中 expatriates 的意思是"移居国外者"、"离乡背井者"。此句也可译为 Overseas Chinese from Fujian。

⑩ "辛苦创业"译为 have started from scratch by the sweat of their brow，其中 to start from scratch 和 by the sweat of one's brow 均为英语成语，分别作"白手起家"和"靠自己辛勤劳动"解。

⑪ "有人从故乡来"也可译为 somebody who has come from Fuzhou，但不如 somebody hailing from Fuzhou 简洁，其中 to hail 作"来自"解。

⑫ "农业科学化了，又在植树造林"译为 people there have gone in for scientific farming and afforestation，其中 to go in for 是成语，作"致力于"、"从事于"解，在译文中是添加成分，原文虽无其词，而有其意。

⑬ "我何尝不想呢"译为 Yes，I am more than eager to do so，其中 more than 作 very 或 extremely 解。

⑭ "把故乡建设得更美好"译为 do my bit to make a

143

still better place of my ancestral home，其中 to do one's bit 为成语，作"尽自己一份力量"、"作一份贡献"解，在译文中是添加成分，原文虽无其词，而有其意。

祖父和灯火管制①

冰　心

一九一一年秋,我们从山东烟台回到福州老家去。在
还乡的路上,母亲和父亲一再地嘱咐我②,"回到福州住在
大家庭里,不能再像野孩子③似的了,一切都要小心。对长
辈们不能没大没小的。祖父是一家之主,尤其要尊敬……"

到了福州,在大家庭里住了下来,我觉得我在归途中的
担心是多余的。祖父、伯父母、叔父母④和堂姐妹兄弟⑤,都
没有把我当作野孩子,大家也都很亲昵平等,并没有什么
"规矩"。我还觉得我们这个大家庭是几个小家庭的很松散
的组合⑥。每个小家庭都是各住各的,各吃各的,各自有自
己的亲戚和朋友,比如说,我们就各自有自己的"外婆
家"⑦!

就在这一年,也许是第二年吧,福州有了电灯公司。我
们这所大房子里也安上电灯,这在福州也是一件新鲜事,我
们这班孩子跟着安装的工人们满房子跑,非常地兴奋欢
喜!我记得这电灯是从房顶上吊下来的,每间屋子都有一
盏,厅堂上和客室里的是五十支光,卧房里的光小一些,厨
房里的就更小了。我们这所大房子里至少也有五六十盏灯,

第一夜亮起来时，真是灯火辉煌，我们孩子们都拍手欢呼！

但是总电门是安在祖父的屋里的。祖父起得很早也睡得很早⑧，每晚九点钟就上床了。他上床之前，就把电闸关上，于是整个大家庭就是黑沉沉的一片！

我们刚回老家⑨，父母亲和他们的兄弟妯娌⑩都有许多别情要叙，我们一班弟兄姐妹，也在一起玩得正起劲⑪，都很少在晚九点以前睡的。为了防备⑫这骤然的黑暗，于是每晚在九点以前，每个小家庭都在一两间屋里，点上一盏捻得很暗的煤油灯。一到九点，电灯一下子都灭了，这几盏煤油灯便都捻亮了，大家相视而笑，又都在灯下谈笑玩耍。

只有在这个时候，我才体会到我们这个大家庭是一个整体，而祖父是一家之主！

Grandpa and Nightly Blackout

Bing Xin

In the autumn of 1911, we returned from Yantai of Shandong Province to our native place Fuzhou. While on the way, my parents warned me again and again, "Since we'll be living in a big family in Fuzhou, remember always to behave properly and never act like a naughty child. Show respect for your elders, particularly your grandpa, who is head of the family...."

After settling down in the big family in Fuzhou, however, I found that my previous worries on the way turned out to be unfounded. My grandpa, uncles, aunties and cousins never thought me a naughty child. We treated each other lovingly and equally. There never existed anything like "family rules of good behaviour". I also found that the big family was a loose community of several smaller ones, which lived and ate separately. They each had their own relatives and friends, for example, their own in-laws.

That year, or the year after, Fuzhou began to have

147

its own power company and electric lights were to be installed in our big house too. That was something new in our home town. We kids, wild with excitement and joy, ran here and there in the house at the heels of the electricians. Each room, I remember, had an electric lamp hanging from the ceiling. The drawing room had a 50-watt bulb; the bedrooms each a lower-wattage one; the kitchens each an even-lower-wattage one. The whole big house at least had a total of some 60 electric lamps. The first evening when they were turned on, the whole house was suddenly ablaze with lights. We kids clapped with joy.

The master switch was fixed in grandpa's room. Grandpa, who kept early hours, would switch off all the lights when he went to bed at 9 o'clock in the evening, thus plunging the whole big house into deep darkness.

Having just set foot in our old home, we seldom slept before 9 o'clock in the evening. For it was but natural that after the long separation, my parents enjoyed hearty chats about the old days with their brothers and in-laws, and we kids of the younger generation played about together to our heart's content. Hence, in anticipation of the sudden blackout at 9 o'clock, each small family would get a dimly-lit kerosene lamp ready in a couple of their rooms. No sooner had the big house been blacked out on the hour than we turned up the wicks of all the kerosene

148

lamps. And, looking and smiling at each other, we would continue to chat and play merrily by the light of the kerosene lamps.

It was then that I realized what a complete whole our big family was, with grandpa as its head.

注　释

　　《祖父和灯火管制》,写于 1982 年 7
月 22 日,是冰心回忆故乡和童年的又一
篇深情佳作。文章娓娓述来,形象地再
现了童年时代的家乡生活片断。

　　① "灯火管制" 本指战时防空停电,作者用它指每夜
定时关灯,有些俏皮。译文结合文章内容增添 Nightly 一
词。在英语中, blackout 一词既可指 "战时灯火管制", 也
可指一般的 "停电", 译文所指是后者。又 blackout 也可换
用 power cut 或 power failure 等。
　　② "一再地嘱咐我" 意即 "一再地告诫我", 译为
warned me again and again, 比 enjoined (或 exhorted) me
again and again 通俗。
　　③ "野孩子" 不宜按字面直译为 wild child。现译为
naughty child, 其中 naughty 常用来指孩子 "不听话"。
　　④ "伯父母、叔父母" 在英语以 uncles 和 aunties 两词
概括即可。
　　⑤ "堂姐妹兄弟" 在英语以 cousins 一词概括即可。
　　⑥ "几个小家庭的很松散的组合" 译为 a loose com-

munity of several smaller ones，其中不妨以 community
代替 combination；community 为近代英语所常用。

⑦"外婆家"指由婚姻而结成的亲戚，如岳父母、妻子
的兄弟姐妹等等，现以 in-laws 一词概括之。

⑧"起得很早也睡得很早"在英语有现成的表达：
kept early hours。如逐字直译为 got up early and went to
bed early 似欠简洁。

⑨"刚回老家"译为 Having set foot in our old home，
其中 set foot in 是成语，作"进入"、"踏上"解。

⑩"娌偄"指兄弟的妻子，以 in-laws 表达即可。

⑪"正起劲"意同"尽情地"，故译 to our heart's con-
tent。

⑫"防备"译为 in anticipation of，意即"预计到……
（而采取措施）"。

话 说 短 文

冰 心

也许是我的精、气、神都不足吧①，不但自己写不出长的东西，我读一本刊物时，也总是先挑短的看，不论是小说、散文或是其他的文学形式，最后才看长的。

我总觉得，凡是为了非倾吐不可而写的作品，都是充满了真情实感的。反之，只是为写作而写作，如②上之为应付编辑朋友③，下之为多拿稿费，这类文章大都是尽量地往长里写，结果是即便有一点点的感情，也被冲洗到水分太多④、淡而无味的地步。

当由一个人物，一桩事迹，一幅画面而发生的真情实感，向你袭来的时候，它就像一根扎到你心尖上⑤的长针，一阵卷到你面前的怒潮，你只能用最真切、最简练的文字，才能描画出你心尖上的那一阵剧痛和你面前的那一霎惊惶！

我们伟大的祖国，是有写短文的文学传统的⑥。那部包括上下数千年的《古文观止》，"上起东周，下迄明末，共选辑文章 220 篇"有几篇是长的⑦？如杜牧的《阿房宫赋》，韩愈的《祭十二郎文》⑧等等，哪一篇不是短而充满了真情实感？今人的巴金的《随感录》，不也是一个实例吗⑨？

A Chat about Short Essays

Bing Xin

Perhaps due to my failing energies, not only have I refrained from writing anything long, but also, in reading a magazine, for example, I usually finish its shorter pieces of writing first, be they fiction, prose or any other forms of literature, before going on to the longer ones.

I always believe that anything written with an irresistible inner urge to unbosom oneself must be full of genuine feelings. On the contrary, if one writes simply for the sake of writing—say, to humour one's editor friends, or worse still, to earn more remuneration, one will most probably make his writings unnecessarily long until they become, despite what little feelings they may contain, inflated and wishy-washy.

When true emotions aroused by a person, an event or a scene come upon you like a pin pricking your heart or an angry tide surging threateningly before you, all you can do is use the most vivid and succinct language to describe the severe pain in your heart or the momentary feeling of panic caused by the angry tide.

Our great motherland is known for its literary tradition of short essays. Do you find anything unduely long in *A Treasury of Best Ancient Chinese Prose* with its 220 essays selected from a period of several thousand years in ancient China from the Eastern Zhou Dynasty down until the end of the Ming Dynasty? Aren't the essays in it, like Du Mu's *Rhapsody on Epang Palace* and Han Yu's *An Elegiac Address to My Nephew Shi'erlang*, all short and yet full of true feelings? Isn't *A Collection of Random Thoughts* by Ba Jin, our contemporary, another like example of pithy writing?

注　释

《话说短文》是冰心写于 1988 年 1 月的随笔。作者一针见血地指出"为写作而写作"的不正之风以及崇尚长文的时弊。

① "也许是我的精、气、神都不足吧" 也可译为 Perhaps due to deficiency in my mental and physical energy，但不如 Perhaps due to my failing energies 简洁。"精、气、神" 在文中显得俏皮，意即 "精力"，故译 energies 即可。

② "如" 即 "比如说"，译为 say。英语中举例时常用 say 这个字，和 for example 同义。

③ "为应付编辑朋友" 的意思是 "迁就编辑朋友之约或要求"，故译为 to humour one's editor-friends。英语 to humour 作 to gratify by compliance 解。

④ "也被冲洗到水分太多" 意即 "变得夸张空洞"，故译为 become inflated。

⑤ "你心尖上" 即 "你的内心深处" 或 "你的心头"，译为 your heart 即可，不宜按字面译为 the tip of your heart。

⑥ "我们伟大的祖国,是有写短文的文学传统的"也可译为 Our great motherland has a literary tradition of short essays,但不如 Our great motherland is known for its literary tradition of short essays 灵活顺口。

⑦ "……有几篇是长的?" 译为 Do you find anything unduely long...,其中 unduely 是添加成份,作 "不适当地" 或 "过分地" 解,原文虽无其词而有其意。

⑧ "《祭十二郎文》" 译为 An Elegiac Address to My Nephew Shi'erlang,其中 My Nephew 是为交待 "十二郎" 何许人而添加的成份,有助于读者的理解,属释义性译文。

⑨ "……不也是一个实例吗?" 译为 Isn't ... another like example of pithy writing?,其中 like 和 of pithy writing 均为添加成份,原文虽无其词而有其意。

路畔的蔷薇

郭　沫　若

　　清晨往松林里去散步，我在林荫路畔发见了一束被人遗弃了的蔷薇。蔷薇的花色还是鲜艳的，一朵紫红，一朵嫩红，一朵是病黄的象牙色中带着几分血晕①。

　　我把蔷薇拾在手里了。

　　青翠的叶上已经凝集着细密的露珠，这显然是昨夜被人遗弃了的。

　　这是可怜的少女受了薄幸的男子的欺绐？还是不幸的青年受了轻狂的妇人的玩弄呢？

　　昨晚上甜蜜的私语，今朝的冷清的露珠……②

　　我把蔷薇拿到家里来了，我想找个花瓶来供养它。

　　花瓶我没有③，我在一只墙角上寻着了一个断了颈子的盛酒的土瓶。

　　——蔷薇哟，我虽然不能供养你以春酒，但我要供养你以清洁的流泉，清洁的素心。你在这破土瓶中虽然不免要凄凄寂寂地飘零④，但比遗弃在路旁被人践踏了的好罢？

Wayside Roses

Guo Moruo

Rambling through a pine forest early in the morning,
I came across a bunch of forsaken roses lying by the shady
wayside. They were still fresh in colour. One was pur-
plish-red, another pink, still another a sickly ivory-yellow slightly tinged with blood-red.

I picked them up in my hand.

The numerous fine dewdrops on the fresh green
leaves clearly showed that the roses had just been cast
away the previous night.

Were they pitiful maidens deflowered by fickle men?
Or were they unlucky young men. fooled by frivolous
women?

Last night's whispers of love; this morning's drops of
cold dew ...

I brought the roses home and tried to find a flower
vase to keep them in.

Flower vase I had none, but I did find in a nook of my
room an empty earthern wine bottle with its neck broken.

158

—O dear roses, though unable to treat you to spring wine, I could offer you limpid spring water and my sincere pure heart. Wouldn't it be better for you to wither away in solitude in this broken earthen wine bottle than to lie abandoned by the roadside and be trodden down upon?

注　释

　　《路畔的蔷薇》是郭沫若(1892—
1978)的早期著名小品，玲珑剔透，饶有
诗意，堪称一首优美的散文诗。

　　①"一朵是病黄的象牙色中带着几分血晕"译为 a
sickly ivory-yellow slightly tinged with blood-red，其中
sickly 作"病态的"解。又，ivory-yellow 和 blood-red 的结
构都是"实物颜色词＋基本颜色词"，为英语颜色词的常见
形式。

　　②"昨晚上甜蜜的私语，今朝的冷清的露珠……"译
为 Last night's whispers of love；this morning's drops of
cold dew...，两个英语并列词组，在用词结构上前后完全
对称，与原文形似，并与原文有同样的言外之意。又，"昨
晚"在这里虽指过去的过去，但仍译为 last night，不译为
the previous night，以求语言生动，这是英语中常见的灵
活用法。

　　③"花瓶我没有"译为 Flower vase I had none，等于
I had no flower vase，其中 none 作形容词用，修饰前面的
Flower vase。这种用法常见于文学语体中，如：Time and

160

money he had none。

④ "飘零" 意即 "凋落"，故译 to wither away。

夕　暮

郭　沫　若

　　我携着①三个孩子在屋后草场中嬉戏着的时候，夕阳正烧着海上的天壁②，眉痕的新月已经出现在鲜红的云③缝里了。

　　草场中牧放着的几条黄牛，不时曳着悠长的鸣声④，好像在叫它们的主人快来牵它们回去。

　　我们的两匹母鸡和几只鸡雏⑤，先先后后地从邻寺的墓地里跑回来了。

　　立在厨房门内的孩子们的母亲向门外的沙地上撒了一握米粒出来。

　　母鸡们咯咯咯地叫起来了⑥，鸡雏们也啁啁地争食起来了。

　　——"今年的成绩真好呢，竟养大了十只⑦。"

　　欢愉的音波，在金色的暮霭中游泳。

Dusk

Guo Moruo

While my three kids, accompanied by myself, were frolicking about on the meadow behind our house, the sky above the distant edge of the sea was aglow with the setting sun and the crescent new moon was already peeping out from behind the scarlet clouds.

A few cows grazing on the pasture let out a long drawn-out moo now and then as if urging their master to lead them home as quickly as possible.

Our two mother hens and their baby chicks were scurrying homewards one after another from the graveyard of the nearby monastery.

The kids' mother, standing by the kitchen door, sprinkled a handful of rice onto the sandy ground in the open.

At the clucking of the hens, the chicks scrambled for the feed, chirping.

"We've done quite well this year, with ten chicks growing fast," beamed my wife.

The joyous sound wave drifted through the golden evening mist.

注　释

《夕暮》是郭沫若的早期小品,充满
诗情画意,堪称一篇玲珑剔透的美文。
文章记述的是真情真事,字里行间流露
出热爱生活的感情。

① "我携着" 译为 accompanied by myself,其中 myself 比 me 更确切,不但读来顺口,且能加强语气,突出
"亲自" 的含义。

② "海上的天壁" 指 "海边的上空",不宜直译,现以
加字法处理:the sky above the distant edge of the sea。

③ "鲜红的云" 译为 the scarlet clouds。颜色词 scarlet 在此比 red 更确切,因 scarlet 的意思是 very bright
red,与原文 "鲜红" 一致。

④ "曳着悠长的鸣声" 中的 "曳" 作 "拖" 或 "拉" 解,
结合上下文译为 let out,意同 utter(发出),为英语常用成
语。又 "鸣声" 译为 moo,为英语拟声词,指牛的叫声,相当
于汉语的 "哞"。

⑤ "我们的两匹母鸡和几只鸡雏" 译为 Our two moth-
er hens and their baby chicks,其中 mother 和 baby 是为

加强译文效果而添加的定语,前者作"母"解,后者作"幼小"解。

⑥"母鸡们咯咯地叫起来了"译为 At the clucking of the hens,其中介词 At 表示时间,即先后两个动作很快相继发生, 或后面一个动作是前面一个动作的反应。在此指母鸡一叫,小鸡立即争食。

⑦"'今年的成绩真好呢,竟养大了十只'"译为 "We've done quite well this year, with ten chicks growing fast," beamed my wife,其中 beamed my wife(妻微笑地或欣喜地说)是添加成分,原文虽无其词而有其意。

白　发

郭　沫　若

　　许久储蓄在心里的诗料①，今晨在理发店里又浮上了心来了。——

　　你年青的，年青的，远隔河山的②姑娘哟，你的名姓我不曾知道，你恕我只能这样叫你了。

　　那回是春天的晚上吧？你替我剪了发，替我刮了面，替我盥洗了③，又替我涂了香膏。

　　你最后替我分头的时候，我在镜中看见你替我拔去了一根白发④。

　　啊，你年青的，年青的，远隔河山的姑娘哟，飘泊者自从那回离开你后又飘泊了三年，但是你的慧心⑤替我把青春留住了。

The White Hair

Guo Moruo

My long pent-up poetic emotion emerged again this morning at a hairdresser's.

O young lady, you young lady of the distant land! Excuse me for addressing you as "young lady ", for your name is still unknown to me.

It was probably on a spring evening. You cut my hair, shaved my face, gave me a shampoo and applied some vanishing cream.

Finally, in the mirror I saw you plucking out a white hair from my head while parting my hair.

O young lady, you young lady of the distant land, I have been leading a wandering life for another three years since I saw you last, but it is your feeling heart that has been the cause of my sustained youth.

注　释

《白发》是郭沫若的早期小品，热情奔放，玲珑而富有诗意，是一首优美的散文诗。

① "许久储蓄在心里的诗料" 译为 My long pent-up poetic emotion。"储蓄在心里" 意即 "被抑制的"，故译为 pent-up。"诗料" 即 "诗情"，故译为 poetic emotion。

② "远隔河山的" 不必按字面直译，现按 "遥远的" 意思译为 of the distant（或 remote）land。

③ "替我舆洗了" 在此指 "替我洗了头"，故译为 gave me a shampoo。

④ "拔去了一根白发" 译为 plucking out a white hair from my head，其中 hair 作可数名词用。

⑤ "慧心" 在这里可按 "温柔体贴"、"富有同情的心" 等含义译为 feeling heart 或 tender heart。

水　墨　画①

郭　沫　若

天空一片灰暗，没有丝毫的日光。

海水的蓝色浓得惊人②，舐岸的微波吐出群鱼喋喋的声韵。

这是暴风雨欲来时的先兆③。

海中的岛屿和乌木的雕刻一样静凝着了。

我携着中食的饭匣向沙岸上走来，在一只泊系着的渔舟里面坐着。

一种淡白无味的凄凉的情趣——我把饭匣打开，又闭上了④。

回头望见松原里的一座孤寂的火葬场⑤。红砖砌成的高耸的烟囱口上，冒出了一笔灰白色的飘忽的轻烟⑥……

An Inkwash Painting

Guo Moruo

The sky was a sheet of murky grey, completely devoid of sunlight.

The sea was a ghastly dark blue. The gentle waves licking at the shore gave forth a humming sound like that of fish in shoals.

All that foreboded a storm.

Some isles in the sea stood quiet and still like ebony sculptures.

I walked towards the sandy beach carrying my lunch-box and then sat inside a fishing boat moored at the seashore.

What an insipid and dreary scene! I opened the lunch-box only to have it covered up again.

Looking back, I caught sight of a lonely crematorium looming out of a pine wood. Its towering red-brick chimney was giving off wisps of greyish smoke.

注　释

《水墨画》是郭沫若的早期小品，玲
珑剔透，是他异乡生活片断的直接记录。

①"水墨画"除译 An Inkwash Painting 外，也可译为
An Ink-and-Wash Painting。

②"海水的蓝色浓得惊人"译为 The sea was a ghastly dark blue，其中 ghastly 的意思是"可怕的"，但兼有
"不正常"的含义。

③"这是暴风雨欲来时的先兆"译为 All that foreboded a storm。"先兆"也可译为 foretold，但不如 foreboded 确切，因后者一般都针对不好的事物。

④"又闭上了"译为 only to have it covered up again，
其中 only（用在不定式前）往往作"结果却"或"却又"解。

⑤"望见松原里的一座孤寂的火葬场"译为 caught
sight of a lonely crematorium looming out of a pine wood，
其中用 looming 代替 standing 等能较好地表达"赫然耸
现"的含义。

⑥"冒出了……轻烟"译为 giving off ... smoke，其
中 to give off 是成语，意同 to send out, to emit 等。

172

墓

郭　沫　若

　　昨朝我一人在松林里徘徊，在一株老松树下戏筑了一座砂丘①。

　　我说，这便是我自己的坟墓了②。

　　我便拣了一块白石来写上了我自己的名字，把来做了墓碑。

　　我在墓的两旁还移种了两株稚松③把它伴守。

　　我今朝回想起来，又一人走来凭吊④。

　　但我已经走遍了这莽莽的松原，我的坟墓究竟往那儿去了呢？

　　啊，死了的我昨日的尸骸哟⑤，哭墓的是你自己的灵魂，我的坟墓究竟往那儿去了呢？

The Grave

Guo Moruo

Yesterday morning, while wandering about alone in a pine forest, I amused myself by piling up a small sandhill under an old pine tree.

"Let this be my own grave," said I.

Picking up a piece of white stone, I scribbled my name on it and said, "Let this be my own gravestone."

On either side of the grave, I transplanted a pine sapling to keep it company.

This morning, recalling the grave, I went to pay a visit to it.

But the grave was nowhere to be found though I searched every nook and corner of the dense forest. Where was it gone to?

O ye remains of my yesterday's dead self, it was your own soul that had come to mourn at the grave! Where was my grave gone to?

注　释

《墓》是郭沫若的早期小品,玲珑而
富有诗情,其中所表现的闲情与哀愁为
他早期短文的特点。

①"戏筑了一座砂丘"的意思是"堆起一座砂丘以自
娱",现译为 I amused myself by piling up a small sandhill, 也可译为 I piled up for fun a small sandhill。"筑"在
这里作"堆积"解,故译为 piling up,不宜按字面译为
building 或 constructing 等。译文中的 small 是添加成分,
原文虽无其词而有其意。

②"这便是我自己的坟墓了"含有说话者的意图,故
译文用祈使句表达: Let this be my own grave, 和 This
shall be my own grave 同义。

③"稚松"即"松树苗",故译为 pine sapling。

④"凭吊"在此作"探望"解,译 to pay a visit to 即
可,不必译为 to pay homage to 或 to pay respects to 等。

⑤"啊,死了的我昨日的尸骸哟"译为 O ye remains
of my yesterday's dead self,其中 ye 作"你"解,属古语,
在此用以烘托散文诗的格调。

想 北 平

老　舍

设若让我写一本小说，以北平作背景，我不至于害怕，因为我可以拣着我知道的写，而躲开我所不知道的。让我单摆浮搁的讲一套北平，我没办法。北平的地方那么大，事情那么多，我知道的真觉太少了，虽然我生在那里，一直到廿七岁才离开。以名胜说，我没到过陶然亭①，这多可笑！以此类推，我所知道的那点只是"我的北平"，而我的北平大概等于牛的一毛。

可是，我真爱北平。这个爱几乎是要说而说不出的。我爱我的母亲。怎样爱？我说不出。在我想作一件事讨她老人家喜欢的时候，我独自微微的笑着；在我想到她的健康而不放心的时候，我欲落泪。言语是不够表现我的心情的，只有独自微笑或落泪才足以把内心揭露在外面一些来。我之爱北平也近乎这个。夸奖这个古城的某一点是容易的，可是那就把北平看得太小了。我所爱的北平不是枝枝节节的一些什么，而是整个儿与我的心灵相粘合的一段历史，一大块地方，多少风景名胜，从雨后什刹海的蜻蜓一直到我梦里的玉泉山的塔影②，都积凑到一块，每一小的事件中有个我，我的每一思念中有个北平，这只有说不出而已。

真愿成为诗人，把一切好听好看的字都浸在自己的心血里，像杜鹃③似的啼出北平的俊伟。啊！我不是诗人！我将永远道不出我的爱，一种像由音乐与图画所引起的爱。这不但是辜负了北平，也对不住我自己，因为我是最初的知识与印象都得自北平，它是在我的血里，我的性格与脾气里有许多地方是这古城所赐给的。我不能爱上海与天津，因为我心中有个北平。可是我说不出来！

伦敦，巴黎，罗马与堪司坦丁堡，曾被称为欧洲的四大"历史的都城"。我知道一些伦敦的情形；巴黎与罗马只是到过而已；堪司坦丁堡根本没有去过。就伦敦，巴黎，罗马来说，巴黎更近似北平——虽然"近似"两字都拉扯得很远——不过，假使让我"家住巴黎"，我一定会和没有家一样的感到寂苦。巴黎，据我看，还太热闹。自然，那里也有空旷静寂的地方，可是又未免太旷④；不像北平那样既复杂而又有个边际⑤，使我能摸着——那长着红酸枣的老城墙！面向着积水滩，背后是城墙，坐在石上看水中的小蝌蚪或苇叶上的嫩蜻蜓，我可以快乐的坐一天，心中完全安适，无所求也无可怕，像小儿安睡在摇篮里。是的，北平也有热闹的地方，但是它和太极拳相似，动中有静。巴黎有许多地方使人疲乏，所以咖啡与酒是必要的，以便刺激；在北平，有温和的香片茶就够了。

论说巴黎的布置已比伦敦罗马匀调的多了，可是比上北平还差点事儿。北平在人为之中显出自然，几乎是什么地方既不挤得慌，又不太僻静：最小的胡同里的房子也有院子与树；最空旷的地方也离买卖街与住宅区不远。这种分配法可以算——在我的经验中——天下第一了。北平的好处不在处处设备得完全，而在它处处有空儿，可以使人自由的喘气；不在有好些美丽的建筑，而在建筑的四周都有空闲的地方，使它们成为美景。每一个城楼，每一个牌楼，都可以从老远就看见。况且在街上还可以看见北山与西山呢！

好学的，爱古物的，人们自然喜欢北平，因为这里书多古物多。我不好学，也没钱买古物。对于物质上，我却喜爱北平的花多菜多果子多。花草是种费钱的玩艺，可是此地的"草花儿"很便宜，而且家家有院子，可以花不多的钱而种一院子花，即使算不了什么，可是到底可爱呀。墙上的牵牛，墙根的靠山竹与草茉莉，是多么省钱省事而也足以招来蝴蝶呀！至于青菜，白菜，扁豆，毛豆角，黄瓜，菠菜等等，大多数是直接由城外担来而送到家门口的。雨后，韭菜叶上还往往带着雨时溅起的泥点，青菜摊子上的红红绿绿几乎有诗似的美丽。果子有不少是由西山与北山来的，西山的沙果，海棠，北山的黑枣，柿子，进了城还带着一层白霜儿呀！哼，美国的橘子包着纸；遇到北平的带霜儿的玉李，还不愧杀！

是的，北平是个都城，而能有好多自己产生的花，菜，水果，这就使人更接近了自然。从它里面说，它没有像伦敦的那些成天冒烟的工厂；从外面说，它紧连着园林、菜圃与农村。采菊东篱下⑥，在这里，确是可以悠然见南山的；大概把"南"字变个"西"或"北"，也没有多少了不得的吧⑦。像我这样的一个贫寒的人，或者只有在北平能享受一点清福了⑧。

好，不再说了吧；要落泪了，真想念北平呀！

Fond Memories of Peiping

Lao She

I have no misgivings about writing a novel with Peiping as its background because I can choose to write about what I am most familiar with while shying away from what is less known to me. But I shall be at a complete loss if I should be called upon to write exclusively about Peiping. Peiping is so big and multifaceted that very little of it, I believe, is known to me though I was born and brought up there and never went away until I was 27. Just fancy that I have neglected to visit even Tao Ran Ting, a local scenic attraction! It follows that, in contrast with Peiping in its entirety, what little I know about it is probably a mere drop in the ocean.

I do cherish, however, a genuine love for Peiping — a love that is almost as inexpressible as my love for mother. I smile by myself when I think of something I can do to please mother; I feel like crying when I worry about mother's health. Words fail me where silent smiles and tears well express my innermost feelings. The same is true of my love for Peiping. I shall fail to do justice to this vast ancient city if I should do no more than extol just one certain aspect of it. The Peiping I love is not something in bits and pieces, but a phase of history and a vast tract of land completely bound up with my heart. Numerous scenic spots and historical sites from Shi Sha Hai Lake with its dragonflies after a rain to the Yu Quan Shan Mountain with the dream pagoda on top — all merge into a single whole. I associate myself with everything in Peiping no matter how trivial it is; Peiping is always in my mind. I can't tell why.

If only I were a poet so that, with all the sweet and beautiful words at my command, I could sing of the grandeur of Peiping in as longing a note as that of a cuckoo! Alas, I am no poet! I shall never be able to express my love — the kind of love as inspired by music or painting. That is quite a letdown to both Peiping and myself, for it is to this ancient city that I owe what I have within me, including my early knowledge and impressions as well as much of my character and temperament. With Peiping possessing my heart, I can never become attached to either Shanghai or Tianjin. I can't tell why.

London, Paris, Rome and Constantinople are known as the four major "historic capitals" of Europe. I know something about London; I have been to Paris and Rome only briefly; I have never visited Constantinople at all. Of

all these cities, Paris has the closest affinity with Peiping
(The word "affinity" may perhaps sound a bit far-
fetched). Nevertheless, if I should make my home in
Paris, I would feel very lonely as if I had no home at all.
As far as I know, Paris is too much of a bustling town. It
does have quiet open spaces, but they smack of mere expanses of vacancy. Peiping is complicated and yet tangible. I can feel it by touch. I can feel the red wild jujubes
growing on its ancient city wall! I can spend a whole day
enjoying myself sitting on a rock to observe tiny tadpoles
in the water or tender dragonflies on reeds while facing
me lies Ji Shui Tan Pond and right behind me rises the
high city wall. I can thus enjoy a perfect inner calm, free
from any desire or fear, like a child sleeping peacefully in
the cradle. There are also bustling places in Peiping, to
be sure, but like the traditional Chinese shadow boxing
Tai Ji Quan, the city retains its stillness in the midst of
motion. While Parisians have to turn to coffee or wine for
the relief of boredom caused by so many wearisome places
in their city, the mild beverage of jasmine tea will be more
than adequate for dwellers of Peiping.

Though Paris has a better layout than London or
Rome, it nevertheless cannot compare with Peiping. In
Peiping, one always finds the natural in the midst of the
artificial. The city as a whole is neither too crowded nor
too secluded. Even houses tucked away in very small

181

lanes have their own courtyards and trees. Even the most secluded places are situated within a stone's throw of business or residential districts. Such a layout is, to my mind, without equal all over the world. However, what distinguishes Peiping is not the perfect layout, but the open spaces here and there where people can breathe freely; not the many beautiful buildings, but the open grounds around each building which add to its architectural beauty. Each gate tower of the city wall and each *pailou* (decorated archway) can be seen from afar. And the Northern and Western hills are visible to people in the open streets.

Those who are fond of studying or collecting curios will naturally be drawn to Peiping, which is remarkable for its rich store of books and curios. Personally I am not given to studying, nor do I have spare money to buy curios. But I am keen on the flowers, vegetables and fruit which grow in rich abundance in Peiping. Gardening is something very expensive. But since flowers of herbaceous plants in Peiping are very cheap and each house has a courtyard of its own, it does not cost very much to plant a whole courtyard to such flowers which, though humble, are nevertheless lovely to look at, such as morning glories on the wall, china pinks at the foot of the wall and marvels-of-Peru. Yes, cheap as they are, they attract butterflies! Green vegetables, cabbages, hyacinth beans, young soya beans, cucumbers, spinach, etc. are often carried straight from the suburbs to your residential quarters for marketing. Often, leeks from rural farms after a rain still have specks of mud on their leaves. The vegetable stalls are so colourful that they present a scene of poetic charm. Fruits come mainly from the western and northern suburbs, such as crab apples and cherry apples from the Western Hills, and jujubes and persimmons from the Northern Hills. Look, how they are still covered with frostlike bloom when they are put on the market! Indeed, America's paper-wrapped oranges will pale beside Peiping's plums bearing a thin coating of frostlike bloom!

The city of Peiping brings its residents into closer contact with nature by growing flowers, vegetables and fruit in large quantities. The city proper is not plagued by factory chimneys such as you find in London giving off volumes of smoke all day long. On the outskirts of the city lie numerous flower gardens, vegetable farms and villages. An ancient Chinese poet by the name of Tao Yuanming says aptly in one of his famous poems, "Plucking chrysanthemums under the eastern hedge, I calmly view the southern hills. " To adapt it to life in Peiping, I might as well substitute the word "western" or "northern" for the word "southern" in the line. Peiping is probably the only place for a man of limited means like me to live an easy and carefree life in.

Now, let me leave off writing, for I am on the point of shedding tears. How I miss Peiping!

注　释

北京于 1930 年改称北平，1949 年新中国成立时恢复旧名。《想北平》是老舍名篇，写于 1936 年。约六十年前的古都风貌和生活情调，时至今日，已发生巨大变化。当时老舍在山东大学任教，正值日寇入侵，国难当头。文章热情颂扬北平，字里行间洋溢着强烈的爱国主义和民族自豪感。

①“我没到过陶然亭”译为 I have neglected to visit even Tao Ran Ting，a local scenic attraction，其中 a local scenic attraction 是添加成份，俾国外读者理解“陶然亭”乃古都一大名胜。又译文中 neglected 一词也可用 failed 来表达。

②“梦里的玉泉山的塔影”译为 the Yu Quan Shan Mountain with the dream pagoda on top，其中 dream 属定语形容词，作“梦一般完美的”解。

③“杜鹃”是一种益鸟，也称“杜宇”、“布谷”或“子规”，英语为 cuckoo。古代诗人认为杜鹃鸣声凄厉，旅人

闻之，不禁产生思家的心情，故常用"啼血"形容其鸣声。"啼血"不宜直译，可结合上下文意译为 its longing note。

④ "可是又未免太旷"译为 but they smack of mere expanses of vacancy，其中 smack of 作"有些像……"解，用以表达原文"未免"的含义；又"太旷"作"大而空"解，故译为 expanses of vacancy。

⑤ "有个边际"意即"可触摸的"或"有实质的"，故译为 tangible 或 palpable。

⑥ "采菊东篱下"出自东晋文学家陶渊明《论酒》诗。本是"采菊东篱下，悠然见南山"，两句相联。现用解释性翻译法，把诗人姓名、时代，以及上下诗句，交代清楚，否则国外读者无法理解。

⑦ "大概把'南'字变个'西'或'北'，也没有多少了不得的吧。"这句紧接上面的诗句，英译时也须灵活处理，交代其内涵：To adapt it to life in Peiping，I might as well substitute the word "western" or "northern" for the word "southern" in the line。

⑧ "清福"可译为 an easy and carefree life 或 a life free from worries and cares。

养　花

老　舍

　　我爱花，所以也爱养花①。我可还没成为养花专家，因为没有工夫去作研究与试验。我只把养花当作生活中的一种乐趣，花开得大小好坏都不计较，只要开花，我就高兴。在我的小院中，到夏天，满是花草，小猫儿们只好上房去玩耍②，地上没有它们的运动场。

　　花虽多，但无奇花异草。珍贵的花草不易养活，看着一棵好花生病欲死是件难过的事。我不愿时时落泪。北京的气候，对养花来说，不算很好。冬天冷，春天多风，夏天不是干旱就是大雨倾盆；秋天最好，可是忽然会闹霜冻。在这种气候里，想把南方的好花养活，我还没有那么大的本事。因此，我只养些好种易活、自己会奋斗的花草③。

　　不过，尽管花草自己会奋斗④，我若置之不理，任其自生自灭⑤，它们多数还是会死了的。我得天天照管它们，像好朋友似的关切它们。一来二去⑥，我摸着一些门道：有的喜阴，就别放在太阳地里，有的喜干，就别多浇水。这是个乐趣，摸住门道，花草养活了，而且三年五载⑦老活着、开花，多么有意思呀！不是乱吹，这就是知识呀！多得些知识，一定不是坏事。

我不是有腿病吗，不但不利于行，也不利于久坐。我不知道花草们受我的照顾，感谢我不感谢；我可得感谢它们。在我工作的时候，我总是写了几十个字，就到院中去看看，浇浇这棵，搬搬那盆，然后回到屋中再写一点，然后再出去，如此循环⑧，把脑力劳动与体力劳动结合到一起，有益身心⑨，胜于吃药。要是赶上狂风暴雨或天气突变哪，就得全家动员⑩，抢救花草，十分紧张⑪。几百盆花，都要很快地抢到屋里去，使人腰酸腿疼，热汗直流。第二天，天气好转，又得把花儿都搬出去，就又一次腰酸腿疼，热汗直流。可是，这多么有意思呀！不劳动，连棵花儿也养不活，这难道不是真理么？

送牛奶的同志，进门就夸"好香"！这使我们全家都感到骄傲。赶到昙花开放的时候，约几位朋友来看看，更有秉烛夜游的神气⑫——昙花总在夜里放蕊。花儿分根了，一棵分为数棵，就赠给朋友们一些；看着友人拿走自己的劳动果实，心里自然特别喜欢。

当然，也有伤心的时候，今年夏天就有这么一回。三百株菊秧还在地上（没到移入盆中的时候），下了暴雨。邻家的墙倒了下来，菊秧被砸死者约三十多种，一百多棵！全家都几天没有笑容！

有喜有忧，有笑有泪，有花有实，有香有色，既须劳动，又长见识，这就是养花的乐趣。

On Growing Flowers

Lao She

I love flowers and hence have taken to growing them. But, short of time to do research and experiment in flower cultivation, I am no gardener at all. I merely take flower cultivation as a pleasure of life. I really don't care whether or not my flowers will put forth plump and nice-looking blossoms. I'll be delighted as long as they can blossom. In summer, flowers and plants growing in luxuriance in my small courtyard will leave little open space as a playground for the little cats, so they have to sport about in our rooms instead.

I grow many flowers, but none of them are exotic or rare ones. It is difficult to grow a precious flower species. And I feel bad to see a good flower dying of illness. I don't want often to shed tears over that. But Beijing's climate is more or less unfit for the growing of flowers. Freezing in winter, windy in spring, and either too dry or too often visited by rainstorms in summer. While autumn is the best of all, it is often plagued by a sudden frost. In a climate like this, it is far beyond my capacity to grow precious flowers of southern breed. Therefore, I only grow flowers and plants that are hardy and enjoy a high survival rate.

Although such flowers are able to weather through by themselves, I, however, never ignore them or abandon them to their own fate, for otherwise most of them will probably end up dead. I have to care for them every day as if they were my close friends. Thus, in the course of time, I've somehow got the hang of flower cultivation. Some flowers which are accustomed to growing in the shade should not be too much exposed to the sun. Those which prefer dryness should not be watered too often. It gives me much pleasure to know the right way of handling them. How interesting it is to be able to keep my flowers and plants alive and watch them thrive and bloom year in year out! It is no exaggeration to say that there is much knowledge involved in this! And the more knowledge one acquires, the better it is of course.

As I have some trouble with my leg, I can't move around easily, nor can I sit too long. I don't know if the flowers under my care are grateful to me or not. However, I wish for my part to acknowledge my thanks to them. I often leave off sedentary work after writing a few dozen words and go to the courtyard to take a look at the flowers, watering them and moving about the potted ones.

Then I'll return to my room to write a bit more. I'll go through the same back-and-forth process again and again, thus combining mental with manual labour. This is a better way to keep me fit in mind and body than taking medicine. In case of a violent storm or a sudden change of weather, however, the whole family will have to turn out to salvage the flowers and plants. Everybody will then feel keyed up. By the time when we have managed to move the several hundred potted flowers to the rooms in a hurry, we will be dog-tired and wet with perspiration. The next day, when the weather is fine, we will have another round of being dog-tired and wet with perspiration in taking all the flowers out to the courtyard again. How interesting it is! Isn't it true that without doing manual labour, we could't even keep a single flower alive?

It filled the whole family with pride whenever the milkman exclaims on entering our gate, "What a sweet smell!" When the night-blooming cereuses are about to be in flower, we will invite some friends to visit us in the evening to feast their eyes on them — in an atmosphere smacking of nocturnal merry-making under candle lights. When the cereuses have branched out, we will pick some of the flowers and give them as a present to our friends. We are of course especially happy to see them take away our fruits of labour.

Of course, there is a time to feel sad too. Last summer, a rainstorm hit us when 300 chrysanthemum seedlings in the courtyard were about to be transplanted to pots. Suddenly, the wall of our neighbour collapsed and crushed more than 100 seedlings of 30 varieties. The whole family were sad-faced for quite a few days!

Joy and sorrow, laughter and tears, flowers and fruit, fragance and colour , manual labour and increased knowledge — all these make up the joy of flower cultivation.

注　释

　　老舍的《养花》于 1956 年 10 月 21 日发表在《文汇报》上。老舍爱花,写出了养花的乐趣,视花儿为自己生命的一部分,人花合一。文章短小简练,朴素隽永,语言白俗。

　　① "所以也爱养花" 译为 hence have taken to growing them,其中动词短语 to take to 的意思是 "开始喜欢"。此句也可译为 are therefore fond of growing flowers。

　　② "只好上房去玩耍" 译为 they have to sport about in our rooms instead,其中动词短语 to sport about 的意思是 "嬉戏"(to play and jump about happily)。

　　③ "我只养些好种易活、自己会奋斗的花草" 译时稍作灵活处理:I only grow flowers and plants that are hardy and enjoy a high survival rate,其中用 enjoy a high survival rate(成活率高)表达 "好种易活";用 hardy(耐寒、耐劳、能吃苦)表达 "会奋斗的"。

　　④ "自己会奋斗" 译为 able to weather through by themselves,其中动词短语 to weather through 的意思是 "对

付困难"、"渡过风暴"等。此句也可译为 able to carry on the struggle for existence by themselves，但用字太大、太多。

⑤"任其自生自灭"不宜按字面直译，现意译为 abandon them to their own fate。

⑥"一来二去"的意思是"经过一定的时间"，故译为 in the course of time。

⑦"三年五载"以灵活的办法译为 year in year out。

⑧"然后再出去，如此循环"不宜按字面直译，现以灵活的办法译为 I'll go through the same back-and-forth process again and again，其中定语 back-and-forth 作"来来往往的"解；go through the same process 作"重复同一过程"解。

⑨"有益身心"可有两种译法：to keep me fit in mind and body 或 to keep me mentally and physically fit。

⑩"就得全家动员"译为 the whole family will have to turn out，其中动词短语 to turn out 的意思是"出动"或"出来参加"。

⑪"十分紧张"译为 feel keyed up，其中动词短语 to key up 的意思是"使紧张"，因此 keyed up 和 excited 、tense 等同义。

⑫"更有秉烛夜游的神气"中的"秉烛夜游"是成语，比喻"及时行乐"，今结合上下文按"夜间秉烛作乐"的意思译为 nocturnal merry-making under candle lights。又"更有……的神气"意即"带有……的味道"，故全句译为 in an atmosphere smacking of nocturnal merry-making under candle lights。

白 杨 礼 赞

茅 盾

白杨树实在是不平凡的,我赞美白杨树!

当汽车在望不到边际的高原上奔驰,扑入你的视野的,是黄绿错综的一条大毡子①;黄的,那是土,未开垦的处女土,几十万年前由伟大的自然力所堆积成功的黄土高原的外壳;绿的呢,是人类劳力战胜自然的成果,是麦田,和风吹送,翻起了一轮一轮的绿波——这时你会真心佩服昔人所造的两个字"麦浪",若不是妙手偶得,便确是经过锤炼的语言的精华;黄与绿主宰着,无边无垠,坦荡如砥②,这时如果不是宛若并肩的远山的连峰提醒了你(这些山峰凭你的肉眼来判断,就知道是在你脚底下的),你会忘记了汽车是在高原上行驶。这时你涌起来的感想也许是"雄壮",也许是"伟大",诸如此类的形容词;然而同时你的眼睛也许觉得有点倦怠,你对当前的"雄壮"或"伟大"闭了眼③,而另一种味儿在你心头潜滋暗长④了——"单调"!可不是,单调,有一点儿吧?

然而刹那间,要是你猛抬眼看见了前面远远地有一排,——不,或者甚至只是三五株,一二株,傲然地耸立,像

195

哨兵似的树木的话,那你的恹恹欲睡⑤的情绪又将如何?我那时是惊奇地叫了一声的!

那就是白杨树,西北极普通的一种树,然而实在不是平凡的一种树!

那是力争上游的一种树,笔直的干,笔直的枝。它的干呢,通常是丈把高,像是加过人工似的,一丈以内,绝无旁枝;它所有的丫枝呢,一律向上,而且紧紧靠拢,也像是加过人工似的,成为一束,绝无横斜逸出⑥;它的宽大的叶子也是片片向上,几乎没有斜生的,更不用说倒垂了;它的皮,光滑而有银色的晕圈,微微泛出淡青色。这是虽在北方的风雪的压迫下却保持着倔强挺立的一种树!哪怕只有碗来精细罢,它却努力向上发展,高到丈许,二丈,参天耸立,不折不挠,对抗着西北风。

这就是白杨树,西北极普通的一种树,然而决不是平凡的树!它没有婆娑的姿态,没有屈曲盘旋⑦的虬枝,也许你要说它不美丽,——如果美是专指"婆娑"或"横斜逸出"之类而言,那么白杨树算不得树中的好女子;但是它却是伟岸⑧,正直,朴质,严肃,也不缺乏温和,更不用提它的坚强不屈与挺拔,它是树中的伟丈夫!当你在积雪初融的高原上走过,看见平坦的大地上傲然挺立这么一株或一排白杨树,难道你觉得树只是树?难道你就不想到它的朴质,严肃,坚强不屈,至少也象征了北方的农民;难道你竟一点也不联想到,在敌后的广大土地上,到处有坚强不屈,就像这白杨树一样傲然挺立的守卫他们家乡的哨兵⑨,难道你又不更远一点想到这样枝枝叶叶靠紧团结,力求上进的白杨树,宛然象征了今天在华北平原纵横激荡⑩,用血写出新中国历史

196

的那种精神和意志。

　　白杨不是平凡的树。它在西北极普遍，不被人重视，就跟北方农民相似；它有极强的生命力⑪，磨折不了，压迫不倒，也跟北方的农民相似。我赞美白杨树，就因为它不但象征了北方的农民，尤其象征了今天我们民族解放斗争中所不可缺的⑫朴质，坚强，以及力求上进的精神。

　　让那些看不起民众，贱视民众，顽固的倒退的人们去赞美那贵族化的楠木⑬（那也是直干秀颀⑭的），去鄙视这极常见、极易生长的白杨罢，但是我要高声赞美白杨树！

Tribute to the White Poplar

Mao Dun

The white poplar is no ordinary tree. Let me sing its praises.

When you travel by car through Northwest China's boundless plateau, all you see before you is something like a huge yellow-and-green felt blanket. Yellow is the soil — the uncultivated virgin soil. It is the outer covering of the loess plateau accumulated by Mother Nature several hundred thousand years ago. Green are the wheat fields signifying man's triumph over nature. They become a sea of rolling green waves whenever there is a soft breeze. One is here reminded of the Chinese expression *mai lang* meaning "rippling wheat" and cannot help admiring our forefathers' ingenuity in coining such a happy phrase. It must have been either the brainwave of a clever scholar, or a linguistic gem sanctioned by long usage. The boundless highland, with dominant yellow and green, is flat like a whetstone. Were it not for the distant mountain peaks standing side by side (which, as your naked eyes tell you, are below where you stand), you would probably forget that you are on the highland . The sight of the scene will probably call up inside you a string of epithets like "spectacular" or "grand". Meanwhile, however, your eyes may become weary of watching the same panorama, so much so that you are oblivious of its being spectacular or grand. And you may feel monotony coming on. Yes, it is somewhat monotonous, isn't it?

Now what will become of your weariness if you suddenly raise your eyes only to catch sight of a distant row of trees (or just a couple of them) standing there proudly like sentries. For my part, I cannot keep from uttering an exclamation of surprise!

They are white poplars. Though very common in Northwest China, they are no ordinary trees!

With straight trunks and branches, white poplars aim high. Their trunks are usually over ten feet tall and, as if wrought by human effort, utterly bare of branches below ten feet. Their twigs, also like things artificially shaped, all reach out towards the sky and grow close together in a cluster without any sideway growth. Their leaves are broad and point upwards with very few slanting sideways, much less upside down. Their glossy barks are a faint light green with hazy silver spots. They stand erect and unbending in face of North China's violent wind and snow. Though they may be only as big as the mouth of a bowl, they strive to grow upwards until they reach the towering height of some twenty feet and stand indomitable against the northwest wind.

They are white poplars. Though very common in Northwest China, they are no ordinary trees! You may call them unattractive because they have neither the graceful carriage of a dancer, nor such branches as can twine and climb. But nevertheless they are big and tall, honest and upright, simple and plain, earnest and unyielding — and not without gentleness and warmth though. They are giants among trees! When you trudge through the melting snow of the highland and see one or a row of white poplars standing proudly on the vast plains, how could you look upon them as nothing but mere trees? How could you forget that with all their simplicity, earnestness and unyieldingness, they are symbolic of our peasants in the North? How could you fail to associate them with our dauntless soldiers guarding our homeland all over the vast rear? How could you fail to see that these trees, ever striving to put out their closely knit branches and leaves in an upward direction, are symbolic of the spirit and will of our men who, fighting heroically all over the northern plains, are writing the history of New China with their own blood?

White poplars are no ordinary trees. But these common trees in Northwest China are as much ignored as our peasants in the North. However, like our peasants in the North, they are bursting with vitality and capable of surviving any hardship or oppression. I pay tribute to them because they symbolize our peasants in the North and, in particular, the spirit of honesty, tenacity and forging ahead — a spirit central to our struggle for national liberation.

The reactionary diehards, who despise and snub the common people, can do whatever they like to eulogize the elite nanmu (which is also tall, straight and good-looking) and look down upon the common, fast-growing white poplar. I, for my part, will be loud in my praise of the latter!

注　释

《白杨礼赞》是茅盾在抗日战争期间1941年3月写的一篇著名散文。作者用象征的手法,通过对白杨树的赞美,热情歌颂中国共产党领导下的人民革命和伟大的民族精神。

①"是黄绿错综的一条大毡子"译为 something like a huge yellow-and-green felt blanket,其中 something like 是为适应英语上下文而增添的成分,变隐喻为明喻,使译文读来更顺当 。又 yellow-and-green(或 yellow and green)和 yellow green 不同,前者为黄绿杂处,构成一种花色,后者为黄绿混合,即绿中带黄。

②"坦荡如砥"意即平坦得像一块磨刀石,现直译为 flat like a whetstone,保留原文的比喻。

③"你对当前的'雄壮'或'伟大'闭了眼"意即你对眼前的景色不再感到"雄壮"或"伟大",现译为 you are oblivious of its being spectacular or grand ,其中 oblivious of 作"忘却"或"不觉得"解 。

④"潜滋暗长"意即"逐渐开始",现译为 coming on.

英语短语 to come on 作 to begin by degrees 解。

⑤ "恹恹欲睡" 作 "困倦" 解，故译为 weariness。

⑥ "横斜逸出" 指树枝从树干的旁边斜伸出来，现译为 sideway growth。

⑦ "屈曲盘旋" 意即弯弯曲曲地向上爬，现译为 twine and climb。

⑧ "伟岸" 意即 "高大"，现译为 big and tall。

⑨ "守卫他们家乡的哨兵" 中的 "哨兵" 实际上指 "士兵" 或 "战士"，不宜译为 sentries。全部短语应译为 soldiers guarding our homeland。

⑩ "纵横激荡" 意即到处同敌人英勇战斗，现译为 fighting heroically。

⑪ "有极强的生命力" 译为 are bursting with vitality，其中 bursting with 意同 full of。

⑫ "我们民族解放斗争中所不可缺的……" 译为 ... central to our struggle for national liberation，其中 central to 意同 essential to。

⑬ "楠木" 是一种常绿乔木，质地坚固，为贵重木材，现译为 nanmu。

⑭ "秀颀" 意即美丽而高大，现译为 good-looking and tall。

故 都 的 秋

郁 达 夫

秋天,无论在什么地方的秋天,总是好的[①];可是啊,北国的秋,却特别地来得清,来得静,来得悲凉。我的不远千里[②],要从杭州赶上青岛,更要从青岛赶上北平来的理由,也不过想饱尝一尝这"秋",这故都的秋味。

江南,秋当然也是有的;但草木凋得慢,空气来得润,天的颜色显得淡,并且又时常多雨而少风;一个人夹在苏州上海杭州,或厦门香港广州的市民中间,浑浑沌沌地过去,只能感到一点点清凉,秋的味,秋的色,秋的意境与姿态,总看不饱,尝不透,赏玩不到十足[③]。秋并不是名花,也并不是美酒,那一种半开,半醉的状态,在领略秋的过程上,是不合适的。

不逢北国之秋,已将近十余年了。在南方每年到了秋天,总要想起陶然亭的芦花,钓鱼台的柳影,西山的虫唱,玉泉的夜月,潭柘寺的钟声[④]。在北平即使不出门去罢,就是在皇城人海之中,租人家一椽破屋来住着,早晨起来,泡一碗浓茶,向院子一坐,你也能看得到很高很高的碧绿的天色,听得到青天下驯鸽的飞声。从槐树叶底,朝东细数着一丝一丝漏下来的日光，或在破壁腰中，静对着像喇叭似的牵牛花（朝荣）的蓝朵，自然而然地也能够感觉到十分的秋意。说到了牵牛花，我以为以蓝色或白色者为佳，紫黑色次之，淡红色最下。最好，还要在牵牛花底教长着几根疏疏落落的尖细且长的秋草，使作陪衬。

北国的槐树，也是一种能使人联想起秋来的点缀。像花而又不是花的那一种落蕊，早晨起来，会铺得满地。脚踏上去，声音也没有，气味也没有，只能感出一点点极微细极柔软的触觉。扫街的在树影下一阵扫后，灰土上留下来的一条条扫帚的丝纹，看起来既觉得细腻，又觉得清闲⑤，潜意识下并且还觉得有点儿落寞，古人所说的梧桐一叶而天下知秋的遥想，大约也就在这些深沉的地方。

秋蝉的衰弱的残声，更是北国的特产；因为北平处处全长着树，屋子又低，所以无论在什么地方，都听得见它们的啼唱。在南方是非要上郊外或山上去才听得到的。这秋蝉的嘶叫，在北平可和蟋蟀耗子一样，简直像是家家户户都养在家里的家虫⑥。

还有秋雨哩，北方的秋雨，也似乎比南方的下得奇，下得有味，下得更像样⑦。

在灰沉沉的天底下，忽而来一阵凉风，便息列索落地下起雨来了。一层雨过，云渐渐地卷向了西去，天又青了，太阳又露出脸来了；著着很厚的青布单衣或夹袄的都市闲人，咬着烟管，在雨后的斜桥影里，上桥头树底下去一立，遇见熟人，便会用了缓慢悠闲的声调，微叹⑧着互答着的说：

"唉，天可真凉了——"

"可不是么？一层秋雨一层凉了！"

北方的果树，到秋来，也是一种奇景。第一是枣子树；屋角，墙头，茅房边上，灶房门口，它都会一株株地长大起来。像橄榄又像鸽蛋似的这枣子颗儿，在小椭圆形的细叶中间，显出淡绿微黄的颜色的时候，正是秋的全盛时期；等枣树叶落，枣子红完，西北风就要起来了⑨，北方便是尘沙灰土的世界，只有这枣子、柿子、葡萄，成熟到八九分的七八月之交，是北国的清秋的佳日，是一年之中最好也没有的golden days。

有些批评家说，中国的文人学士，尤其是诗人，都带着很浓厚的颓废色彩，所以中国的诗文里，颂赞秋的文字特别的多。但外国的诗人，又何尝不然？我虽则外国诗文念得不多，也不想开出账来，做一篇秋的诗歌散文钞，但你若去一翻英德法意等诗人的集子，或各国的诗文的 anthology 来，总能够看到许多关于秋的歌颂与悲啼。各著名的大诗人的长篇田园诗或四季诗里，也总以关于秋的部分，写得最出色而最有味。足见有感觉的动物，有情趣的人类，对于秋，总是一样的能特别引起深沉，幽远，严厉，萧索的感触来的。不单是诗人，就是被关闭在牢狱里的囚犯，到了秋天，我想也一定会感到一种不能自已的深情⑩；秋之于人，何尝有国别，更何尝有人种阶级的区别呢？不过在中国，文字里有一个"秋士"⑪的成语，读本里又有着很普遍的欧阳子的秋声⑫与苏东坡的《赤壁赋》⑬等，就觉得中国的文人，与秋的关系特别深了。可是这秋的深味，尤其是中国的秋的深味，非要在北方，才感受得到底。

南国之秋，当然是也有它的特异的地方的，比如廿四桥的明月，钱塘江的秋潮，普陀山的凉雾，荔枝湾的残荷等等，可是色彩不浓,回味不永。比起北国的秋来,正像是黄酒之与白干,稀饭之与馍馍,鲈鱼之与大蟹,黄犬之与骆驼。

秋天,这北国的秋天,若留得住的话,我愿把寿命的三分之二折去,换得一个三分之一的零头。

Autumn in Peiping

Yu Dafu

Autumn, wherever it is, always has something to recommend itself. In North China, however, it is particularly limpid, serene and melancholy. To enjoy its atmosphere to the full in the onetime capital, I have, therefore, made light of travelling a long distance from Hangzhou to Qingdao, and thence to Peiping.

There is of course autumn in the South too, but over there plants wither slowly, the air is moist, the sky pallid, and it is more often rainy than windy. While muddling along all by myself among the urban dwellers of Suzhou, Shanghai, Xiamen, Hong Kong or Guangzhou, I feel nothing but a little chill in the air, without ever relishing to my heart's content the flavour, colour, mood and style of the season. Unlike famous flowers which are most attractive when half opening, or good wine which is most tempting when one is half drunk, autumn, however, is best appreciated in its entirety.

It is more than a decade since I last saw autumn in

the North. When I am in the South, the arrival of each autumn will put me in mind of Peiping's Tao Ran Ting with its reed catkins, Diao Yu Tai with its shady willow trees, Western Hills with their chirping insects, Yu Quan Shan Mountain on a moonlight evening and Tan Zhe Si with its reverbrating bell. Suppose you put up in a humble rented house inside the bustling imperial city, you can, on getting up at dawn, sit in your courtyard sipping a cup of strong tea, leisurely watch the high azure skies and listen to pigeons circling overhead. Saunter eastward under locust trees to closely observe streaks of sunlight filtering through their foliage, or quietly watch the trumpet-shaped blue flowers of morning glories climbing half way up a dilapidated wall, and an intense feeling of autumn will of itself well up inside you. As to morning glories, I like their blue or white flowers best, dark purple ones second best, and pink ones third best. It will be most desirable to have them set off by some tall thin grass planted underneath here and there.

Locust trees in the North, as a decorative embellishment of nature, also associate us with autumn. On getting up early in the morning, you will find the ground strewn all over with flower-like pistils fallen from locust trees. Quiet and smelless, they feel tiny and soft underfoot. After a street cleaner has done the sweeping under the shade of the trees, you will discover countless lines left by his broom in the dust, which look so fine and quiet that somehow a feeling of forlorness will begin to creep up on you. The same depth of implication is found in the ancient saying that a single fallen leaf from the *wutong* tree is more than enough to inform the world of autumn's presence.

The sporadic feeble chirping of cicadas is especially characteristic of autumn in the North. Due to the abundance of trees and the low altitude of dwellings in Peiping, cicadas are audible in every nook and cranny of the city. In the South, however, one cannot hear them unless in suburbs or hills. Because of their ubiquitous shrill noise, these insects in Peiping seem to be living off every household like crickets or mice.

As for autumn rains in the North, they also seem to differ from those in the South, being more appealing, more temperate.

A sudden gust of cool wind under the slaty sky, and raindrops will start pitter-pattering. Soon when the rain is over, the clouds begin gradually to roll towards the west and the sun comes out in the blue sky. Some idle townsfolk, wearing lined or unlined clothing made of thick cloth, will come out pipe in mouth and, loitering under a tree by the end of a bridge, exchange leisurely conversation with acquaintances with a slight touch of regret at the passing of time:

"Oh, real nice and cool —"

"Sure! Getting cooler with each autumn shower!"

Fruit trees in the North also make a wonderful sight in autumn. Take jujube trees for example. They grow everywhere — around the corner of a house, at the foot of a wall, by the side of a latrine or outside a kitchen door. It is at the height of autumn that jujubes, shaped like dates or pigeon eggs, make their appearance in a light yellowish-green amongst tiny elliptic leaves. By the time when they have turned ruddy and the leaves fallen, the northwesterly wind will begin to reign supreme and make a dusty world of the North. Only at the turn of July and August when jujubes, persimmons, grapes are 80-90 percent ripe will the North have the best of autumn — the golden days in a year.

Some literary critics say that Chinese literati, especially poets, are mostly disposed to be decadent, which accounts for predominence of Chinese works singing the praises of autumn. Well, the same is true of foreign poets, isn't it? I haven't read much of foreign poetry and prose, nor do I want to enumerate autumn-related poems and essays in foreign literature. But, if you browse through collected works of English, German, French or Italian poets, or various countries' anthologies of poetry or prose, you can always come across a great many literary pieces eulogizing or lamenting autumn. Long pastoral poems or songs about the four seasons by renowned poets are mostly distinguished by beautiful moving lines on autumn. All that goes to show that all live creatures and sensitive humans alike are prone to the feeling of depth, remoteness, severity and bleakness. Not only poets, even convicts in prison, I suppose, have deep sentiments in autumn in spite of themselves. Autumn treats all humans alike, regardless of nationality, race or class. However, judging from the Chinese idiom *qiushi* (autumn scholar, meaning an aged scholar grieving over frustrations in his life) and the frequent selection in textbooks of Ouyang Xiu's *On the Autumn Sough* and Su Dongpo's *On the Red Cliff*, Chinese men of letters seem to be particularly autumn-minded. But, to know the real flavour of autumn, especially China's autumn, one has to visit the North.

Autumn in the South also has its unique features, such as the moon-lit Ershisi Bridge in Yangzhou, the flowing sea tide at the Qiantangjiang River, the mist-shrouded Putuo Mountain and lotuses at the Lizhiwan Bay. But they all lack strong colour and lingering flavour. Southern autumn is to Northern autumn what yellow rice wine is to *kaoliang* wine, congee to steamed buns, perches to crabs, yellow dogs to camels.

Autumn, I mean Northern autumn, if only it could be made to last forever! I would be more than willing to

keep but one-third of my life-span and have two-thirds of
it bartered for the prolonged stay of the season!

注　释

《故都的秋》是郁达夫(1896—1945)
的名篇,1934年8月写于北平。文章通
过对北国特有风物的细腻描绘,抒发作
者对故都之秋的无比眷恋之情。

① "总是好的" 不宜照字面直译。现译为 always has something to recommend itself, 其中 to have ... to recommend ... 作 "有……可取之处" 解。

② "不远千里,要从杭州赶上青岛……" 译为 have made light of travelling a long distance from Hangzhou to Qingdao ..., 其中 to make light of 是成语,作 "对…… 不在乎" 解。

③ "总看不饱,尝不透,赏玩不到十足" 不宜逐字直译。译文 without ever relishing to my heart's content ... 中用 relishing to my heart's content 概括原文中的 "看……饱"、"尝……透"、"赏玩……" 等。

④ "每年到了秋天,总要想起陶然亭的芦花……" 译为 the arrival of each autumn will put me in mind of Peiping's Tao Ran Ting with its reed catkins ..., 其中 to

214

put one in mind of ... 是成语，作"使人想起……"解。译文中的 Peiping's 是添加成分，以便国外读者理解句中所列各景点的所在地是北平。

⑤"既觉得细腻，又觉得清闲"中的"清闲"意同"幽静"，故译 quiet。

⑥"可和蟋蟀耗子一样，简直像是家家户户都养在家里的家虫"译为 seem to be living off every household like crickets or mice，其中 to live off(＝to live on) 是成语，作"靠……生活"解，用以表达"养在……的家虫"。

⑦"更像样"意即"更有节制"，故译为 more temperate。

⑧ 根据上下文，"微叹"是为"感怀时光的消逝"，故以释义方法译为 with a slight touch of regret at the passing of time。

⑨"西北风就要起来了"译为 the northwesterly wind will begin to reign supreme，其中 to reign supreme 强调"占优势"之意。

⑩"感到不能自已的深情"译为 have deep sentiments ... in spite of themselves，其中 in spite of oneself 是成语，作"不由自主地"解。

⑪"秋士"是古汉语，指"士之暮年不遇者"，现译为 qiushi (autumn scholar, meaning an aged scholar grieving over frustrations in his life)。

⑫"欧阳子的秋声"即"欧阳修所作的《秋声赋》"，现译为 Ouyang Xiu's On the Autumn Sough。

⑬《赤壁赋》为苏东坡所作，借秋游赤壁，抒发自己的

人生感慨。可译为 *On the Red Cliff* 或 *Fu on the Red Cliff*。

谈 结 婚

郁 达 夫

前些日子,林语堂先生似乎曾说过①女子的唯一事业,是在结婚。现在一位法国大文豪来沪,对去访问他的新闻记者的谈话之中,又似乎说,男子欲成事业,应该不要结婚。

华盛顿·欧文②是一个独身的男子,但《见闻短记》里的一篇歌颂妻子的文章③,却写得那么的优美可爱。同样查而斯·兰姆④也是个独身的男子,而爱丽亚的《独身者的不平》⑤一篇,又冷嘲热讽,将结婚的男女和婚后必然的果子——小孩们——等,俏皮到了那一步田地。

究竟是结婚的好呢,还是不结婚的好?这问题似乎同先有鸡呢还是先有鸡蛋一样⑥,常常有人提起,而也常常没有人解决过的问题⑦。照大体看来,想租房子的时候,是无眷莫问的,想做官的时候,又是朝里无裙⑧莫做官的,想写文章的时候,是独身者⑨不能写我的妻的,凡此种种似乎都是结婚的好。可是要想结婚,第一要有钱,第二要有闲,第三要有职,这潘驴⑩……的五个条件,却也很不容易办到⑪。更何况结婚之后,"儿子自己要来"⑫,在这世界人口过剩,经济恐慌,教育破产,世风不古的时候,万一不慎,同兰姆所说的一样，儿子们去上了断头台⑬，那真是连祖宗三代的楣都要倒尽，那里还有什么"官人请！娘子请！"的唱随之乐⑭可说呢？

左思右想，总觉得结婚也不好的，不结婚也是不好的。

A Chat about Marriage

Yu Dafu

The other day, Mr. Lin Yutang said something to
the effect that women's only career lies in matrimony.
Now, an eminent French writer declared at a press interview after arriving in Shanghai that men should stay bach-
elors if they want to achieve success in life.

Washington Irving was a confirmed bachelor, but in
his *Sketch Book* there is an article extolling the wife as a
graceful and lovely life-long partner. Charles Lamb, also a
single man, in *A Bachelor's Complaint of the Behaviour of
Married People*, one of his essays signed *"Elia"*, speaks
mockingly of married people with their inevitable post-
nuptial fruits — the children.

Marriage or no marriage, which is more desirable?
That sounds like the chicken-and-egg question, which,
though often discussed, remains a perpetual puzzle. Generally speaking, one who has no family dependants is not
supposed to rent a house, one who has no petticoat influence in the government should refrain from becoming an

219

official, an unmarried male writer is in no position to writer about "my wife". All these seem to hint at the advantages of marriage. But, to get married, you need to have five prerequisites, namely, money, leisure, employment, good looks and potentness, of which all are not always available. What is more, after your marriage, your offspring will come to this world of themselves. And in a world with overpopulation, economic crisis, educational bankruptcy and deteriorating public morals, they may, just as Charles Lamb says, through their own acts of indiscretion, be sent to the gallows. With such a terrible misfortune befalling your family, how could you still have wedded bliss to speak of?

Thinking the matter over and over again, I cannot but come to the conclusion that neither matrimony nor bachelorship has anything to recommend itself.

注　释

郁达夫,一生短暂,在恋爱与婚姻上有很多坎坷经历。小品文《谈结婚》寥寥数语,看似游戏笔墨,但庄谐并出,寓理于趣,感叹人生多苦难,对现实百态深表不满。

① "似乎曾说过……"意即"说过一些话,大意是……",译为 said something to the effect that ...,其中 to the effect that ... 作"大意是……"解。

② "华盛顿·欧文"是美国作家 Washington Irving (1783—1859)。《见闻短记》(*Sketch Book*)为其著名代表作。

③ "一篇歌颂妻子的文章"的篇名为 *The Wife*。

④ "查而斯·兰姆"是英国散文家 Charles Lamb (1775—1834)。笔名爱丽亚(Elia),著有《爱丽亚散文集》(*Essays of Elia*)。

⑤ "《独身者的不平》"指《爱丽亚散文集》中的一篇,名为 *A Bachelor's Complaint of the Behaviour of Married People*。

⑥ "这问题似乎同先有鸡呢还是先有鸡蛋一样"译为 That sounds like the chicken-and-egg question，其中 chicken-and-egg（或 chicken and egg）是成语，作"鸡与蛋孰先难定的"或"因果难定的"解。

⑦ "常常没有人解决过的问题"可译为 has never been resolved，现译 remains a perpetual puzzle，变反说为正说。

⑧ "裙"指"裙带关系"，意即"藉以相互依靠的姻亲关系"，现译为 petticoat influence。

⑨ "独身者"指"独身男作家"，故译为 An unmarried male writer。

⑩ "潘驴"源自《金瓶梅》第三回，指"潘安的貌"和"驴大行货"，在文中分别指第四、第五两个条件。现分别译为 good looks 和 potentness。

⑪ "却也很不易办到"意即"却也不易都具备"，译为 of which all are not always available，等于 of which not all are always available。

⑫ "儿子自己要来"译为 your offspring will come to this world of themselves，其中短语 of themselves 和 automatically 同义。

⑬ "走上了断头台"，本可译为 be sent to the guillotine，但因兰姆文中说的是绞刑架，故译为 be sent to the gallows。

⑭ "'官人请！娘子请！'的唱随之乐"不宜逐字直译，现意译为 wedded bliss（闺房之乐），简单明了。

永远的憧憬①和追求

一九一一年，在一个小县城里边，我生在一个小地主的家里。那县城差不多就是中国的最东最北部——黑龙江省——②所以一年之中，倒有四个月飘着白雪。

父亲常常为着贪婪而失掉了人性。他对待仆人，对待自己的儿女，以及对待我的祖父都是同样的吝啬而疏远，甚至于无情③。

有一次，为着房屋租金的事情，父亲把房客的全套的马车赶了过来。房客的家属们哭着诉说着④，向我的祖父跪了下来，于是祖父把两匹棕色的马⑤从车上解下来还了回去。

为着这匹马，父亲向祖父起着终夜的争吵⑥。"两匹马，咱们是算不了什么的，穷人，这匹马就是命根。⑦"祖父这样说着，而父亲还是争吵。九岁时，母亲死去。父亲也就更变了样⑧，偶然打碎了一只杯子，他就要骂到使人发抖的程度。后来就连父亲的眼睛也转了弯，每从他的身边经过，我就像自己的身上生了针刺一样⑨；他斜视着你，他那高傲的眼光从鼻梁经过嘴角而后往下流着⑩。

所以每每在大雪中的黄昏里⑪，围着暖炉，围着祖父，

223

听着祖父读着诗篇,看着祖父读着诗篇时微红的嘴唇⑫。

父亲打了我的时候,我就在祖父的房里,一直面向着窗子,从黄昏到深夜——窗外的白雪,好像白棉花一样飘着;而暖炉上水壶的盖子,则像伴奏的乐器似的振动着⑬。

祖父时时把多纹的两手放在我的肩上,而后又放在我的头上,我的耳边便响着这样的声音:

"快快长吧!长大就好了。"

二十岁那年,我就逃出了父亲的家庭。直到现在还是过着流浪的生活。

"长大"是"长大"了,而没有"好"。

可是从祖父那里,知道了人生除掉了冰冷和憎恶而外,还有温暖和爱。

所以我就向这"温暖"和"爱"的方面,怀着永久的憧憬和追求。

My Everlasting Dream and Pursuit

Xiao Hong

In 1911, I was born into a petty Landlord family in a remote county town in Heilongjiang Province — a town situated virtually at the northeastern tip of China. We had snow there for as long as one third of a year.

Father, driven by avarice, often became very unfeeling. He would treat his servants, his own children and even my grandpa alike with meanness and indifference, not to say with ruthlessness.

Once, due to a dispute over house rent, he took away by force a tenant's horse-drawn cart and drove it home. The tenant's family came to see grandpa and, dropping to their knees, tearfully related their troubles. Grandpa unharnessed the two chestnut horses and returned them to the tenant.

That touched off a night-long quarrel between father and grandpa. "The two horses mean nothing to us, but everything to the poor," argued grandpa. Father, however, refused to listen. Mother died when I was nine. From

225

then on father went from bad to worse. Even a mere cup accidentally broken by someone would send him into such a violent rage that we all shivered with fear. Later, whenever I happened to walk past him, he would even have his eyes directed sideways, which made me feel like being pricked all over on thorns. When he looked askance at me, superciliousness gushed from his eyes down the bridge of his nose and then off the corners of his mouth.

Often of a snowy evening, we children would hang about grandpa by a heating stove, listening to him reading poems aloud and meanwhile watching his busy ruddy lips.

Whenever father had given me a beating, I would seek solace in grandpa's room where I would stay gazing out of the window from dusk till late into the night while snowflakes were flying like cotton and the lid of the kettle over the heating stove rattling like a musical instrument playing an accompaniment.

Grandpa would place his wrinkled hand on my shoulder and then on my head, saying,

"Grow up quick, poor child! You'll be all right after you've grown up."

I fled from home at twenty. And so far I still live the life of a vagrant.

True, I've "grown up", but I'm not yet "all right".

Nevertheless, from grandpa I've learned that apart from coldness and hatred, there is also warmth and love in life.

Hence my everlasting dream and pursuit of this "warmth" and "love".

注　释

萧红(1911—1942),黑龙江省呼兰县人,官僚地主家庭出身,是才华横溢的女作家。《永远的憧憬和追求》是她应美国友人斯诺之约而写的小传。文章诉说她如何在祖父的关怀和抚育下度过寂寞的幼女时代。

①"憧憬"译为 dream,和 aspiration、longing、yearning 等同义。

②"那县城差不多就是中国的最东最北部——黑龙江省——"意即"那小县城在黑龙江省,差不多位于中国的东北角"。现译为 in a remote town in Heilongjiang Province—a town situated virtually at the northeastern tip of China,其中以 remote(偏僻的、边远的)表达"小",便于烘托原文的气氛;at the northern tip of China 比 in China's northeastern part 灵活顺口。

③"甚至于无情"译为 not to say with ruthlessness,其中 not to say 是英语成语,意即 and almost 或 and perhaps even。

228

④ "哭着诉说着"译为 tearfully related their troubles，其中 related 意同 told。

⑤ "棕色的马"译为 chestnut horses。英语常用 chestnut 指马的棕色，或棕色的马。

⑥ 译文 touched off 是成语，作"激起"、"引起"解。

⑦ "穷人，这匹马就是命根"译为 they mean everything to the poor，其中 everything 和前面的 nothing 相呼应。

⑧ "父亲也就更变了样"译为 From then on father went from bad to worse，其中 From then on 是连接上句的添加成分。又 went from bad to worse 是成语，作"越来越坏"、"每况愈下"解。

⑨ "就像自己的身上生了针刺一样"译为 feel like being pricked all over on thorns，其中 feel like 是短语动词，作"如同"解，又介词 on 常用来指人体受到伤害的原因，如：He cut his finger *on* the broken glass。

⑩ 译文 superciliousness gushed from his eyes... 是隐喻。

⑪ 译文 Often of a snowy evening 中的 of 等于 on，但有"经常"的含义。

⑫ "围着暖炉，围着祖父，听着祖父读着诗篇，看着祖父读着诗篇时微红的嘴唇"译为 would hang about grandpa by a heating stove, listening to him reading poems aloud and meanwhile watching his busy ruddy lips，其中 hang about 或 hang around 为动词短语，作"待在……身边"解，通常有亲密、友好的含义。又 busy 一字描述祖父的

229

嘴唇不断张合，以代替"读着诗篇时"。

⑬ "暖炉上水壶的盖子，则像伴奏乐器似的振动着"译为 and the lid of the kettle over the heating stove rattling like a musical instrument playing an accompaniment，其中用 rattling 表达"振动"，而不用 vibrating 等，因 to rattle 不仅指"振动"，且指格格作响声，与"伴奏乐器"的比喻相呼应。

当　铺

萧　红

　　"你去当吧！你去当吧，我不去！"

　　"好，我去，我就愿意进当铺①，进当铺我一点也不怕，理直气壮。"

　　新做起来的我的棉袍，一次还没有穿，就跟着我进当铺去了！在当铺门口稍微徘徊了一下，想起出门时郎华要的价目②——非两元不当。

　　包袱送到柜台上，我是仰着脸，伸着腰，用脚尖站起来送上去的，真不晓得当铺为什么摆起这么高的柜台③！

　　那戴帽头的人翻着衣裳看，还不等他问，我就说了：

　　"两块钱。"

　　他一定觉得我太不合理，不然怎么连看我一眼也没看，就把东西卷起来，他把包袱仿佛要丢在我的头上，他十分不耐烦的样子④。

　　"两块钱不行，那么，多少钱呢？"

　　"多少钱不要。"他摇摇像长西瓜形的脑袋，小帽头顶尖的红帽球，也跟着摇了摇。

　　我伸手去接包袱，我一点也不怕，我理直气壮，我明明知道他故意作难⑤，正想把包袱接过来就走。猜得对对的，他并不把包袱真给我⑥。

"五毛钱！这件衣服袖子太瘦，卖不出钱来……"

"不当。"我说。

"那么一块钱，……再可不能多了，就是这个数目。"他把腰微微向后弯一点，柜台太高，看不出他突出的肚囊……一只大手指，就比在和他太阳穴一般高低的地方。

带着一元票子和一张当票，我快快地走，走起路来感到很爽快，默认自己是很有钱的人。菜市，米店我都去过，臂上抱了很多东西，感到非常愿意抱这些东西，手冻得很痛，觉得这是应该，对于手一点也不感到可惜，本来手就应该给我服务，好像冻掉了也不可惜。走在一家包子铺门前，又买了十个包子，看一看自己带着这些东西，很骄傲，心血时时激动，至于手冻得怎样痛，一点也不可惜。路旁遇见一个老叫化子，又停下来给他一个大铜板，我想我有饭吃，他也是应该吃啊！然而没有多给，只给一个大铜板，那些我自己还要用呢⑦！又摸一摸当票也没有丢，这才重新走，手痛得什么心思也没有了，快到家吧！快到家吧。但是，背上流了汗，腿觉得很软，眼睛有些刺痛⑧，走到大门口，才想起来从搬家还没有出过一次街，走路腿也无力，太阳光也怕起来。

又摸一摸当票才走进院去。郎华仍躺在床上，和我出来的时候一样，他还不习惯于进当铺。他是在想什么。拿包子给他看，他跳起来了：

"我都饿啦，等你也不回来。"

十个包子吃去一大半，他才细问："当多少钱？当铺没欺负你？"

把当票给他,他瞧着那样少的数目:

"才一元,太少。"

虽然说当得的钱少,可是又愿意吃包子,那么结果很满足⑨。他在吃包子的嘴⑩,看起来比包子还大,一个跟着一个,包子消失尽了。

The Pawnshop

Xiao Hong

"You go and do the pawning! You go, but not me!"

"OK, I go. I wouldn't mind. I'm not afraid at all. I don't see anything wrong about it."

Thus, my newly-made cotton-padded gown, which had not been worn even once, accompanied me to the pawnshop. At the door of the pawnshop I hesitated for a while, recalling the asking price suggested by Lang Hua when I left home—"Nothing less than two yuan."

I stood on tiptoe, face upward and back straightened, to hand the cloth-wrapped bundle onto the counter. How strange the pawnbroker should have put up a counter so forbiddingly high!

A man in a skullcap turned the gown over and over to examine it. Before he could open his mouth, I said,

"Two yuan."

He must have thought me too unreasonable, for he rolled up the gown without even taking a look at me. Impatience was written all over his face as if he were about

234

to throw the bundle onto my head.

"If two yuan won't do, then how much?"

"We won't take it for anything," said he, shaking his longish watermelon-shaped head, the decorative red bead on top of his skullcap swaying.

I was aware that he was out to make things difficult for me. Therefore, bold and confident, I reached out my hand for the bundle. But, just as I had been doubly sure, he simply wouldn't let go of it.

"Fifty cents! The sleeves are too tight. The gown won't fetch much...."

"I won't pawn it," said I.

"Well, how about one yuan?... Can't give you any more. That's final." He leaned back a little bit, his bulging paunch concealed behind the high counter.... Meanwhile, to signal "one yuan", he gestured with a finger raised as high as his temples.

Armed with a one-dollar note and a pawn ticket, I, unhappy as I was, walked with a light step and felt like one of the rich. I visited the food market and the grain shop. I did not tire of carrying an armful of purchases. My hands ached with cold, but this was as it should be. I felt no pity for them. It was their bounden duty to wait on me — even at the cost of suffering frostbite. I also bought ten steamed stuffed buns at a pastry shop. I was proud of my shopping. Again and again I felt so thrilled that I completely forgot all the pain in my frostbitten hands. When I saw an old beggar by the roadside, I stopped to give him a copper coin. Why, if I had food to eat, he certainly had no reason to go hungry! But I couldn't afford to give him more , for I needed the rest of the money for keeping my own body and soul together! Before I walked on again, I put my hand on the pawn ticket in my pocket to make sure that it was still there. By then, the pain in my hands had become the only thing I was conscious of. So I was anxious to be home again. My back sweated, my legs felt like jelly, my eyes stung. At the gate of my home, it suddenly occurred to me that this was the first time I had ever been out to town since I moved here and that accounted for my legs feeling so weak and my eyes being so shy of light.

On entering the courtyard, I touched the pawn ticket again. Lang Hua was still lying on the bed with the same aversion to a pawnshop. I wondered what was now in his mind. The moment I produced the buns, he jumped up from his bed,

" I'm so hungry. I've been long waiting for you to come back. "

It was not until he had gulped down more than half of the buns that he began to question me closely, "How much did you pawn it for? Did they cheat you?"

I showed him the pawn ticket and he eyed the pitifully small sum scratched on it.

"Only one yuan? Too little!"

True, the money was too little, but the buns were good to eat, so that all's well that ended well. One after another vanished the buns into his cavernous mouth — a mouth that looked even bigger than a bun.

注　释

萧红是有才华的女作家。从 1932
到 1934 年她与作家萧军在哈尔滨共同
度过了一段极艰苦的日子。《当铺》一文
所反映的即当时的生活情景。

①"我就愿意进当铺"译为 I wouldn't mind，所采用
的是正反表达法，把原文从正面表达的句子，在译文中从反
面来表达，以便提高译文的效果。

②"要的价目"译为 the asking price，为英语常用语，
是从 to ask a price 转过来的。

③"这么高的柜台"译为 a counter so forbiddingly
high，其中 forbiddingly 作"令人生畏"或"难以靠近"
（unfriendly 或 unapproachable）解，原文虽无其词而有其
意。

④"十分不耐烦的样子"译为 Impatience was written
all over his face，其中 to be written all over（或 on）作"显
露"解，为英语惯用表达法。

⑤"他故意作难"译为 he was out to make things difficult for me，其中 to be out to do（或 for）something 作

238

"企图"（to intend 或 want）解，为英语惯用表达法。

⑥ "他并不把包袱真给我"译为 he simply wouldn't let go of it，其中 let go of 是英语习用短语，作"放手"（to stop holding）解。

⑦ "然而没有多给……那些我自己还要用呢！"译为 But I couldn't afford to give him more, for I needed the rest of the money to keep my own body and soul together!，其中 to keep my own body and soul together 作"勉强维持生活"（just to make both ends meet）解，是译文中的添加成分，原文虽无其词，而有其意。

⑧ "背上流了汗，腿觉得很软，眼睛有些刺痛"译为 My back sweated, my legs felt like jelly, my eyes stung，三句并列，都用不及物动词，并采用连词省略法（asyndeton），有助于提高译文的表达效果。

⑨ "那么结果很满足"译为 so that all's well that ended well，其中 all's well that ends well 是英语谚语，作"有了好结果就行了"（It is the end that matters）解。

⑩ "嘴"译为 cavernous mouth，其中 cavernous 是为衬托原意而添加的成分，作"大而深"（very large and deep）解。

239

野　草

夏　衍

有这样一个故事。

有人问：世界上什么东西的气力最大①？回答纷纭的很，有的说"象"，有的说"狮"，有人开玩笑似的说：是"金刚"，金刚②有多少气力，当然大家全不知道。

结果，这一切答案完全不对③，世界上气力最大的，是植物的种子。一粒种子所可以显现出来的力，简直是超越一切，这儿又是一个故事。

人的头盖骨，结合得非常致密与坚固，生理学家和解剖学者用尽了一切的方法，要把它完整地分出来④，都没有这种力气，后来忽然有人发明了一个方法，就是把一些植物的种子放在要解剖的头盖骨里，给它以温度与湿度，使它发芽⑤，一发芽，这些种子便以可怕的力量，将一切机械力所不能分开的骨骼，完整地分开了。植物种子力量之大，如此如此。

这，也许特殊了一点，常人不容易理解，那么，你看见笋的成长吗？你看见过被压在瓦砾和石块下面的一颗小草的生成吗？它为着向往阳光，为着达成它的生之意志⑥，不管

240

上面的石块如何重，石块与石块之间如何狭，它必定要曲曲折折地，但是顽强不屈地透到地面上来，它的根往土壤钻，它的芽往地面挺，这是一种不可抗拒的力阻止它的石块，结果也被它掀翻，一粒种子的力量的大，如此如此。

没有一个人将小草叫做"大力士"⑦，但是它的力量之大，的确是世界无比，这种力，是一般人看不见的生命力，只要生命存在，这种力就要显现，上面的石块，丝毫不足以阻挡，因为它是一种"长期抗战"的力，有弹性，能屈能伸的力，有韧性，不达目的不止的力⑧。

种子不落在肥土而落在瓦砾中，有生命力的种子决不会悲观和叹气，因为有了阻力才有磨炼。生命开始的一瞬间就带了斗争来的草，才是坚韧的草，也只有这种草，才可以傲然地对那些玻璃棚中养育着的盆花哄笑。

Wild Grass

Xia Yan

There is a story which goes like this:

Someone asked, "What has the greatest strength on earth?" The answers varied. Some said, "The elephant." Some said, "The lion." Some said jokingly, "The fierce-browed guardian gods to Buddha." But nobody of course could tell how strong the guardian gods were supposed to be.

All the answers turned out to be wide of the mark. The mightiest thing on earth is the seed of a plant. The great strength which a seed is capable of is simply matchless. Here goes another story:

The bones forming a human skull are so tightly and perfectly fit together that all physiologists or anatomists, hard as they try, are powerless to take them apart without damaging them. It so happened that, at the suggestion of someone, some seeds of a plant were placed inside a human skull awaiting dissection before heat and moisture were applied to cause them to grow. Once they started to grow, they let loose a terrific force to separate all the skull bones, leaving each of them intact. This would have been impossible with any mechanical power under the sun. See, how powerful the seeds of a plant can be!

This story may be somewhat too unusual for you to understand. Well, have you ever seen the growth of a bamboo shoot? Or the growth of tender grass from under a heap of rubble or rocks? Seeking sunlight and survival, the young plant will labour tenaciously through twists and turns to bring itself to the surface of the ground no matter how heavy the rocks overhead may be or how narrow the opening between them. While striking its roots deep into the soil, the young plant pushes its new shoots aboveground. The irresistible strength it can muster is such as to overturn any rock in its way. See, how powerful a seed can be!

Though nobody describes the little grass as a "husky", yet its herculean strength is unrivalled. It is the force of life invisible to the naked eye. It will display itself so long as there is life. The rock is utterly helpless before this force — a force that will forever remain militant, a force that is resilient and can take temporary setbacks calmly, a force that is tenacity itself and will never give up until the goal is reached.

When a seed falls under debris instead of on fertile soil, it never sighs in despair because to meet with obstruction means to temper itself. Indomitable is the grass that begins its very life with a tough struggle. It is only fit and proper that the proud grass should be jeering at the potted flowers in a glass house.

注　释

　　　　《野草》是夏衍(1900—1995)于抗
　　战期间写的一篇寓理散文,赞颂小草的
　　那种为常人看不见的顽强生命力,以象
　　征手法鼓舞国人坚定抗战胜利的信心。
　　文章包含的深理对处于任何困难环境中
　　的革命者都有启发性。

　　①"世界上什么东西的气力最大"译为 What has the greatest strength on earth,其中 on earth 和 in the world 同义,但在此句用 on earth 较为合适,因 on earth 为成语,通常用于疑问词或最高级词后加强语气。

　　②"金刚"是"金刚力士"之略,指守护佛法的天神,常怒目作勇猛之相。现把它意译为 the fierce-browed guardian gods to Buddha,其中 fierce-browed 的意思是"怒目横眉"。

　　③"结果,这一切答案完全不对"译为 All the answers turned out to be wide of the mark,其中 wide of the mark 或 far from the mark 为成语,意即"离谱"、"不正确"。

④ "把它完整地分出来"即"把它完好无损地分开"，故译为 to take them apart without damaging them。

⑤ "使它发芽"的译文为 to cause them to grow。也可译为 to cause them to put out fresh shoots。

⑥ "为着向往阳光，为着达成它的生之意志"实际上的意思是"为了争取阳光和生存"，故译为 Seeking sunlight and survival 即可。

⑦ "没有一个人将小草叫做'大力士'"译为 Though nobody describes the little grass as a "husky"，其中 describes ...as 的意思是 "把……说成"、"把……称为"；husky 的意思是 "高大强壮的人"。

⑧ "有韧性，不达目的不止的力"译为 a force that is tenacity itself and will never give up until the goal is reached，其中 itself 一词用来加强前面的抽象名词 tenacity，属习惯用法。

恋爱不是游戏

庐　　隐

没有在浮沉的人海中①，翻过筋斗的和尚，不能算善知识②；

没有受过恋爱洗礼的人生，不能算真人生。

和尚最大的努力，是否认现世而求未来的涅槃③，但他若不曾了解现世，他又怎能勘破现世④，而跳出三界⑤外呢？

而恋爱是人类生活的中心，孟子说："食色性也。"所谓恋爱正是天赋之本能；如一生不了解恋爱的人，他又何能了解整个的人生？

所以凡事都从学习而知而能，只有恋爱用不着学习，只要到了相当的年龄，碰到合式（适）的机会，他和她便会莫名其妙地恋爱起来。

恋爱人人都会⑥，可是不见得人人都懂⑦；世俗大半以性欲伪充恋爱，以游戏的态度处置恋爱，于是我们时刻可看到因恋爱而不幸的记载。

实在的恋爱绝不是游戏，也绝不是堕落的人生所能体验出其价值的，它具有引人向上的鞭策力，它也具有伟大无私的至上情操，它更是美丽的象征。

在一双男女正纯洁热爱着的时候，他和她内心充实着惊人的力量；他们的灵魂是从万有的束缚中，得到了自由，不怕威胁，不为利诱，他们是超越了现实，而创造他们理想的乐园。

不幸物欲充塞的现世界，这种恋爱的光辉，有如萤火之微弱，而且"恋爱"有时适成为无知男女堕落之阶，使维纳斯不禁深深地叹息："自从世界人群趋向灭亡之途，恋爱变成了游戏，哀哉！"

Love Is Not a Game

Lu Yin

A Buddhist monk without having experienced ups and downs in the sea of mortals will have no claim to true wisdom.

Likewise, one who has never gone through the baptism of romantic love will have little genuine knowledge of life.

Buddhist monks exert every effort to renounce this life in favour of future nirvana. But, without a full knowledge of this life, how could they see through the vanity of human society and make a clean break with this mortal world?

Romantic love is the core of human life. Mencius says, "The desire for food and sex is nature." In other words, love is innate. If one remains a lifelong stranger to love, how can he thoroughly understand life?

Man becomes capable through learning. But love is an exception. Boy and girl, when they are of age and meet at an opportune moment, will become mysteriously attached to each other.

Though people love by instinct, yet all cannot understand it correctly. More often than not, love is but carnal
desire in disguise and is treated as a mere game. That is
why we so often hear tragic stories of love.

True love is not a game. Nor can its true value be appreciated by the morally degenerate. True love spurs one
on to higher attainment. It embodies the supreme quality
of selflessness, and is, above all, symbolic of beauty.

When a man and woman are deeply immersed in true
love, they are full of amazing inner strength. Their souls
are freed from all bondage. They are unyielding before
threats and incorruptible before any promise of material
gain. They transcend the reality to create an ideal par-
adise of their own.

Unfortunately, in this present world overflowing
with material desires, this kind of true love is as rare as
the feeble light of fireflies. What is more, "love" sometimes even leads to moral degeneration on the part of ignorant men and women. Over this, Venus cannot help
lamenting with a deep sigh, "Love has become a mere
game ever since humanity set out on its way to extinction.
O what a sad story!"

注　释

　　女作家庐隐(1898—1934)，福建闽
侯人，早期与冰心齐名。她的杂文短小精
悍，直爽坦率，笔锋锐利，在这篇《恋爱不
是游戏》中也有所反映。

　　①"浮沉的人海中"译为 ups and downs in the sea of
mortals，其中 ups and downs 意同 vicissitudes（兴败、盛
衰）；the sea of mortals 意同 the sea of the living。
　　②"不能算善知识"意即"没有资格称为智者"，现译
为 will have no claim to true wisdom，其中 have no claim
to 本作"对……没有提出要求的权利"解，现作"没有资格
称为……"解。此句也可译为 will have no true wisdom to
speak of，但与原意稍有出入。
　　③"涅槃"为佛经用语，指信教者经过长期"修道"所
达到的最高境界。后世也称僧人逝世为"涅槃"（又称"入
灭"或"圆寂"）。英语称之为 virvana，源于印度梵语。
　　④"勘破现世"意同"看破红尘"，现译为 see through
the vanity of human society。
　　⑤"跳出三界"中的"三界"也是佛教用语，指"众生

所住的世界"，现按"与现世一刀两断"的意思把"跳出三界"译为 make a clean break with this mortal world。

⑥ "恋爱人人都会"意即"恋爱出于本能"，故译 People love by instinct。

⑦ "可是不见得人人都懂"译为 yet all cannot understand it correctly，等于 yet not all can understand it correctly。

我 若 为 王

聂 绀 弩

在电影刊物上看见一个影片的名字:《我若为王》①。从这影片的名字,我想到和影片毫无关系的另外的事②。我想,自己如果作了王,这世界会成为一种怎样的光景呢?这自然是一种完全可笑的幻想,我根本不想作王③,也根本看不起王,王是什么东西呢?难道我脑中还有如此封建的残物么?而且真想作王的人,他将用他的手去打天下,决不会放在口里说的。但是假定又假定,我若为王,这世界会成为一种怎样的光景?

我若为王,自然我的妻就是王后了。我的妻的德性,我不怀疑,为王后只会有余的。但纵然没有任何德性,纵然不过是个娼妓,那时候,她也仍旧是王后。一个王后是如何地尊贵呀,会如何地被人们像捧着天上的星星一样捧来捧去呀,假如我能够想象,那一定是一件有趣的事情。

我若为王,我的儿子,假如我有儿子,就是太子或王子了。我并不以为我的儿子会是一无所知,一无所能的白痴④,但纵然是一无所知一无所能的白痴,也仍旧是太子或王子。一个太子或王子是如何地尊贵呀,会如何地被人们

253

像捧天上的星星一样地捧来捧去呀。假如我能想象,倒是件不是没有趣味的事。

我若为王,我的女儿就是公主,我的亲眷都是皇亲国戚。无论他们怎样丑陋,怎样顽劣,怎样……⑤也会被人们像捧天上的星星一样地捧来捧去,因为她们是贵人。

我若为王,我的姓名就会改作:"万岁",我的每一句话都成为:"圣旨"。我的意欲,我的贪念,乃至每一个幻想,都可竭尽全体臣民的力量去实现,即使是无法实现的。我将没有任何过失,因为没有人敢说它是过失;我将没有任何罪行,因为没有人敢说它是罪行。没有人敢呵斥我,指摘我,除非把我从王位上赶下来。但是赶下来,就是我不为王了。我将看见所有的人们在我面前低头,鞠躬,匍匐⑥,连同我的尊长,我的师友,和从前曾在我面前昂头阔步耀武扬威的人们。我将看不见一个人的脸,所看见的只是他们的头顶或帽盔。或者所能够看见的脸都是谄媚的,乞求的,快乐的时候不敢笑,不快乐的时候不敢不笑,悲戚的时候不敢哭,不悲戚的时候不敢不哭的脸。我将听不见人们的真正的声音,所能听见的都是低微的,柔婉的,畏葸⑦和娇痴的,唱小旦的声音:"万岁,万岁!万万岁!"这是他们的全部语言。"有道明君!伟大的主上啊!"这就是那语言的全部内容。没有在我之上的人了,没有和我同等的人了,我甚至会感到单调,寂寞和孤独。

为什么人们要这样呢?为什么要捧我的妻,捧我的儿女和亲眷呢?因为我是王,是他们的主子,我将恍然大悟:我生活在这些奴才们中间,连我所敬畏的尊长和师友也无一不是奴才,而我自己也不过是一个奴才的首领。

254

我是民国国民,民国国民的思想和生活习惯使我深深地憎恶一切奴才或奴才相⑧,连同敬畏的尊长和师友们。请科学家们不要见笑,我以为世界之所以还有待于改进者⑨,全因为有这些奴才的缘故。生活在奴才们中间,作奴才们的首领,我将引为生平的最大耻辱,最大的悲哀。我将变成一个暴君,或者反而是明君:我将把我的臣民一齐杀死,连同尊长和师友,不准一个奴种留在人间。我将没有一个臣民,我将不再是奴才们的君主。

我若为王,将终于不能为王⑩,却也真地为古今中外最大的王了。"万岁,万岁,万万岁!"我将和全世界的真的人们一同三呼。

If I Were King

Nie Gannu

Recently in a movie magazine I came across the title of a film: *If I Were King*. It has put me in mind of something entirely foreign to the film in question. I wonder what would become of this world if I myself were king. This is of course a ridiculous fancy, for being a king is the last thing I aspire to and also a thing I utterly despise. What the hell is a king? How can I still be so feudalistic in my mind? Moreover, if one is really bent on being a king, he will try to carry out his design by deeds instead of by words. But, to put it hypothetically, suppose I were king, what would this world look like?

If I were king, my wife would of course be queen. With all her moral excellence, of which I make no doubt, she would be more than qualified for being a queen. But even if she had no virtue to speak of, or were just a whore, she would be queen all the same. Imagine how noble and dignified a queen would be and how people would keep lauding her to the skies like mad! It is indeed great fun for me to visualize all of this.

If I were king, my son, if any, would be crown prince or prince. I don't think my son will be ignorant or worthless in every way like an idiot. But, even if that were not the case, he would still be crown prince or prince. Imagine how noble and dignified a crown prince or prince would be and how people would keep lauding him to the skies like mad! It is indeed great fun for me to visualize all of this.

If I were king, my daughters would be princesses, and my relatives by marriage would all become members of the royal family. No matter how ugly or perverse or whatnot they were, people would keep lauding them to the skies like mad just the same because they were dignitaries.

If I were king, I would be addressed as "Your Majesty" and every word of mine would become a "royal edict". All my subjects would leave no stone unturned to carry out every will, every avaricious desire and even every whim of mine, even though they were all beyond the possible. I would do no wrong simply because no one dared to call it a wrong. I would commit no crime simply because no one dared to call it a crime. No one would dare to berate or find fault with me unless I was removed from the throne, which meant that I was no longer the king. I would see all people hang their heads, bow low or prostrate themselves at my feet, including my respected elders, teachers, friends and even those who had used to swagger arrogantly in front of me. I could see none of their faces; all I could see were the tops of their heads or the hats or helmets on their heads. The only faces I could see would be ingratiating or supplicating — faces that dared not smile to express joy; faces that dared not refrain from a forced smile when there was no joy at all to justify a smile; faces that dared not cry to express sorrow; faces that dared not refrain from a feigned cry when there was no sorrow to justify a cry. I could hear no true voices of my people. All I could hear would be the feeble, soft, timid and affected voice, like that of a female Peking opera singer, chanting, "Long live the King!" That would be their language in toto. "Great is the King, our enlightened lord!" That would be the sole content of their language. There would be no one above me or on an equal footing with me. I would even feel bored, lonely and isolated.

Why would people behave like that? Why would they flatter my wife, my children and my relatives? Because I was king, their master. It would suddenly dawn on me that living among these flunkeys, including my esteemed elders, teachers and friends, I myself, too, was nothing but a mere head flunkey.

I am the citizen of the Republic. Being accustomed to

the mode of thinking and living of a republican citizen, I would deeply abhor all servility and flunkeys, including my esteemed elders, teachers and friends. Dear scientists, please don't laugh at me. Methinks the world is very much in need of reform simply because of the presence of these flunkeys. I would regard it as the deepest disgrace and sorrow of my life to live among the flunkeys and become their chief. I would rather become a tyrant or an enlightened king so that I could kill off all my subjects, among them my respected elders, teachers and friends, and have the flunkey species exterminated once for all. Then, with all my subjects gone, I would no longer be the king of flunkeys.

If I were king and ultimately ended up becoming no king at all, I would indeed be the greatest king that had ever breathed since time immemorial. I would join true people all the world over in giving three cheers for myself.

注　释

　　《我若为王》是中国现代杰出杂文家聂绀弩(1903—1986)写于1941年的一篇杂文,文字通俗易懂,内容讽刺辛辣,流露了对专制统治者和奴才的蔑视。

　　①“我若为王”译为 If I Were King,其中 King 的前面省略了冠词 a。在指职位、头衔、等级等的名词前面大多不用冠词 a 或 an。

　　②“和影片毫无关系的另外的事”译为 something entirely foreign to the film in question,其中 foreign to 为成语,作 having no relation to 或 unconnected with 解。又 in question 是添加成分,作 being talked about（正被谈论的）解。

　　③“我根本不想作王”译为 being a king is the last thing I aspire to,其中 last 一词作 least likely 或 most un-likely（最不可能的）解。

　　④“一无所知,一无所能的白痴”译为 ignorant or worthless in every way like an idiot,其中 in every way 作“完全”或“彻头彻尾”解。

⑤"无论他们怎样丑陋,怎样顽劣,怎样……"中的最后一个"怎样……"意即"诸如此类的事"或"等等",现译为 or whatnot。英语 whatnot 作 other such things 解,为 what may I not say? 的省略。

⑥"匍匐"在此指俯伏或拜倒动作(表示顺从),现译为 prostrate。

⑦"畏葸"作"胆怯"解,现译为 timid。

⑧"奴才相"译为 servility。英语 servility 意即 slavishness 或 slave-like deference。

⑨"我以为世界之所以大有待于改进者"译为 Methinks the world is very much in need of reform,其中 Methinks 等于 I think 或 It seems to me,为无人称动词,本为古体词,现常作诙谐打趣用语。

⑩"我若为王,将终于不能为王"译为 If I were king and ultimately ended up becoming no king at all,其中 ended up 是成语,作"告终"解。例如:He never dreamed that he would end up owning such a big fortune。

清　贫

方 志 敏

　　我从事革命斗争，已经十余年了。在这长期的奋斗中，我一向是过着朴素的生活，从没有奢侈过。经手的款项，总在数百万元；但为革命而筹集的金钱，是一点一滴地用之于革命事业。这在国民党的伟人们①看来，颇似奇迹，或认为夸张；而矜持不苟，舍己为公，却是每个共产党员具备的美德。所以，如果有人问我身边有没有一些积蓄，那我可以告诉你一桩趣事②：

　　就在我被俘的那一天——一个最不幸的日子，有两个国民党军的兵士，在树林中发现了我，而且猜到我是什么人的时候，他们满肚子热望在我身上搜出一千或八百大洋③，或者搜出一些金镯金戒指一类的东西，发个意外之财④。那知道从我上身摸到下身，从袄领捏到袜底，除了一只时表和一枝自来水笔之外，一个铜板都没有搜出。他们于是激怒起来了，猜疑我是把钱藏在那里，不肯拿出来。他们之中有一个左手拿着一个木柄榴弹，右手拉出榴弹中的引线⑤，双脚拉开一步，作出要抛掷的姿势，用凶恶的眼光钉住我，威吓地吼道：

262

"赶快将钱拿出来,不然就是一炸弹,把你炸死去!⑥"

"哼!你不要作出那难看的样子来吧!我确实一个铜板都没有存;想从我这里发洋财,是想错了。⑦"我微笑着淡淡地说。

"你骗谁!⑧像你当大官的人会没有钱!⑨"拿榴弹的兵士坚不相信。

"决不会没有钱的⑩,一定是藏在那里,我是老出门的⑪,骗不得我。"另一个兵士一面说,一面弓着背重来一次将我的衣角裤裆过细的捏,总企望着有新的发现。

"你们要相信我的话,不要瞎忙吧⑫!我不比你们国民党当官的,个个都有钱,我今天确实是一个铜板也没有,我们革命不是为着发财啦!"我再向他们解释。

等他们确知在我身上搜不出什么的时候,也就停手不搜了;又在我藏躲地方的周围,低头注目搜寻了一番,也毫无所得,他们是多么地失望呵!那个持弹欲放的兵士,也将拉着的引线,仍旧塞进榴弹的木柄里,转过来抢夺我的表和水笔。后彼此说定表和笔卖出钱来平分,才算无话。他们用怀疑而又惊异的目光,对我自上而下地望了几遍,就同声命令地说:"走吧!"

是不是还要问问我家里有没有一些财产?请等一下,让我想一想,啊,记起来了,有的有的,但不算多。去年暑天我穿的几套旧的汗褂裤,与几双缝上底的线袜,已交给我的妻放在深山坞里保藏着——怕国民党军进攻时,被人抢了去,准备今年暑天拿出来再穿;那些就算是我唯一的财产了。但我说出那几件"传世宝"来,岂不要叫那些富翁们齿冷三天?⑬!

清贫,洁白朴素的生活,正是我们革命者能够战胜许多困难的地方!

Honest Poverty

Fang Zhimin

I have been engaged in the revolutionary struggle for more than a decade. During these long militant years, I have lived a plain life with no luxuries to speak of. Millions of dollars passed through my hands, but I always saw to it that every single cent of the money raised for the revolution was spent for no other purposes. This may sound like a miracle or an exaggeration to Kuomintang VIPs. Self-discipline and self-sacrifice, however, are the virtue characteristic of a Communist. Therefore, should anyone inquire of me about my personal savings, let him read the following amusing episode:

On the day of my capture — a most inauspicious day it was — two Kuomintang soldiers discovered me in a wood. Sizing me up, they thought they had come upon a windfall and started making a frantic body search, hopefully to find on me hundreds of silver dollars or some jewellery like gold bracelets or rings. They frisked me from top to toe and passed their hands over everything on me from the collar of my jacket to the soles of my socks, but, contrary to their expectation, they found nothing at all, not even a single copper, except a watch and a fountain pen. They were exasperated, suspecting that I had my money hidden somewhere and refused to give it up. One of the two men had in his left hand a wooden-handled grenade. He pulled out the cord from inside the wooden handle and moved his legs one step apart as if he was about to throw the grenade. Glowering at me ferociously, he threatened loudly,

"Out with your money quick, or you die!"

"Hey!" I said drily with a faint smile. "Don't you put on such nasty airs! True I haven't got a single copper with me. You're barking up the wrong tree to seek a fortune from me."

"Shit! Nobody can ever believe a big shot like you ain't got no money!" the soldier with the grenade remained wholly incredulous.

"No money?" the other soldier joined in. "Impossible! It must be hidden somewhere. No fooling an old hand like me." Meanwhile, he bent low to pass his hand again meticulously over every nook and corner of my clothes and the crotch of my trousers, still holding out high hopes of making a new discovery.

"You should believe me and stop messing around!" I explained again. "Unlike your Kuomintang officials

266

who're rolling in money, I'm really penniless. We join the
revolution not for personal gain. "

Finally, when they knew for certain that there was
no money on me, they gave up the body search. Nevertheless, they lowered their heads to scan here and there
the place where I had hidden myself, but again in vain.
How frustrated they must have felt! The soldier holding
the grenade pushed the cord back into its wooden handle,
and turned round to scramble for my watch and fountain
pen. The two men, however, settled their dispute by a-
greeing to divide the money equally between them after
selling the spoils. They eyed me up and down with suspi-
cion and amazement before barking out in chorus, "Come
along!"

Dear readers, maybe you wish to know if I have any
private property at home. Just a minute! Let me see ....
Ah, here it is, but nothing much though. I have left with
my wife for safekeeping a few changes of used underwear
and a few pairs of socks with mended soles, all of which I
used to wear last summer. She has now put them away in
a remote mountain valley to prevent them from being
stolen in case of Kuomintang attack, so that I may wear
them again this summer. These are all the property I have
to my name. But wouldn't the declaration of my "family
treasures" make myself an object of lively ridicule to the
rich?

To remain honest though poor, to live a clean and simple life — that is what we revolutionries count on to overcome innumerable difficulties!

注　释

　　《清贫》是方志敏烈士 1935 年英勇就义前在江西国民党监狱中写下的不朽散文。文章通过真人真事表达作者清廉朴素的生活和崇高的人生目的,情挚意深,爱憎分明。

　　① "国民党伟人们"指"国民党要人们",故译为 Kuomintang VIPs。

　　② "一桩趣事"可译为 amusing event、occurrence、episode 等,但以 episode 较为合适,因它指一系列事件中的一件。

　　③ "一千或八百大洋"中的"大洋"指"银元",故译为 silver dollars。

　　④ "发个意外之财"译为 had come upon a windfall,其中 windfall 本指 a piece of fruit blown off a tree by the wind,现指 a piece of unexpected fortune。

　　⑤ "拉出手榴弹中的引线"中的"引线"不是"引信"(fuse),故译为 cord。

　　⑥ "不然就是一炸弹,把你炸死去"本可按字面直译

为 or the bomb finishes you off，现译为 or you die，简洁明白，较口语化。又动词 die 用现在不定式，不用将来式 will die，是为了表达一种必然将发生的事（a certainty）。

⑦ "想从我这里发财,是想错了"译为 You're barking up the wrong tree to seek a fortune from me，其中 to bark up the wrong tree 是常见于口语的习语,意即 "找错地方" 或 "找错人"。

⑧ "你骗谁"是粗鲁话,相当于 "胡说"，不宜直译,现译为 Shit。

⑧ "像你当大官的人会没有钱"译为 A big shot like you ain't got no money?，其中 ain't 等于 hasn't，常见于口语。又译句中用两个否定（double negative）表达一个否定,为文化低的人所用的不规范英语。

⑩ "决不会没有钱的"是恶狠狠的话,不宜逐字直译,现根据人物对话情景译为 No money? Impossible，取其神似。

⑪ "老出门的"意即 "老手"，故译为 an old hand。

⑫ "不要瞎忙吧"意即 "别胡闹",可译为 don't act or speak stupidly，但欠口语化,现译为 stop messing around 或 stop mucking around。

⑬ "叫那些富翁们齿冷三天"意即 "被那些有钱人尽情嘲笑",现译为 make myself an object of lively ridicule to the rich。

离　别①

郑　振　铎

　　别了，我爱的中国，我全心爱着的中国，当我倚在高高的船栏上，见着船渐渐的离岸了②，船与岸间的水面渐渐的阔了③，见着许多亲友挥着白巾，挥着帽子，挥着手，说着Adieu, adieu！听着鞭炮劈劈拍拍的响着，水兵们高呼着向岸上的同伴告别时，我的眼眶是润湿了，我自知我的泪点已经滴在眼镜面了，镜面是模糊了，我有一种说不出的感动！

　　船慢慢的向前驶着，沿途见了停着的好几只灰色的白色的军舰。不，那不是悬着我们国旗的，它们的旗帜是"红日"④，是"蓝白红"⑤，是"红蓝条交叉着"的联合旗⑥，是有"星点红条"的旗⑦！

　　两岸是黄土和青草，再过去是两条的青痕，再过去是地平线上的几座小岛山，海水满盈盈的照在夕阳之下，浪涛如顽皮的小童似的跳跃不定。水面上现出一片的金光。

　　别了，我爱的中国，我全心爱着的中国！

　　我不忍离了中国而去⑧，更不忍在这大时代中放弃每人应做的工作而去⑨，抛弃了许多亲爱的勇士们在后面，他们是正用他们的血建造着新的中国，正在以纯挚的热诚，争

271

斗着，奋击着。我这样不负责任的离开了中国，我真是一个罪人！

然而我终将在这大时代中工作着的，我终将为中国而努力，而呈献了我的身，我的心；我别了中国，为的是求更好的经验，求更好的奋斗的工具。暂别了，暂别了[⑩]，在各方面争斗着的勇士们，我不久即将以更勇猛的力量加入你们当中了。

当我归来时，我希望这些悬着"红日"的，"蓝白红"的，有"星点红条"的，"红蓝条交叉着"的一切旗帜的白色灰色的军舰都已不见了[⑪]，代替它们的是我们的可喜爱的悬着我们的旗帜的伟大的舰队。

如果它们那时还没有退去中国海[⑫]，还没有为我们所消灭，那末，来，勇士们，我将加入你们的队中，以更勇猛的力量，去压迫它们，去毁灭它们！

这是我的誓言！

别了，我爱的中国，我全心爱着的中国！

Parting Sorrows

Zheng Zhenduo

Farewell, China, my beloved homeland! Leaning over the high railing, I watched the ship tearing itself away slowly from the shore, leaving a widening expanse of water in between. Many relatives and friends of mine were waving their hats and white handkerchiefs amidst shouts of "Adieu, adieu!" Firecrackers were crackling and spluttering, and sailors shouting goodbye to their buddies on the shore. I was seized with violent emotion, tears welling up in my eyes and blurring my eyeglasses.

While the ship was steering ahead slowly, I saw on the way many warships in gray or white lying at anchor and flying flags other than our national ones. They were flying the red sun, the tricolour, the union jack or the stars and stripes.

The banks with their yellowish soil and green grass receded into two greenish strips until they became some mere islets on the horizon. The waters of the sea glistened under the setting sun and kept leaping like romping urchins. The water surface was a vast expanse of gold.

Farewell, China, my beloved homeland!

I cannot find it in my heart to leave China, much less during these stormy times when I have to abandon my bounden duty and leave behind so many dear brave fighters — men who are building a new China with their own blood and struggling and battling in all earnest. To quit China at this moment means to dodge my responsibility, and that makes me feel very guilty indeed!

Nevertheless, I shall eventually answer the call of the times and devote myself heart and soul to my motherland. I am parting from China to acquire more experience and search for better ways of struggle. Dear brave fighters of every field, I shall be separated from you only for the present and will soon return to join your ranks with redoubled strength.

On my return, I hope, I shall see no more gray or white warships plying our territorial waters with flags of the red sun, the tricolour, the union jack or the stars and stripes. I hope I shall see instead our lovely great fleet flying our national colours.

Dear brave fighters, if the foreign warships by that time still hang on to their presence in our territorial waters, I will join you to do my bit in getting rid of them.

That is my pledge!

Farewell, China, my beloved homeland!

274

注　释

郑振铎(1898—1958)是我国现代作家、学者。为躲避国民党当局的政治迫害，他于1927年8月乘船远离祖国，前往法国巴黎和英国伦敦游学，1929年10月归国。《离别》一文写于这一时期，内分三部分，其中第一部分抒发即将去国的志士情怀。现将此部分译成英文。

① 题目《离别》译为 Parting Sorrows，不仅表示告别，且同时把离愁别绪也作了交代。如译为 Parting from Homeland 或 Farewell to China 似缺内涵。

② "见着船渐渐的离岸了"译为 I watched the ship tearing itself away slowly from the shore，其中 tearing itself away 也可用 moving away 表达，但缺少惜别的感情色彩。

③ "船与岸间的水面渐渐的阔了"译为 leaving a widening expanse of water in between，其中 in between 指 between the ship and the shore。

④ "红日"指日本国旗，译为 the red sun，后面未加

275

flag，是为配合造句。否则也可译为 the sun flag (hino-maru) 或 the rising-sun flag。

⑤ "蓝白红"指法国国旗，英语中常以 the tricolour 表达。

⑥ "'红蓝条交叉着'的联合旗"指英国国旗，英语中以 the union jack 或 the union flag 表达。

⑦ "'星点红条'的旗"即美国国旗，英语中称之为 the stars and stripes。

⑧ "我不忍离了中国而去"译为 I cannot find it in my heart to leave China，其中 to find it in one's heart to ... 是成语，作 "不忍作……"解。此句也可译为 I cannot bear to leave China。

⑨ "更不忍在这大时代中放弃每人应做的工作而去"译为 much less during these stormy times when I have to abandon my bounden duty，其中 much less 是成语，常跟在否定句后面，作 "更不" (and certainly not) 解。又，"这大时代"按内涵译为 these stormy times，未按字面直译为 the great times。

⑩ "暂别了"译为 I shall be separated from you only for the present，其中 for the present 和 for the time being 同义，都作 "暂时"、"眼下"解。

⑪ "白色灰色的军舰都已不见了"译为 I shall see no more gray or white warships plying our territorial waters，其中 plying our territorial waters（往返于我国领海）是添加成分，原文虽无其字，但有其意。

⑫ "如果它们那时还没有退去中国海"译为 if the for-

eign warships by that time still hang on to their presence in our territorial waters，其中 hang on to 是成语，作"抓住不放"、"不肯放弃"解。又 presence 一词现常用来指(军、政)"势力"、"存在"。

时间即生命

梁 实 秋

　　最令人怵目惊心的一件事,是看着钟表上的秒针一下
一下的移动,每移动一下就是表示我们的寿命已经缩短了
一部分。再看看墙上挂着的可以一张张撕下的日历,每天
撕下一张就是表示我们的寿命又缩短了一天。因为时间即
生命。没有人不爱惜他的生命,但很少人珍视他的时间。如
果想在有生之年做一点什么事,学一点什么学问,充实自
己,帮助别人,使生命成为有意义,不虚此生,那么就不可浪
费光阴。这道理人人都懂①,可是很少人真能积极不懈的善
为利用他的时间。

　　我自己就是浪费了很多时间的一个人②。我不打麻将,
我不经常的听戏看电影,几年中难得一次,我不长时间看电
视,通常只看半个小时,我也不串门子闲聊天。有人问我:
"那么你大部分时间都做了些什么呢?"我痛自反省,我发
现,除了职务上的必须及人情上所不能免的活动之外,我的
时间大部分都浪费了。我应该集中精力,读我所未读过的
书,我应该利用所有时间,写我所要写的东西。但是我没能
这样做。我的好多的时间都糊里糊涂的混过去了,"少壮不

努力,老大徒伤悲。"

例如我翻译莎士比亚,本来计划于课余之暇每年翻译两部,二十年即可完成,但是我用了三十年,主要的原因是懒。翻译之所以完成,主要的是因为活得相当长久,十分惊险③。翻译完成之后,虽然仍有工作计划,但体力渐衰,有力不从心之感④。假使年轻的时候鞭策自己,如今当有较好或较多的表现。然而悔之晚矣。

再例如,作为一个中国人,经书不可不读。我年过三十才知道读书自修的重要⑤。我披阅,我圈点,但是恒心不足,时作时辍。五十以学易,可以无大过矣⑥,我如今年过八十,还没有接触过《易经》,说来惭愧。史书也很重要。我出国留学的时候,我父亲买了一套同文石印的前四史⑦,塞满了我的行箧的一半空间,我在外国混了几年之后又把前四史原封带回来了。直到四十年后才鼓起勇气读了《通鉴》⑧一遍。现在我要读的书太多,深感时间有限。

无论做什么事,健康的身体是基本条件。我在学校读书的时候,有所谓"强迫运动",我踢破过几双球鞋,打断过几只球拍。因此侥幸维持下来最低限度的体力。老来打过几年太极拳,目前则以散步活动筋骨而已。寄语年轻朋友,千万要持之以恒的从事运动,这不是嬉戏,不是浪费时间。健康的身体是作人做事的真正的本钱⑨。

Time Is Life

Liang Shiqiu

It is most startling to hear a watch or clock clicking away the seconds, each click indicating the shortening of one's life by a little bit. Likewise, with each page torn off the wall calendar, one's life is shortened by another day. Time, therefore, is life. Nevertheless, few people treasure their time as much as their life. Time must not be wasted if you want to do your bit in your remaining years or acquire some useful knowledge to improve yourself and help others, so that your life may turn out to be significant and fruitful. All that is foolproof, yet few people really strive to make the best use of their time.

Personally, I am also a fritterer. I don't play mahjong. I seldom go to the theatre or cinema — I go there maybe only once every few years. I seldom spend long hours watching TV — usually I watch TV for no more than 30 minutes at a sitting. Nor do I go visiting and gossiping from door to door. Some people asked me, "Then what do you do with most of your time?" Introspecting with remorse, I found that apart from the time earmarked for my job and unavoidable social activities, most of my time had been wasted. I should have concentrated my energies on reading whatever books I have not yet read. I should have utilized all my time in writing anything I want to write. But I've failed to do so. Very much of my time has been frittered away aimlessly. As the saying goes, "One who does not work hard in youth will grieve in vain in old age."

Take the translation of Shakespeare for example. I had initially planned to spend 20 years of my spare time in doing the translation, finishing two plays a year. But I spent 30 years instead, due primarily to my slothfulness. The whole project would probably have fallen through had it not been for my fairly long life. After that I had other plans for work, but, because of my approaching senility, somehow I failed to do what I had wished to. Had I spurred myself on in my youth, I would have done more and better work. Alas, it is too late to repent.

Another example. The reading of Chinese classics is a must for all Chinese. But it was not until I was over 30 that I came to realize the importance of self-study in the matter of classics. I did read carefully though, marking words and phrases for special attention with small circles and dots. But my efforts at self-study were off and on. Confucius says, "I shall be free of great faults if I can live long enough to begin the study of *Yi*① at the age of 50. " I feel ashamed to admit that I haven't even touched *Yi* though I'm now over 80. Chinese history books are equally important. When I was leaving China to study abroad, father bought a set of the Tong Wen lithographic edition of the First Four Books of History②, and crammed them into my travelling box, taking up half of its space. Several years later, however, after drifting along abroad, I returned home carrying with me the same books all unread. It was not until 40 years later that I plucked up enough courage to read through *Tong Jian*③. So many books still remain to be read, and I much regret not having enough time to do it.

Whatever you do, you need a sound body first of all. In my school days, in response to the so-called "compulsory physical exercises", I went in for many sports at the expense of many pairs of sneakers and rackets, thus luckily building up a minimum of good physique. When I was approaching old age, I did *tai ji quan* (shadow boxing) for several years. Now I only do some walking exercises.

---

① *Yi* — *The Book of Changes.*
② the First Four Books of History — *The Historical Records, The Book of Han, The Book of Later Han* and *The Annals of the Three Kingdoms.*
③ *Tong Jian* — the 294-volume chronicle by Sima Guang.

Dear young friends, my advice to you is: Do physical exercises perseveringly. That has nothing to do with merrymaking or time-wasting. Good health is the wherewithal for a successful life and career.

注　释

梁实秋(1902—1987)为我国著名现代作家、翻译家、教育家，一生致力于英国文学研究。《时间即生命》一文选自他的散文集《雅舍小品》。

①"这道理人人都懂"译为 All that is foolproof，其中 foolproof 作 very simple to understand 解，意同"不言而喻"或"简单明了"。此句也可译为 All that is self-evident。

②"我自己就是浪费了很多时间的一个人"译为 Personally, I am also a fritterer，其中 fritterer 一词在用法上既可泛指"时间、金钱等等的浪费者"，又可专指"不爱惜时间的人"(a person who wastes time)。

③"翻译之所以完成，主要的是因为活得相当长久，十分惊险"的意思是"幸亏自己命长，否则可能完成不了莎士比亚的翻译"。其中"十分惊险"的意思是"险些完成不了"。现全句译为 The whole project would probably have fallen through had it not been for my fairly long life。

④"但体力渐衰，有力不从心之感"译为 because of

my approaching senility, somehow I failed to do what I had wished to，其中 senility 指因年迈而导致身心两方面的衰退。

⑤ "才知道读书自修的重要"中的"读书"，根据上下文应指"读经书"，故此句译为 came to realize the importance of self-study in the matter of classics，其中 in the matter of 作 in relation to 或 in regard to（就……而论）解。

⑥ "五十以学易，可以无大过矣"出自《论语·述而》中的"子曰，加我数年，五十以学易，可以无大过矣。"其意为"让我再多活几年，到五十岁时去学习《易经》，就可以没有多大的过错了。"现按此意用加字法译为 Confucius says, "I shall be free of great faults if I can live long enough to begin the study of *Yi* at the age of 50."

⑦ "前四史"指《史记》、《汉书》、《后汉书》以及《三国志》。

⑧ "《通鉴》"即《资治通鉴》，详见译文脚注。

⑨ "健康的身体是作人做事的真正的本钱"译为 Good health is the wherewithal for a successful life and career，其中 the wherewithal 意同 the necessary means（必要的资金、手段等）。又"作人做事"指"生活"与"事业"两方面，故参照上下文译为 a successful life and career。

学问与趣味

梁 实 秋

前辈的学者常以学问的趣味启迪后生，因为他们自己实在是得到了学问的趣味，故不惜现身说法，诱导后学①，使他们也在愉快的心情之下走进学问的大门②。例如，梁任公先生就说过③："我是个主张趣味主义④的人，倘若用化学化分'梁启超'这件东西⑤，把里头所含一种原素名叫'趣味'的抽出来，只怕所剩下的仅有个零了。"任公先生注重趣味，学问甚是渊博，而并不存有任何外在的动机，只是"无所为而为"⑥，故能有他那样的成就。一个人在学问上果能感觉到趣味，有时真会像是着了魔一般⑦，真能废寝忘食，真能不知老之将至，苦苦钻研，锲而不舍，在学问上焉能不有收获？不过我尝想，以任公先生而论，他后期的著述如历史研究法，先秦政治思想史，以及有关墨子佛学陶渊明的作品，都可说是他的一点"趣味"在驱使着他，可是在他在年青的时候，从师受业，诵读典籍⑧，那时节也全然是趣味么？作八股文，作试帖诗⑨，莫非也是趣味么？我想未必。大概趣味云云，是指年长之后自动作学问之时⑩而言，在年青时候为学问打根底之际恐怕不能过分重视趣味。学问没有根底，趣味也很难滋生。任公先生的学问之所以那样的博大精深,涉笔成趣,左右逢源,不能不说的一大部分得力于他的学问根底之打得坚固。

我尝见许多年青的朋友,聪明用功,成绩优异,而语文程度不足以达意,甚至写一封信亦难得通顺,问其故则曰其兴趣不在语文方面。又有一些位,执笔为文,斐然可诵,而视数理科目如仇雠,勉强才能及格,问其故则亦曰其兴趣不在数理方面,而且他们觉得某些科目没有趣味,便撇在一旁视如敝屣[11],怡然自得,振振有词,略无愧色,好像这就是发扬趣味主义。殊不知天下没有没有趣味的学问[12],端视吾人如何发掘其趣味,如果在良师指导之下按部就班的循序而进,一步一步的发现新天地,当然乐在其中,如果浅尝辄止,甚至躐等躁进,当然味同嚼蜡,自讨没趣。一个有中上天资的人,对于普通的基本的文理科目,都同样的有学习的能力,绝不会本能的长于此而拙于彼。只有懒惰与任性,才能使一个人自甘暴弃的在"趣味"的掩护之下败退[13]。

由小学到中学,所修习的无非是一些普通的基本知识。就是大学四年,所授课业也还是相当粗浅的学识。世人常称大学为"最高学府",这名称易滋误解,好像过此以上即无学问可言。大学的研究所才是初步研究学问的所在,在这里作学问也只能算是粗涉藩篱,注重的是研究学问的方法与实习。学无止境,一生的时间都嫌太短[14],所以古人皓首穷经,头发白了还是在继续研究,不过在这样的研究中确是有浓厚的趣味。

在初学的阶段,由小学至大学,我们与其倡言趣味,不如偏重纪律。一个合理编列的课程表,犹如一个营养均衡的食谱，里面各个项目都是有益而必需的，不可偏废，不可再有选择。所谓选修科目也只是在某一项目范围内略有拣选余地而已。一个受过良好教育的人，犹如一个科班出身的戏剧演员，在坐科的时候他是要服从严格纪律的，唱工作工武把子都要认真学习，各种脚色的戏都要完全谙通，学成之后才能各按其趣味而单独发展其所长。学问要有根底，根底要打得平正坚实，以后永远受用。初学阶段的科目之最重要的莫过于语文与数学。语文是阅读达意的工具，国文不通便很难表达自己，外国文不通便很难吸取外来的新知。数学是思想条理之最好的训练。其他科目也各有各的用处，其重要性很难强分轩轾，例如体育，从另一方面看也是重要得无以复加。总之，我们在求学时代，应该暂且把趣味放在一旁，耐着性子接受教育的纪律，把自己锻炼成为坚实的材料。学问的趣味，留在将来慢慢享受一点也不迟。

Learning and Personal Inclination

Liang Shiqiu

Scholars of the older generation often urge young people to develop interest in learning because they themselves have been enjoying the real pleasure of academic studies. And they are ever ready to cite their own example by way of advice, in hopes of enabling young people to gain access to scholarship in an enjoyable way. For example, the distinguished scholar Liang Qichao once said wittily, "I always stand for interest-ism. If you broke down Liang Qichao's stuff into its component parts, there would be nothing left except an element named 'Interest'." Mr. Liang was a man of profound learning who attached much importance to interest. He attained great academic success because he pursued scholarly study solely for its own sake, without any ulterior motive. A man who is really interested in learning sometimes does act like one possessed. He forgets his approaching old age and works hard even to the neglect of his meals and sleep. Isn't it but natural for a man of such devotion to have great scholarly achievements? But, though Mr. Liang's later works, such as those on method of historical studies, political and ideological history of the pre-Qin days, as well as those on Mohism, Buddhism and Tao Yuanming, were motivated by his personal inclination, can the same be said of his younger days when he was a pupil chanting ancient Chinese books under a private tutor? Was he motivated by his personal inclination while learning to write stereotyped essays and poems prescribed for the imperial civil service examinations? No, I think not. Generally speaking, the so-called interest begins to exist only when one is mature enough to engage in independent studies. It is improper, I am afraid, for young people to overstress the importance of interest while they are still in the period of learning the basics of knowledge. Interest will never develop where no solid foundation has been laid for learning. There is no denying the fact that Mr. Liang owed his wide erudition and unusual literary talent, for the most part, to his good grasp of foundation knowledge.

I have come across a great many bright and diligent young friends who have done exceedingly well in their studies, but are rather weak in Chinese. They cannot even write a letter in correct Chinese. When I asked them why, they said they were not interested in the Chinese language. Some, though they can write beautifully, detest the study of mathematics and physics, and barely managed to pass the examinations in them. When I asked them why, they said they were not interested in them. They cast away whatever subjects they dislike like something utterly worthless. They are so smug and thick-skinned that they speak volubly in defence of their own attitude like champions of interest-ism. They hardly realize that there is no learning but is capable of engendering interest and that all depends on how to search for it. You will develop a liking for learning if, under the guidance of a good teacher, you study to discover new horizons opening up before you one after another by following the proper order and advancing step by step. On the other hand, you will find learning as dry as sawdust and feel frustrated if you refuse to go into a subject in depth or even make impetuous advances without following the proper order. People with an average natural gift are equally capable of mastering the basics of liberal arts and natural science. They are never predetermined by nature to be good in one subject and poor in another. It is laziness and waywardness, however, that causes one to give himself up as hopeless and back down on the pretext of "no interest".

Primary and secondary school will impart to you only some rudiments of knowledge. Even what you learn during the four years of university will be something quite superficial too. A university has often been misleadingly referred to as "the highest seat of learning", which sounds as if there were no more learning to speak of beyond it. The research institute of a university, however, is the place for preliminary scholarship. But even there you get only the first taste of learning and the emphasis is on research methodology and practice. Art is long, life is short. That is why some of our ancients continued to study even when they were hoaryheaded. They were, of course, motivated by an enormous interest in their studies.

During the preliminary stage of learning, from primary school to college, it is better to advocate discipline than interest. A properly arranged school curriculum, like a cookbook on nutritionally well-balanced food, must include all the useful and indispensable courses — courses which are equally important and obligatory. The so-called electives mean only some little option within the scope of a certain item. A well-educated person is like a professionally trained Peking opera singer. While undergoing the training, he must observe a most exact discipline. He must pay equal attention to singing, acting and acrobatic skills, and learn to play different roles. It is not until he has finished the all-round training that he begins to develop his own speciality according to his personal disposition. Laying a solid foundation for learning will be of great lifelong benefit to you. Of all the school subjects during the preliminary stage of learning, languages and mathematics are the most important. Languages serve as a tool for reading and communication. Without a good knowledge of Chinese, you will find it difficult to express yourself. Without a good knowledge of a foreign language, you will find it difficult to absorb new knowledge from abroad. Mathematics makes for logical thinking. Other subjects also have their respective uses. It is hard to say which is more important. Physical education, for example, is also extremely important from another point of view. In short, while in school, we should temporarily put aside our personal liking and patiently observe school discipline so that we may temper ourselves and become solid stuff. Don't hurry — there *will* be a time for you to find relish in learning in the days to come.

注　释

梁实秋在《学问与趣味》一文中论述
做学问的方法,教诲青年学子在初学阶
段应着重打根底,不宜过分强调趣味。

①"不惜现身说法,诱导后学"译为 And they are ever ready to cite their own example by way of advice。"不惜"原意"舍得",在此可作"乐于"解,故译为 ever ready, 等于 always prepared。"诱导后学"译为 by way of advice 即可,其中 by way of 是成语,作"为了"解,等于 for the purpose of。

②"走进学问的大门"也可直译为 to enter the gate of learning。现译为 to gain access to scholarship, 其中 to gain access to 是惯用搭配,作"进入"、"到达"等解。

③"梁任公先生就说过"译为 the distinguished scholar Liang Qichao once said wittily。梁启超号"任公",现译梁的全名为 Liang Qichao,并在前面加 distinguished scholar,便于外国读者理解梁为何许人。译文还针对上下文添加 wittily(风趣地)一词。

④"趣味主义"译为 interest-ism,其中 ism 乃表达

"主义"而采用的英语后缀。

⑤ "倘若用化学化分'梁启超'这件东西"译为 If you broke down Liang Qichao's stuff into its component parts，其中短语动词 broke down 意即"分解"（to decompose），例如：Water can be broken down into hydrogen and oxygen。

⑥ "只是'无所为而为'"意即"只是为研究学问而研究学问"，故译为 solely for its own sake，等于 solely for the sake of scholarly study。

⑦ "像是着了魔一般"译为 like one possessed，其中 possessed（为过去分词)作"着迷"、"鬼迷心窍"解。

⑧ "从师受业，诵读典籍"译为 he was a pupil chanting ancient Chinese books under a private tutor，其中 a pupil...under a private tutor 表示"从师受业"。"师"指"塾师"，译为 private tutor。又 chanting ancient Chinese books 表示"诵读典籍"。

⑨ "试帖诗"为科举考试所采用的诗体，其格式限制比一般诗严格，现和"八股文"一并以释义法译为 stereotyped（或 rigid-style）essays and poems prescribed for the imperial civil service examination。

⑩ "年长之后自动作学问之时"中的"自动作学问"实际上指"独立作学问"，故译为 independent studies，不宜按字面直译为 engage in voluntary studies 等。又"年长之后"不仅指"成年"，还包含智力成熟之意，故译为 when one is mature enough。

⑪ "便撇在一旁视如敝屣"也可直译为 cast away...

like a pair of worn-out shoes，保持原文的形象比喻。现意译为 cast away…like something utterly worthless，似较明白易懂。

⑫ "没有没有趣味的学问"译为 there is no learning but is capable of engendering interest，其中 but 是关系代词，常用于否定词后，相当于 that not。

⑬ "在'趣味'的掩护之下败退"的意思是"借口'缺乏趣味'而放弃不干"，故译为 back down on the pretext of "no interest"，其中 back down 是成语，意同 beat a retreat。

⑭ "学无止境，一生的时间都嫌太短"译为 Art is long，life is short，其中 Art 为古词，作"学问"、"知识"解，和 learning、scholarship 同义。Art is long 一句见于美国十九世纪诗人 Longfellow 名著 *A Psalm of Life*，今借用之。"学无止境"也可译为 There is no limit to learning。

枣　核

萧　乾

　　动身访美之前，一位旧时同窗写来封航空信，再三托付我为他带几颗生枣核①。东西倒不占分量，可是用途却很蹊跷。

　　从费城出发前，我们就通了电话。一下车，他已经在站上等了。掐指一算，分手快有半个世纪了，现在都已是风烛残年。

　　拥抱之后，他就殷切地问我："带来了吗?"我赶快从手提包里掏出那几颗枣核②。他托在掌心③，像比珍珠玛瑙还贵重。

　　他当年那股调皮颈显然还没改。我问起枣核的用途，他一面往衣兜里揣，一面故弄玄虚地说④："等会儿你就明白啦。"

　　那真是座美丽的山城，汽车开去，一路坡上坡下满是一片嫣红。倘若在中国，这里一定会有枫城之称。过了几个山坳，他朝枫树丛中一座三层小楼指了指说："喏，到了。"汽车拐进草坪，离车库还有三四米，车库门就像认识主人似的自动掀启。

朋友有点不好意思地解释说,买这座大房子时,孩子们还上着学,如今都成家立业了。学生物化学的老伴儿在一家研究所里做营养试验。

他把我安顿在二楼临湖的一个房间后,就领我去踏访他的后花园⑤。地方不大,布置得却精致匀称⑥。我们在靠篱笆的一张白色长凳上坐下,他劈头就问我:"觉不觉得这花园有点家乡味道?"经他指点,我留意到台阶两旁是他手栽的两株垂杨柳,草坪中央有个睡莲池。他感慨良深地对我说:"栽垂柳的时候,我那个小子才五岁,如今在一条核潜艇上当总机械长了。姑娘在哈佛教书。家庭和事业都如意,各种新式设备也都有了。可是我心上总像是缺点什么。也许是没出息⑦,怎么年纪越大,思乡越切。我现在可充分体会出游子的心境了。我想厂甸,想隆福寺。这里一过圣诞,我就想旧历年。近来,我老是想总布胡同院里那棵枣树。所以才托你带几颗种籽,试种一下。"

接着,他又指着花园一角堆起的一座假山石说⑧:"你相信吗⑨?那是我开车到几十里以外,一块块亲手挑选,论公斤买下⑩,然后用汽车拉回来的。那是我们家的'北海'。"

说到这里,我们两人都不约而同地站了起来。沿着草坪旁用卵石铺成的小径,走到"北海"跟前⑪。真是个细心人呢,他在上面还嵌了一所泥制的小凉亭,一座红庙,顶上还有尊白塔。朋友解释说,都是从旧金山唐人街买来的。

他告诉我,时常在月夜,他同老伴儿并肩坐在这长凳上,追忆起当年在北海泛舟的日子。睡莲的清香迎风扑来,眼前仿佛就闪出一片荷塘佳色。

改了国籍,不等于就改了民族感情;而且没有一个民族像我们这么依恋故土的。

Date Stones

Xiao Qian

Before I set out for the US, a former schoolmate of
mine wrote me by airmail, asking me in all earnest to
bring him some raw date stones. They were not heavy in
weight, yet I was curious about their use.

At Philadelphia, shortly before starting out for my
friend's place, I called him up. So when I got off the train
at the destination, I found him already waiting for me at
the station. It was about half a century since we last met,
and we were now both in our declining years.

After hugging each other, he asked me eagerly,
"Have you brought them with you?" I immediately fished
out the date stones from my handbag. He fondled them in
his palm as if they were something more valuable than
pearls or agates.

Obviously he was just as childlike as before. When I
asked about the use of the date stones, he put them into
his pocket and replied by way of fooling me deliberately,
"Yor'll understand soon."

It was really a beautiful mountain city. As we drove on, an expanse of rich crimson up and down the slope came into sight. In China a place like this would have been described as a maple city. After passing through several cols, my friend said pointing to a three-storied house amidst the maple trees, "Here we are." The car turned into a lawn and when it was three or four meters away from the garage, its door automatically opened as if it recognized its own master.

My friend looked somewhat ill at ease when he told me this: At the time when he bought this big house, his children had all been at school. Now they had their own homes and jobs. His wife, a biochemist, was a dietician at a research institute.

After assigning me a room on the second floor facing a lake, he showed me around his back garden, which, though not too big, was exquisite and nicely arranged. The moment we sat down on a white bench close to a hedge, he asked me, "Don't you find something here smacking of our native place in China?" At this, I noticed a weeping willow, planted by himself, on either side of a flight of steps as well as a water-lily pond in the middle of the garden. He said with deep feeling, "When I planted the willows, my son was only five. Now he serves as head of chief mechanics in a nuclear submarine. My daughter teaches at Harvard University. I'm happy with my family and my career. I own all modern household facilities I need. But I still feel something lacking. Maybe I'm a bit too foolish. How come the older I become, the more I think of my homeland. Now I fully understand the frame of mind of one residing in a place far away from home. I always think of Changdian and Longfusi. Every time Christmas is celebrated here in America, I think of the lunar New Year back in China. I can never forget the date tree in the courtyard of the house on Zongbu Hutong. That's why I've asked you to bring me some date stones. I'll try to plant them here."

Then he said pointing to a jumble of rockery standing in a corner of the garden, "Believe it or not, the rocks, hand-picked by me, were bought by the kilogram. I drove dozens of kilometers away to haul them back in my car. Look, that's Beihai in our home."

Thereupon, we rose to our feet simultaneously and walked along a cobbled footpath beside the lawn towards the miniature Beihai. What a careful man my friend was! He had had the artificial hill inlaid with a clay pavilion and a red temple, with a white pagoda on top. He said he had bought the decorative objects from China Town in San Francisco.

He also told me that on a moonlit night he and his wife would sit side by side on the bench recalling how they had used to go boating on the Beihai Lake. Mean-

302

while, as I smelled the faint scent of the water-lilies carried to us by the breeze, I felt as if the beautiful scene of a Chinese lotus pond were flashing past my eyes.

The change of nationality doesn't mean the change of national feeling. No other nation has such a strong attachment for the native land as we Chinese.

　　萧乾(1910—1999)，作家、文学翻译家，曾任《大公报》记者，以散文、特写著称。曾任人民文学出版社顾问。《枣核》以平易简洁的文字，叙述一个长期侨居国外的旧时同窗，尽管已改变了国籍，不忘自己是炎黄子孙，一往情深地眷恋故乡故土和本民族。

　　①"再三托付我为他带几颗生枣核"中的"再三"作"恳切"解，不能按字面理解为"一次又一次"或"重复"。因此全句译为 asking me in all earnest to bring him some raw date stones，其中 in all earnest 是成语，作"认真地"或"恳切地"解。

　　②"我赶快从手提包里掏出那几颗枣核"中的"掏出"译为 fished out 比 took out 贴切，因前者有"搜寻"的含义。

　　③"他托在掌心"译为 He fondled them in his palm，比 He held them in his palm 贴切，因 to fondle 表达了原文的内涵"爱抚"。

　　④"故弄玄虚地说"中的"故弄玄虚"作"故意把……

搞得神秘化"解，通常可译为 deliberately to make a mystery of...。现全句按"故意开玩笑地说"的意思译为 replied by way of fooling me deliberately，其中 by way of 是成语，其意思是"为了"或"意在"（with the intention of）。

⑤ "领我去踏访他的后花园"译为 he showed me around his back garden，其中 to show around 是短语动词，作"带领某人参观某地"解。

⑥ "布置得却精致匀称"译为 was exquisite and nicely arranged，其中 nicely 的意思是"恰到好处"或"恰恰合适"。

⑦ "也许是没出息"不宜按字面直译，现按"也许是自己有些傻"译为 Maybe I'm a bit too foolish。

⑧ "堆起的一座假山石"译为 a jumble of rockery，其中 jumble 的意思是"杂乱的一堆"。

⑨ "你相信吗？"本可译为 Don't you believe it?。现译为 Believe it or not，为具有同样意思的常用口头语。

⑩ "论公斤买下"即"按公斤计算买下"，译为 bought by the kilogram。注意这里介词 by 和后面的定冠词 the 属习惯搭配。

⑪ "走到'北海'跟前"译为 Walked... towards the miniature Beihai，其中 miniature（微型的）是译者添加的成分，用以表达原文中加引号的北海。

黎明前的北京[①]

季羡林

　　前后加起来，我在北京已经住了四十多年，算是一个老北京了[②]。北京的名胜古迹，北京的妙处[③]，我应该说是了解的；其他老北京当然也了解。但是有一点，我相信绝大多数的老北京并不了解[④]，这就是黎明时分以前的北京。

　　多少年来，我养成了一个习惯：每天早晨四点在黎明以前起床工作。我不出去跑步或散步，而是一下床就干活儿。因此我对黎明前的北京的了解是在屋子里感觉到的。我从前在什么报上读过一篇文章[⑤]，讲黎明时分天安门广场上的清洁工人。那情景必然是非常动人的，可惜我从未能见到，只是心向往之而已。

　　四十年前，我住在城里在明朝曾经是特务机关的东厂里面。几座深深的大院子，在最里面三个院子里只住着我一个人。朋友们都说这地方阴森可怕，晚上很少有人敢来找我，我则恰然自得[⑥]。每当夏夜，我起床以后，立刻就闻到院子里那些高大的马缨花树散发出来的阵阵幽香，这些香气破窗而入，我于此时神清气爽，乐不可支，连手中那一支笨拙的笔也仿佛生了花。

几年以后,我搬到西郊来住,照例四点起床,坐在窗前工作。白天透过窗子能够看到北京展览馆那金光闪闪的高塔的尖顶,此时当然看不到了⑦。但是,我知道,即使我看不见它,它仍然在那里挺然耸入天空,仿佛想带给人以希望,以上进的劲头。我仍然是乐不可支,心也仿佛飞上了高空。

　　过了十年,我又搬了家。这新居既没有马缨花,也看不到金色的塔顶。但是门前却有一片清碧的荷塘。刚搬来的几年,池塘里还有荷花。夏天早晨四点已经算是黎明时分。在薄暗中透过窗子可以看到接天莲叶,而荷花的香气也幽然袭来⑧,我顾而乐之,大有超出马缨花和金色塔顶之上的意味了。

　　难道我欣赏黎明前的北京仅仅由于上述的原因吗?不是的。三十几年以来,我成了一个"开会迷"⑨。说老实话,积三十年之经验,我真有点怕开会了。在白天,一整天说不定什么时候就会接到开会的通知。说一句过火的话,我简直是提心吊担,心里不得安宁。即使不开会,这种惴惴不安的心情总摆脱不掉。只有在黎明以前,根据我的经验,没有哪里会来找你开会的⑩。因此,我起床往桌子旁边一坐,仿佛有什么近似条件反射的东西立刻就起了作用,我心里安安静静,一下子进入角色,拿起笔来,"文思"⑪(如果也算是文思的话)如泉水喷涌,记忆力也像刚磨过的刀子,锐不可当。此时,我真是乐不可支,如果给我机会的话,我简直想手舞足蹈了。

　　因此,我爱北京,特别爱黎明前的北京。

Predawn Beijing

Ji Xianlin

I've been in Beijing altogether for over 40 years. So I can well call myself a long-timer of Beijing. Like all other long-timers of the city, I'm supposed to be very familiar with its scenic spots and historical sites, nay, its superb attractions. But I believe there is one thing lying unknown to most of the long-time residents—the predawn hours of Beijing.

For many years, I have been in the habit of getting up before daybreak to start work at four. Instead of going out for a jog or walk, I'll set about my work as soon as I'm out of bed. As a result, it is from inside my study that I've got the feel of predawn Beijing. Years ago, I hit upon a newspaper article about street cleaners in Tian'anmen Square at daybreak. It must have been a very moving scene, but what a pity I haven't seen it with my own eyes. I can only picture it in my mind longingly.

Forty years ago, I lived downtown in Dongchang, a compound which had housed the secret service of the

Ming Dynasty. There were inside it several deep spacious courtyards one leading into another. I was the sole dweller of the three innermost courtyards. My friends, calling this place too ghastly, seldom dared to come to see me in the evening whereas I myself found it quite agreeable. In summer, the moment I got out of bed before daybreak, I would smell the delicate fragrance of the giant silk trees coming from outside my window. Thereupon, I would feel refreshed and joyful, and the clumsy pen in my hand would seem to have become as agile as it could.

Several years later when I moved to the western suburbs, I kept my habit of rising at four to begin work at the window. The glittering spire atop the tower of the Beijing Exhibition Center, which I could see in the daytime through my window, would no longer be visible now in the early morning haze. Nevertheless I knew that, though invisible, it remained there intact, towering to the skies to inspire people with hope and the urge for moving ahead. At this, I would be beside myself with joy and feel as if my heart were also flying high up into the skies.

Ten years after, I moved again. In the new home of mine, I had no silk trees, nor could I get sight of the glittering spire from afar. There was, however, a lotus pond of limpid blue in front of my door. In the first few years after I moved there, lotus flowers continued to blossom on the surface of the pond. In the summertime, when day broke early at four, a vast stretch of lotus leaves looking skywards outside my window came dimly into sight while the quiet fragrance of the lotus flowers assailed my nose. All that delighted me even more than the silk trees and the glittering spire.

Is it exclusively due to the above-mentioned that I've developed a liking for predawn Beijing? No. For 30 years, I've been bogged down in the mire of meetings. To tell you the truth, with the experience accumulated over the 30 years, I'm now scared of meetings. In the daytime, there is no telling when I may be served a notice for attending a meeting. To exaggerate it a bit, that keeps me in constant suspense and makes me fidgety. Even when no meeting is to take place, I feel restless all the same. However, my experience tells that it is only during the predawn hours that I can be truly havened from any involvement in meetings. As soon as I sit at my desk before dawn, something similar to the conditioned reflex will begin to function within me: Instantly I'll pick up my pen to play my proper part with perfect peace of mind. Then inspiration comes gushing to my mind and my memory becomes as quick as a newly-sharpened knife. I'll feel overjoyed, almost to the point of waving my arms and stamping my feet.

In short, I love Beijing, especially predawn Beijing.

注　释

　　季羡林(1911—　　　)，著名教育家、印度学家、梵文文学翻译家、散文家，自1948 年起任北京大学东方语言文学系教授兼系主任。《黎明前的北京》是他写于 1985 年 2 月 11 日的一篇小品文。文章叙述他喜爱黎明前的北京有诸多原因，其中主要的一条是在黎明以前他可免除种种会议的困扰，"安安静静"从事脑力劳动。作者现身说法，对建国以来长期流行的"文山会海"提出含蓄的批评。

　　① "黎明前的北京"除译为 Predawn Beijing 外，也可译为 Beijing Before Dawn 或 Beijing before Daybreak。

　　② "算是一个老北京了"除译为 I can well call myself a long-timer of Beijing 外，也可译为 I'm eligible for being called a long-timer of Beijing。又 long-timer 也可用 old-timer 代替。

　　③ "北京的妙处"是上句"北京的名胜古迹"的补充，

故译为 nay，its superb attractions，其中 nay 是副词，作"不仅如此"解，是译文中添加的成分。

④ "有一点……老北京并不了解"译为 there is one thing lying unknown to... long-time residents，其中 lying 和 remaining 同义。

⑤ "在什么报上读过一篇文章"译为 I hit upon a newspaper article，其中 to hit upon 是成语，作"偶然发现"解，和 to come across、to find by chance 等同义。

⑥ "我则怡然自得"意即"我却觉得很惬意"，故译为 whereas I myself find it quite agreeable。

⑦ "此时当然看不到了"译为 would no longer be visible now in the morning haze，其中 in the morning haze（在朦胧的清晨）是译义中的添加成分，原文虽无其词而有其意。

⑧ "香气幽然袭来"意即"香气悄悄地扑鼻而来"，故译为 the quiet fragrance... assailed my nose（或 nostrils）。

⑨ "开会迷"在文中并不指"对开会着迷"或"特别爱好开会"。它的真正意思却是"陷入繁多的会议之中"或者"疲于应付各种会议"，因此可译为 I've been bogged down in the mire of meetings 或 I'v been bogged down in meetings。

⑩ "只有在黎明以前……没有哪里会找你开会的"译为 it is only during the predawn hours that I can be havened from any involvement in meetings，灵活处理，其中 havened 是由名词 haven（避难所）转化为动词的。因此

be havened from 的意思是"免受……之扰"。

　⑪"'文思'如泉水喷涌"中的"文思"实际上指"灵感",现将全句译为 Then inspiration comes gushing to my mind。

文学批评无用论

季 羡 林

读最近一期的《文学评论》，里面有几篇关于"红学"①的文章，引起了我的注意。有的作者既反省②，又批判。有的作者从困境中找出路。有的作者慨叹，"红学"出了危机。如此等等，煞是热闹。文章的论点都非常精彩，很有启发。但是，我却忽然想到了一个怪问题：这样的"红学"有用处吗？对红学家本身，对在大学里和研究所里从事文学理论研究的人，当然有用。但是对广大的《红楼梦》的读者③呢？我看④是没有用处。

《红楼梦》问世二百年以来⑤，通过汉文原文和各种译文读过本书的人，无虑多少个亿。这样多的读者哪一个是先看批评家的文章，然后再让批评家牵着鼻子走，按图索骥地去读原作呢⑥？我看是绝无仅有⑦。一切文学作品，特别是像《红楼梦》这样伟大的作品⑧，内容异常地丰富，涉及到的社会层面异常地多，简直像是一个宝山，一座迷宫。而读者群就更为复杂，不同的家庭背景，不同的社会经历，不同的民族，不同的国家，不同的文化传统，不同的心理素质，不同的年龄，不同的性别，不同的职业，不同的爱好——还可以这样"不同"下去,就此打住——,他们来读《红楼梦》,会各就自己的特点,欣赏《红楼梦》中的某一个方面,受到鼓舞,受到启发,引起了喜爱;也可能受到打击⑨,引起了憎恶,总之是千差万别。对这些读者来说,"红学家"就好像是住在"太虚幻境"⑩里的圣人、贤人,与自己无关。他们不管"红学家"究竟议论些什么,只是读下去,读下去。

因此我说,文学批评家无用。

不但对读者无用,对作者也无用。查一查各国文学史,我敢说,没有哪一个伟大作家是根据文学批评家的理论来进行创作的。

那么,文学批评家的研究不就是毫无意义了吗?也不是的。他们根据自己的文学欣赏的才能,根据不同的时代潮流,对文学作品提出自己的看法,互相争论,互相学习,互相启发,互相提高,这也是一种创作活动,对文学理论的建设会有很大的好处。只是不要幻想,自己的理论会对读者和作者有多大影响。这样一来,就可以各安其业,天下太平了。

上面这些话其实只有幼儿园的水平⑪。可是还没有见有什么人这样坦率地说了出来。就让我当一个"始作俑者"吧⑫!

On the Futility of Literary Criticism

Ji Xianlin

In the latest issue of the *Literary Review*, several articles on Redology have attracted my attention. Some of the authors are introspective as well as critical; some try to find a way out of their academic predicament; some sigh with regret that Redology is faced with a crisis; and so on and so forth. The discussion is quite animated. The arguments set forth in the articles are very interesting and enlightening. Nevertheless, a strange question has occurred to me: Is this kind of Redology of any use at all? It is of course useful to the Redologists themselves as well as to those engaged in the study of literary theory at universities and research institutes. But, to my mind, it is of little use to readers of *A Dream of Red Mansions* at large.

Ever since the publication of this novel some 200 years ago, hundreds of millions of people have read its Chinese original or its translations in various languages. Of these innumerable people, how many have read the novel by starting with a perusal of the critics' articles and allowing themselves to be led by the nose by the critics as to how to read the novel? Next to none. All literary works, especially a monumental one like *A Dream of Red Mansions*, are extremely rich in content and involve diverse social strata — to such an extent that they virtually resemble a mountain of treasure or a labyrinth. And the readers are even more complicated, differing from each other in family background, social experience, nationality, country, cultural tradition, psychological condition, age, sex, profession, hobby, etc., etc. The list could go on endlessly, so I wouldn't mind stopping here. They will each appreciate a certain aspect of the novel according to their own individuality. They may feel inspired and enlightened, and hence love it, or they may feel hurt, and hence loathe it. In short, the reactions vary. To them, the Redologists seem to be sages and men of virtue residing in the "Illusory Land of Great Void" and having nothing whatsoever to do with them. They just read on and on, caring not what the Redologists may say.

Therefore, I reiterate, literary criticism is useless.

It is useless not only to the readers, but also to writers. Looking up the literary history of each and every country, I dare say that none of the world's great literary figures ever did their writing in line with the theory of literary critics.

On the other hand, however, does it follow that the

research done by literary critics is totally meaningless? No, that is not true either. In accordance with their own capacity for literary appreciation and the different historical trends, the views they put forward for mutual discussion, study, inspiration and improvement are also something creative and conducive to the development of literary theory. Only they should be under no illusion about their theories exerting powerful influence on the readership or writers. That is the way for each to have a role of his own to play and for peace to reign under heaven.

What I've said above is only skin-deep, of kindergarten level. But so far none else have ventured to be equally candid. Therefore, let me be reconciled to being saddled with the epithet of "originator of a bad practice".

注　释

《文学批评无用论》是季羡林写于
1989 年 1 月 26 日的一篇小品文。

① "红学"指研究古典文学《红楼梦》的学问，可译为
Hongloumeng scholarship，但不如 Redology 简洁。Redo-
logy 是由 Red 加词尾 ology（学）构成。

② "反省"译为 introspective，和 self-examining 同义。

③ "广大的……读者"译为 readers of... at large，其
中 at large 是成语，和 as a whole 或 in general 同义。

④ "我看"意即"我认为"，现用成语 to my mind 表达。

⑤ "问世二百年以来"实际上是"问世约二百年以
来"，故译为 Ever since the publication of... some 200
years ago，其中 some 是添加的成分，作"大约"解。

⑥ "哪一个是先看批评家的文章，然后再让批评家牵
着鼻子走，按图索骥地去读原作呢？"译为 how many have
read the novel by starting with a perusal of the critics' articles and allowing themselves to be led by the nose by the
critics as to how to read the novel？"按图索骥"在这里指
"按批评家的指点去读原作"，其意思已包括在上面译文中，

故略而不译。

⑦ "绝无仅有"作"极其少有"解,译为 Next to none,和 Almost none 同义。

⑧ "特别是像《红楼梦》这样伟大的作品"译为 especially a monumental one like *A Dream of Red Mansions*,其中 monumental 比 great 更有力,有不朽(immortal)的意思。

⑨ "也可能受到打击"中的"打击"作"刺痛"或"感情受到创伤"等解,不宜按字面直译为 feel attacked。现全句译为 or they may feel hurt。

⑩ "太虚幻境"引自《红楼梦》第五回,曾被译为 Great Void Illusion Land 和 Illusory Land of Great Void 等。

⑪ "上面这些话其实只有幼儿园的水平"译为 What I've said above is only skin-deep, of kindergarten level,其中 skin-deep(肤浅的)是添加成分,用以衬托 of kindergarten level。

⑫ "就让我当一个'始作俑者'吧!"语气幽默,意即"姑且接受'始作俑者'的称号吧!"现按此意译为 Therefore, let me be reconciled to being saddled with the epithet of "originator of a bad practice"。

父　亲

鲁　彦

　　"父亲已经上了六十岁了，还想作一点事业，积一点钱，给我造起屋子来①。"一个朋友从北方来，告诉了我这样的话。

　　他的话使我想起了我的父亲②。我的父亲正是和他的父亲完全一样的。

　　我的父亲曾经为我苦了一生，把我养大，送我进学校，为我造了屋子，买了几亩田地。六十岁那一年，还到汉口去做生意，怕人家嫌他年老，只说五十几岁③。大家都劝他不要再出门，他偏背着包裹走了。

　　"让我再帮儿子几年④！"他只是这样说。

　　后来屋子被火烧掉了，他还想再做生意，把屋子重造起来。我安慰他说，三年以后我自己就可积起钱造屋了⑤，还是等一等吧。他答应了。他给我留下了许多造屋的材料，告诉我这样可以做什么那样可以做什么。他死的以前不久，还对我说：

　　"早一点造起来吧，我可以给你监工⑥。"

　　但是他终于没有看见屋子重造起来就死了。他弥留的时候对我说，一切都满足了。但是我知道他倘能再活几年，我把屋子造起来，是他所最心愿的。我听到他弥留时的呻吟和叹息，我相信那不是病的痛苦的呻吟和叹息。我知道他还想再活几年，帮我造起屋子来。

现在我自己已是几个孩子的父亲了。我爱孩子，但我没有前一辈父亲的想法，帮孩子一直帮到老，帮到死还不足。我赞美前一辈父亲的美德，而自己却不能跟着他们的步伐走去。

我觉得我的孩子累我，使我受到极大的束缚。我没有对他们的永久的计划，甚至连最短促的也没有。

"倘使有人要，我愿意把他们送给人家！"我常常这样说，当我厌烦孩子的时候。

唉，和前一辈做父亲的一比，我觉得我们这一辈生命力薄弱得可怜，我们二三十岁的人比不上六七十岁的前辈，他们虽然老的老死的死了，但是他们才是真正活着到现在到将来。

而我们呢，虽然活着，却是早已死了。

Father

Lu Yan

"Father is now over sixty, but he still wants to work to save up for a house to be built for me," a friend of mine from North China told me.

That put me in mind of my father. My father was very much like his.

Father went through untold hardships for me all his life. He brought me up, sent me to school, had a house built for me and bought me a few *mu* of land. He went to Hankou to engage in trade the year when he was already sixty. And he tried to make out that he was still in his fifties lest people should consider him too old to be of much use. We had all tried to dissuade him from going out to Hankou, but he simply wouldn't listen and left home carrying the luggage on his back.

"Let me toil a few more years for my son's sake!" That was what he said.

It happened afterwards that the house was burned down. And he wanted to go back to his business in order to have the house rebuilt. I tried to console him, saying that there was no need for him to do it because in three years' time I myself would have laid by enough money for a new house. He agreed. Then he gave me a lot of building materials and told me what to do with them. Shortly before his death, he urged me,

"You'd better get started right away so that I can watch to see that everything is done properly."

Unfortunately he didn't live long enough to see the new house. He told me on his deathbed that he had nothing to feel sorry about. But I knew he would be much happier if he could live a few more years just to see the new house put up. When I heard his dying groans and sighs, I believed they were caused not by physical pain, but by regret for not being able to live a few more years to help me with the new house.

Now I myself am a father of several children. Though I love my kids, I do not share the idea of father and people of his time that one can never do too much in his lifetime to help his children. Much as I admire father and people of his time for their moral excellence, I can never follow in their footsteps.

I think of my children as an encumbrance to me. I haven't worked out a long-term plan for them, nay, not even a short-term one.

"I'd like to give away my kids to anyone who's will-

324

ing to take them!" That's what I say whenever I am fed up with them.

Alas, compared with father and people of his time, the present generation, I think, have pitifully low vitality. We in our twenties or thirties cannot compare with our elders in their sixties or seventies. Today they may be advanced in years or even no more, but they will, nevertheless, live forever and ever.

As for us, though still alive, we have long been dead.

注　释

《父亲》是我国近代优秀作家鲁彦
(1901—1944)写的一篇散文。文章追叙父
亲为儿子劳碌一生，是对父爱的赞颂。原
文风格朴素，英译时文字也应力求通俗。

①"积一点钱,给我造起屋子来"译为 to save up for a house to be built for me, 其中 to save up for 是成语,作"为……而把钱存起来"解。

②"他的话使我想起了我的父亲"译为 That put me in mind of my father, 等于 That reminded me of my father。To put one in mind of. . . 是成语。

③"只说五十几岁"译为 tried to make out that he was still in his fifties, 其中 to make out 是成语,作"声称"或"假装"等解。

④"让我再帮儿子几年！"译为：Let me toil a few more years for my son's sake! 如把原文中的"帮"字直译为 help, 则欠达意。

⑤"就可积起钱造屋了"译为 would have laid by enough money for a new house, 其中 laid by 是成语,作

326

"积蓄"解。

⑥ "早一点造起来吧，我可以给你监工。"如逐字硬译为 Let the construction of the house get started as soon as possible so that I can oversee the work for you 则欠口语化。现用意译法灵活处理为 You'd better get started right away so that I can watch to see that everything is done properly。

母亲的回忆

朱　　德

得到母亲去世的消息，我很悲痛。我爱我母亲，特别是她勤劳一生，很多事情是值得我永远回忆的。

我家是佃农，祖籍广东韶关客籍人，在"湖广填四川"①时迁移四川仪陇县马鞍场。世代为地主耕种，家境是贫苦的②，和我们来往的朋友也都是老老实实的贫苦农民。

母亲一共生了十三个儿女，因为家境贫穷，无法全部养活，只留下八个，以后再生下的被迫溺死了。这在母亲心里是多么惨痛、悲哀和无可奈何的事啊！母亲把八个孩子一手养大成人。可是她的时间大半给家务和耕种占去了，没法多照顾孩子，只好让孩子们在地里爬着。

母亲是个"好劳动"③。从我能记忆时起，总是天不亮就起床。全家二十口人，妇女们轮班煮饭，轮到就煮一年。母亲把饭煮了，还要种田种菜，喂猪养蚕，纺棉花。因为她身材高大结实，还能挑水挑粪。

母亲这样地整日劳碌着，我们到四五岁时就很自然地在旁边帮她的忙，到八九岁时就不单能挑能背，还会种地了。记得那时我从学堂回家，母亲总在灶上汗流满面地烧饭,我就悄悄把书本一放,挑水或放牛去了。有的季节里,我上午读书下午种地,一到农忙便整月停在地里跟着母亲劳动。这个时期母亲教给我许多生产知识。

佃农家庭的生活自然是很苦的。可是由于母亲的聪明能干,却很舒服。我们把桐子榨油来点灯。吃的是豌豆饭,菜饭,红薯饭,杂粮饭,把菜籽榨出的油放在饭里做调料,这种地主富人家看也不看的饭食,母亲却能做得使一家吃起来有滋味。赶上丰年,才能缝上一些新衣服,衣服也是自己生产出来的。母亲亲手纺出线,请人织成布,染了颜色,我们叫做"家织布",有铜钱那样厚,一套衣服老大穿过了,老二老三接下来穿还穿不烂④。

劳动的家庭是有规律有组织的。我的祖父是一个中国标本式的农民,到八九十岁还非耕田不可,不耕田就会害病,直到临死前不久还在地里劳动。祖母是家庭的组织者,一切生产事务由她管理分派。每年除夕,分派好一年的工作以后,天还没亮,母亲就第一个起身烧火做饭去了,接着听见祖父起来的声音,接着大家都离开床铺,喂猪的喂猪,砍柴的砍柴,挑水的挑水。母亲在家庭里极能够任劳任怨,她的和蔼的性格使她从没有打骂过我们一次,而且也没有和任何人吵过架⑤。因此,虽在这样的大家庭里,长幼叔伯妯娌相处都很和睦。母亲同情贫苦的人——这是她朴素的阶级意识——虽然自己不富裕,还周济和照顾比自己更穷的亲戚⑥。她自己是很节省的。父亲有时吸点旱烟,喝点酒,母亲管束着我们,不允许我们沾染上一点。母亲那种劳动简朴的习惯,母亲那种宽厚仁慈的态度,至今还在我心中留有深刻的印象。

但是灾难不因为中国农民的和平就不降临到他们的身上。庚子(一九〇〇)后前后,四川连年旱灾,很多农民饥饿破产。农民不得不成群结队去"吃大户"。我亲眼见到六七百著得破破烂烂的农民和他们的妻子儿女,被所谓"官兵"一阵凶杀毒打,血溅四五十里,哭声动天。在这样的年月里,我家也遭受更多的困难,仅仅吃些小菜叶,高粱,通年没有吃过白米。特别是甲辰(一九〇四)那一年,地主欺压佃户,要在租种地上加租子,因为办不到,就趁大年除夕,威胁着我家要退佃,逼着我们搬家。在悲惨的情况下,我们一家人都哭泣着连夜分散。从此我家被迫分两处住下,人手少了,又遭天灾,庄稼没有收成,这是我家最悲惨的一次遭遇。母亲没有灰心,她对穷苦农民的同情,和对为富不仁者的反感却更加强烈了。母亲沉痛的三言两语的诉说,以及我亲眼看见到的许多不平事实,启发了我幼年时期反抗压迫追求光明的思想,使我决心寻找新的生活。

　　我不久就离开了母亲,因为我读了书。我是一个佃农家庭的子弟,本来是没钱读书的。那时乡间豪绅地主的欺压,衙门差役的横蛮,逼得母亲和父亲决心要节衣缩食培养出一个读书人来"支撑门户"⑦。我念过私塾,光绪三十一年(一九〇五)考了科举,以后又到更远的顺庆和成都去读书。这个时期的学费,都是东挪西借来的,总共用了二百多块钱,直到我后来在当护国军旅长时才还清。

　　光绪三十四年(一九〇八),我从成都回来,在仪陇县办高等小学,一年回家二三次去看母亲。那时新旧思想冲突很厉害,我们抱了科学民主的思想想在家乡做点事情,守旧的豪绅们便出来反对我们。我下决心瞒着慈爱的母亲脱离家乡，远走云南参加了新军和同盟会。我到云南后，从家信中知道⑧，我母亲对我这一举动不但不反对，还给我许多慰勉。

从宣统元年（一九〇九）到现在，我再没有回过家一次，只在民国十年（一九二一），我曾经把父亲和母亲接出去，但是他俩劳动惯了，离开土地就不舒服⑨，所以还是回了家，父亲就在回家途中死了，母亲回家继续劳动一直到最后⑩。

中国革命继续向前发展，我的思想也继续的向前进步。当我发现中国革命的正确道路时，我便加入了中国共产党。大革命失败了，我和家庭完全隔绝了。母亲就靠那三十亩地独立支持一家人生活。抗战以后，我才能和家里通信。母亲知道我们所做的事业，她期望着中国民族解放的成功。她知道我们党的困难，依然在家里过着劳苦的农妇生活。七年中间，我曾寄回几百元钱和几张自己的照片给母亲。母亲年老了，但她永远想念着我，如同我永远想念着她一样。去年收到侄儿的来信说："祖母今年已八十有五，精神不如昨年之健康，饮食起居亦不如前，甚望见你一面，聊叙别后情景。……"但我献身于民族抗战事业，竟未能报答母亲的希望。

母亲最大的特点，是一生不曾脱离过劳动。母亲生我前一分钟还在灶上煮饭。虽到老年，仍然热爱生产。去年另一封外甥的家信中说："外祖母大人因年老关系，近年不比往年健康，但仍不辍劳作，尤喜纺棉。……"

我应该感谢母亲，她教给我与困难作斗争的经验，我在家庭生活中已经饱尝艰苦，这使我在三十多年的军事生活和革命生活中，再没有感到困难和被困难吓倒。母亲又给我一个强健的身体和一个劳动的习惯，使我从来没有感到过劳累。

我应该感谢母亲，她教给了我生产的知识和革命的意志，鼓励我走上以后的革命道路，在这条路上我一天比一天更加认识了：只有这种知识，这种意志，才是世界上最可宝贵的财产。

　　母亲现在离我而去了，我将永不能再见她一面了，这个悲哀是无法补救的。母亲是一个"平凡"的人，她只是中国千百万劳动人民中的一员，但是正是这千百万人创造了和创造着中国的历史。我用什么方法来报答母亲的深恩呢？我将继续尽忠于我们的民族和人民，尽忠于我们的民族和人民的希望——中国共产党，使和母亲同样生活着的人能够过一个快乐的生活，这就是我所能做的和我一定做的。

　　愿母亲在地下安息！

Loving Memories of Mother

Zhu De

I was deeply grieved to learn of mother's death. I love my mother. Of her hardworking life, in particular, a great many things will forever be cherished in my memory.

I come from a tenant farmer's family. My original family home was Shao Guan, Guangdong Province, into which my ancestors had moved from another province as settlers. During the mass migration of peasants from Huguang to Sichuan Province, my ancestors moved to Ma An Chang, Yi Long County, Sichuan. From generation to generation, they tilled land for landlords only to eke out a bare subsistence. People who associated with them as friends were likewise honest impoverished peasants.

Mother gave birth to thirteen children in all. But only the first eight of them survived while the next five were drowned at birth by my parents against their will because they were too poor to raise them all. How anguished, sad and helpless mother must have felt ! She did manage, however, to have the eight children brought up all by herself. But she was too busily occupied with household chores and farming to look after the kids so that they were left alone crawling about in the fields.

Mother was a hardworking woman. As far as I can remember, she would always get up before daybreak. In our household of more than twenty members, all women would take turns to do cooking for one year. Apart from cooking, mother did farming, planted vegetables, fed pigs, raised silkworms and spinned cotton into yarn. Tall and of strong build, she could carry two buckets of water or manure on a shoulder pole.

Mother worked hard from dawn till dusk. When we kids were four or five years old, we found ourselves automatically helping her with farm work. At the age of eight or nine, I could not only carry heavy loads on a shoulder pole or on my back, but also knew how to farm the land. I remember whenever I came back from school and saw mother busy cooking in the kitchen with sweat streaming down her face, I would immediately lay down my books and sneak out to carry water on a shoulder pole or graze the cattle. In some seasons, I would study in the morning and work in the fields in the afternoon. During the busy season, I would spend all day working by the side of mother. It was then that she taught me a lot about the knack of farming.

The life of a tenant farmer's family was of course hard, but we somehow managed to scrape along because mother was a clever and able woman. We used oil squeezed from seeds of tung trees to light our lamps. We ate rice cooked with peas, vegetables, sweet potatoes or coarse grain, and all seasoned with rapeseed oil — food which landlords and rich people would scorn to eat. Nevertheless, mother's cooking was done so well that everybody ate with gusto. Only in a good year, could we afford to have some home-made new clothes to wear. Mother would spin cotton into yarn and then asked somebody to have it woven into fabric and dyed. We called it "home-spun fabric". It was as thick as a copper coin and was so durable that after the eldest brother had grown out of the home-spun garment, it could still be used by the second and third brothers in turn without being worn out.

It was characteristic of an industrious household to be well-regulated and well-organized. My grandfather was a typical Chinese farmer. He went on doing farm work even when he was an octogenarian. He would feel unwell without doing farm labour. He was found still working on the farm even shortly before his death. Grandmother was the organizer of the household. She was in charge of all the farm affairs, assigning tasks to each member of the household. On each New Year's Eve, she would work out all job assignments for the coming

335

new year. Mother would be the first to get up before day-break. Soon grandfather would be heard to rise from his bed, followed by the rest of the household. Some went about feeding pigs, some cutting firewood, and some carrying water on a shoulder pole. Mother always worked without complaint despite hardships. Amiable by nature, she never beat or scolded us, let alone quarreled with anybody. Consequently, large as it was, the whole household, old and young, uncles and sisters-in-law, lived in perfect harmony. Out of her naive class consciousness, she showed sympathy for the poor. Despite her own straitened circumstances, she often went out of her way to help out those relatives who were even more needy than herself. She lived a very frugal life. Father would occasionally smoke a long-stemmed Chinese pipe or drink some wine. To prevent us from falling into the same habit, mother kept us children under strict control. Her diligence and frugality, her generosity and kindhearted-ness — all have left a lasting impression on my mind.

Chinese peasants were honest and peaceable, but disaster befell them just the same. Around 1900, when Sichuan Province was hit by successive years of drought, numerous poverty-stricken peasants went hungry and had to go out in crowds to seize food from the homes of landlords. Thereupon I saw with my own eyes how a group of shabbily-dressed peasants and their families were savagely

336

beaten up or slain by government troops, the road stained with their blood for some 40 *li* and their cries rending the air. In those days, my family also met with increasing difficulties. All the year round, we went without rice to eat, and simply lived on edible wild herbs and *kaoliang*. In 1904, especially, when landlords, riding rough shod over tenants, pressed for higher rents on the let-out pieces of land, we, unable to meet their demands, had our tenancy cancelled by them and were forced to move house on New Year's Eve. On that miserable night, my family tearfully separated and thenceforth had to live in two different places. Shorthandedness and crop failure due to the natural calamity brought misfortune on my family. Mother, however, did not lose heart. Adversity had deepened her sympathy for the poor and needy as well as her aversion to the heartless rich. The painful complaint she had uttered in one or two words and the innumerable injustices I had witnessed aroused in me a spirit of revolt and a desire for a bright future. I made up my mind to seek a new life.

Not long afterwards, I had to tear myself away from mother when I began my schooling. As the son of a tenant, I of course could not afford to go to school. My parents, however, faced with the bullying and oppression of the local evil gentry, landlords and *yamen* bailiffs, decided to scrape up enough money by living a very frugal life to pay for my education so that they could make a scholar

337

of me for the family to keep up appearances. At first I was sent to an old-style private school and in 1905 I took the imperial examination. Later, I went farther away from home to study in Shunqing and Chengdu, both in Sichuan Province. All the tuition fees were paid with borrowed money, totalling more than 200 silver dollars. The debt was not repaid until later I became a brigade commander of the Hu Guo Army[1].

In 1908, I came back from Chengdu to set up a higher primary school in Yi Long County. While teaching school, I went home to see mother two or three times a year. In those days, there was a sharp conflict between old and new ideologies. Due to our leaning towards science and democracy, we met with opposition from the local conservative influential gentry in whatever we attempted for the benefit of our home town. So I decided to leave, without my mother's knowledge, for the faraway province of Yunnan, where I joined the New Army[2] and Tongmenhui[3]. On my arrival in Yunnan, I learned from my home letters that mother, instead of frowning upon my new move, gave me a lot of encouragement and comfort.

From 1909 up to now, I have never paid a visit to my home town. In 1921, however, I had my parents come out to live with me. But, as confirmed farm laborers, they felt unwell without land to till and subsequently had to return home. Father died on the way back, and mother continued to do farm work at home to the very last.

As the Chinese revolution continued to develop, I became more and more politically aware. I joined the Chinese Communist Party as soon as I discovered the correct orientation of the Chinese revolution. When the Great Revolution of 1924-1927 failed in China, I completely lost contact with my family. Mother alone supported the whole family by working on the 30 *mu* of land. I did not hear from her until the outbreak of the War of Resistance to Japan. When she was informed of the great cause in which I was engaged, she eagerly looked forward to the success of China's national liberation. While living the hard life of a peasant woman at home, she was aware of the difficulties and hardships that our Party was then undergoing. During the seven years after the outbreak of the War, I managed to send her several hundred *yuan* and some photos of myself. Mother was getting old. She was always thinking of me as I was of her. Last year, a letter from my nephew says, "Grandma is 85. She's no longer as vigorous and healthy as before. She's eager to see you and chat about things that have happened since you left home...." But I never lived up to her expectations because of my dedication to the cause of the War of Resistance Against Japan.

The most prominent characteristic of mother was her

lifelong participation in physical labour. She did cooking in the kitchen just one minute before giving birth to me. Her ardent love for agricultural production remained undiminished even in her old age. My nephew says in another letter to me last year, "Because of old age, grandma is no longer in good health, but she still does manual labour, and is particularly fond of spinning cotton into yarn...."

I owe mother a debt of gratitude because she taught me how to cope with the numerous difficulties that I ran into at home so that later during my over 30 years of military and revolutionary life I have never bowed down to any difficulty. She also bequeathed me a strong constitution as well as a strong inclination for labour so that I have been able to work untiringly.

I owe mother a debt of gratitude because she imparted to me knowledge of productive labour and a revolutionary will, thus enabling me to take to the revolutionary path. By keeping to this path, I have come to realize more and more clearly that this knowledge of productive labour and this revolutionary will are the most valuable assets in the world.

Mother is gone and I shall never see her again. This is an ever-lasting sorrow. Mother is an "ordinary" person and one of the millions of labouring people who have made and are still making Chinese history. What can I do to repay her my debt of deep gratitude? I swear to remain ever loyal to our nation and the people, ever loyal to the Chinese Communist Party — the hope of our nation and the people, so that all those who share the same lot with my mother may live a happier life. That is what I can do and what I am certainly able to do.

May mother rest in peace !

---

① The troops that rallied against Yuan Shikai when he attempted to restore monarchy in 1916.

② Western-style army organized toward the end of the Qing Dynasty.

③ The United League of China (1905—1912), the antecedent of the Kuomintang.

注　释

《母亲的回忆》出自当代伟人朱德之
手，1944 年 4 月 5 日发表在《解放日报》
上。文章就母子之情，侃侃谈心，感情真
挚，语言平实简约。

① "湖广填四川"译为 the mass migration of peasants from Huguang to Sichuan Province。"湖广"为旧时一个省份。元代湖广相当于今两湖、两广。明、清时湖广专指两湖。四川曾因天灾人祸，人口锐减，湖广农民乃大批迁入。

② "世代为地主耕种，家境是贫苦的"译为 From generation to generation，they tilled land for landlords only to eke out a bare subsistence，其中 only 用于不定式前作"结果却……"解，往往表示一种不幸的结果。又 to eke out 是成语，后面常跟 a bare subsistence 或 a living、an existence、a livelihood 等，作"勉强糊口"解。

③ "母亲是个'好劳动'"不宜照字面直译，现按"母亲是一个勤劳的妇女"译为 Mother was a hardworking woman。

④ "一套衣服老大穿过了"意即"衣服因老大长大了

342

而不能继续穿下去"，故译为 after the eldest brother had grown out of the home-spun garment，其中 had grown out of 是习用短语，作 had grown too large to fit (clothes) 解。

⑤ "她的和蔼的性格使她从没有打骂过我们一次，而且也没有和任何人吵过架"译为 Amiable by nature, she never beat or scolded us, let alone quarreled with anybody，其中根据上下文的内涵，把"而且"译为 let alone，作"更不用说"解，是英语成语。

⑥ "还周济和照顾比自己更穷的亲戚"译为 she often went out of her way to help out those relatives who were even more needy than herself，其中 went out of her way 是成语，作"特地"、"不怕麻烦地"(to make a special effort, especially in spite of difficulties) 解。

⑦ "培养出一个读书人来'支撑门户'"译为 so that they could make a scholar of me for the family to keep up appearances，其中 to keep up appearances 是英语成语，作"装门面"(to keep up or maintain an outward show) 解。又，为了把原文的意思交代清楚，译文中出现添加成份 for the family。

⑧ "从家信中知道"译为 I learned from my home letters，其中 my home letters 等于 my letters from home。

⑨ "但是他俩劳动惯了，离开土地就不舒服"译为 But, as confirmed farm labourers, they felt unwell without land to till，其中 confirmed 作"成习惯的"(habitual) 解。

⑩ "母亲回家继续劳动一直到最后"译为 mother con-

tinued to do farm work at home to the very last，其中 to
the last（或 till the last）是成语，意即 to the end 或 till
death。

巷

柯　灵

　　巷，是城市建筑艺术中一篇飘逸恬静①的散文，一幅古雅冲淡的图画。

　　这种巷，常在江南的小城市中②，有如古代的少女，躲在僻静的深闺，轻易不肯抛头露面。你要在这种城市里住久了，和它真正成了莫逆，你才有机会看见她，接触到她优娴贞静的风度。它不是乡村的陋巷③，湫隘破败④，泥泞坎坷，杂草乱生，两旁还排列着错落的粪缸。它不是上海的里弄，鳞次栉比的人家，拥挤得喘不过气；小贩憧憧来往，黝暗的小门边，不时走出一些趿着拖鞋的女子，头发乱似临风飞舞的秋蓬⑤，眼睛里网满红丝，脸上残留着不调和的隔夜脂粉，颓然⑥地走到老虎灶上去提水。也不像北地的胡同，满目尘土，风起处刮着弥天的黄沙。

　　这种小巷，隔绝了市廛的红尘，却又不是乡村的风味。它又深又长，一个人耐心静静走去，要老半天才走完。它又这么曲折，你望着前面，好像已经堵塞了⑦，可是走了过去，一转弯，依然是巷陌深深，而且更加幽静。那里常是寂寂的，寂寂的⑧，不论什么时候，你向巷中踅去，都如宁静的黄昏,可以清晰地听到自己的足音。不高不矮的围墙挡在两边,斑斑驳驳的苔痕,墙上挂着一串串苍翠欲滴的藤萝,简直像古朴的屏风。墙里常是人家的竹园,修竹森森,天籁细细⑨;春来时还常有几枝娇艳的桃花杏花,娉娉婷婷,从墙头殷勤地摇曳红袖,向行人招手。走过几家墙门,都是紧紧关着,不见一个人影,因为那都是人家的后门。偶然躺着一只狗,但是决不会对你猖猖地狂吠。

小巷的动人处就是它无比的悠闲。无论谁,只要你到巷里去踯躅一会,你的心情就会如巷尾不波的古井,那是一种和平的静穆,而不是阴森和肃杀⑩。它闹中取静,别有天地,仍是人间。它可能是一条现代的乌衣巷⑪,家家有自己的一本哀乐帐,一部兴衰史,可是重门叠户,讳莫如深,夕阳影里,野花闲草,燕子低飞,寻觅归家。只是一片澄明如水的气氛,净化一切,笼罩一切,使人忘忧。

你是否觉得劳生草草⑫,身心两乏?我劝你工余之暇,常到小巷里走走,那是最好的将息,会使你消除疲劳,紧张的心弦得到调整。你如果有时情绪烦燥,心情悒郁,我劝你到小巷里负手行吟一阵,你一定会豁然开朗,怡然自得,物我两忘。你有爱人吗?我建议不要带了她去什么名园胜景,还是利用晨昏时节,到深巷中散散步。在那里,你们俩可以随便谈谈,心贴得更近,在街上那种贪婪的睨视,恶意的斜觑,巷里是没有的;偶然呀的一声,墙门口显现出一个人影,又往往是深居简出⑬的姑娘,看见你们,会娇羞地返身回避了。

巷,是人海汹汹中的一道避风塘,给人带来安全感;是城市喧嚣扰攘中的一带洞天幽境⑭,胜似皇家的阁道⑮,便于平常百姓徘徊徜徉。

爱逐臭争利,锱铢必较的,请到长街闹市去;爱轻嘴薄舌的,争是论非的,请到茶馆酒楼去;爱锣鼓钲镗,管弦嗷嘈的,请到歌台剧院去;爱宁静淡泊,沉思默想的,深深的小巷在欢迎你。

The Lane

Ke Ling

The lane, in terms of the art of urban architecture, is like a piece of prose of gentle gracefulness or a painting of classic elegance and simplicity.

Often tucked away in a small town south of the Yangtse River, the lane, like a maiden of ancient times hidden away in a secluded boudoir, is reluctant to make its appearance in public. You'll never have an apportunity to see it and savour its gentle poise until you have become truly attached to the small town after living there for a long time. The lane has nothing in common with the mean rural alleys, which are narrow and low-lying, muddy and bumpy, overgrown with wild weeds and lined here and there with manure vats. Nor has it anything in common with *lilong* (meaning alleys) in Shanghai, which are literally packed with dwellings and their residents. Over there, you'll see vendors hawking their wares here and there. From time to time, women are seen emerging from inside some dingy small gates and shuffling languidly in their slippers towards a *laohuzao*, the shop specializing in selling boiled water, their hair dishevelled like wind-blown withered grass in autumn, their eyes blood-shot, their faces betraying traces of overnight make-up. Nor has the lane anything in common with *hutong* (also meaning alleys) in North China, which are dusty on every side, especially when a wind rises.

The lane, though cut off from the hustle and bustle of busy cities, does not taste of the countryside at all. It is long and deep, so it will take you a long while to walk patiently and quietly through it from end to end. It is also so winding that it seems to be a blind alley when you look far ahead, but if you keep walking until you take a turning, you'll find it again lying endless and still more quiet. There is nothing but stillness there. At any hour of day, you can even distinctly hear in the dusk-like quiet your own footsteps. On either side of the lane stand enclosing walls of medium height, which, moss-covered and hung with clusters of fresh green wistaria, look almost like screens of primitive simplicity. Inside the walls are residents' gardens with dense groves of tall bamboos as well as soft sounds of nature. In spring, beautiful peach and apricot blossoms atop the walls, like graceful girls waving their red sleeves, will sway hospitably to beckon the pedestrians. You'll find the doors in the walls close shut without a soul in sight because they are back doors

349

to some households. Occasionally, you may come upon a dog lying there, which, however, never gives a bark at you.

The charm of the lane lies in its absolute serenity. No matter who you are, if you loiter around in the lane for a while, your mind will become as unruffled as the ancient well at the end of the lane. There you will experience a kind of peaceful calmness rather than gloomy sternness. There reigns peace and quiet in the midst of noisy bustle. It is a world of its own on earth. It may be a modern version of *Wu Yi Xiang*, a special residential area of nobility in the Jin Dynasty southeast of today's Nanjing, where each family, secluded behind closed doors, has its own covered-up story of joys and sorrows, and rise and decline. When the sun is setting, swallows will fly low over wild flowers and grass on their way to their nests. The all-pervading and all-purifying atmosphere of water-like placidness makes one forget all cares and worries.

Aren't you weighed down with cares in this life of hard toil and exhausted physically and mentally? I would like to advise you often to take a walk in the lane in your off-duty hours. That is the best way to take a rest. It will dissipate your fatigue and relieve your nervous tension. When you are fidgety or depressed, go to the lane and wander around reciting or composing poems with your hands crossed behind your back. You will then suddenly fall into a bright mood and enjoy inner peace, forgetting both yourself and the external world. Don't you have a sweetheart? Let me suggest that, instead of accompanying her on a visit to a famous park or scenic spot, you take her with you for a stroll in the lane at dawn or dusk. Over there, you two can chat freely and with even deeper affection, free from greedy sidelong glances or malicious squints such as you often meet with in busy streets. Suddenly, at a creaking sound, there may appear a figure by a door — usually an unsophisticated young girl. She will, at the sight of you, withdraw coyly into the house.

The lane is a safe haven for those struggling in the turbulent sea of humans to enjoy a sense of security. It is a heavenly abode in the midst of confusion. Unlike the erstwhile plank-paved path used exclusively by the imperial family for their vehicles to move on smoothly, the lane is a place for the common people to roam about leisurely.

Those who strive after fame and gain, and haggle over every penny, please go to the downtown area! Those who are sharp-tongued and quarrelsome, please go to the teahouse or restaurant! Those who love deafening gongs and drums as well as noisy wind and string instruments, please go to the opera house or theatre! Those who are given to profound meditation and a quiet life without worldly desires, welcome to the lane!

注　释

　　《巷》是柯灵（1909—　　　）写于
1930年秋的一篇著名小品散文。作者以
沉挚细腻的笔调叙述江南小城市中的小
巷，向往那里悠闲宁静的情调，流露出对
大都市喧闹纷争的生活的厌恶。

　　① "飘逸恬静" 译为 gentle gracefulness，把原文两个
并列形容词转变为英语 "定语＋抽象名词" 的形式，内容不
变。这是文学翻译时的常用方法。

　　② "常在江南的小城市中" 译为 Often tucked away in
a small town south of the Yangtse River，其中动词短语
to tuck away 作 "使隐藏"、"把……置放在隐蔽的地方"
解，是添加成分，原文虽无其词而有其意。

　　③ "它不是乡村的陋巷" 意即 "它和乡村的陋巷不
同"，因此全句译为 The lane has nothing in common with
the mean rural alleys，其中成语 in common 的意思是 "共
同"。

　　④ "湫隘破败" 译为 narrow and low-lying，未交代
"破败"，因它的意思已包含在句中 "陋"、"坎坷" 等形容词

352

中。但如照译不误，也无不可：narrow, low-lying and in bad condition (out of repair)。

⑤"头发乱似临风飞舞的秋蓬"中的"蓬"是一种草，即"蓬蒿"，秋时干枯，临风飞舞，现将此句译为 dishevelled like wind-blown withered grass in autumn。

⑥"颓然"意即"没精打采"或"慢吞吞"，译为 languidly 或 sluggishly。

⑦"好像已经堵塞了"意即"好像是死胡同"，故译为 it seems to be a blind alley。

⑧"那里是寂寂的，寂寂的"语气强调，故相应译为 There is nothing but stillness there。

⑨"修竹森森，天籁细细"中的"修"作"高"解；"森森"作"茂密"解；"天籁"作"自然界的音响"解。两句一并译为 dense groves of tall bamboos as well as soft sounds of nature。

⑩"阴森和肃杀"译为 gloomy sternness，也是把原文两个并列形容词转化为英语"定语＋抽象名词"的形式。

⑪"乌衣巷"在今南京市东南，东晋时为望族居住的地方，现采取释义法把它译为 Wu Yi Xiang, a special residential area of nobility in the Jin Dynasty southeast of today's Nanjing。

⑫"你是否觉得劳生草草"中的"劳生"作"辛劳的生活"解；"草草"作"忧虑"解。现全句译为 Aren't you weighed down with cares in this life of hard toil...，其中动词短语 to weigh down 作"使苦恼"解。

⑬"深居简出"可译为 secluded，现译为 unsophisti-

353

cated，是按"不懂世故"之意作灵活处理。

⑭ "洞天幽境"中的"洞天"本指上天群仙居住之处，现按"超凡的住所"把全文译为 heavenly abode。

⑮ "阁道"指古代皇家楼阁之间以木架空的通道，现以释义法把它译为 the erstwhile plank-paved path used exclusively by the imperial family for their vehicles to move smoothly。

第二次考试

何　为

　　著名的声乐专家苏林教授发现了一件奇怪的事情:在这次参加考试的二百多名合唱训练班学生中间,有一个二十岁的女生陈伊玲,初试时的成绩十分优异:声乐、视唱、练耳和乐理等课目都列入优等,尤其是她的音色美丽和音域宽广令人赞叹。而复试时却使人大失所望。苏林教授一生桃李满天下,他的学生中间不少是有国际声誉的,但这样年青而又有才华的学生却还是第一个,这样的事情也还是第一次碰到。

　　那次公开的考试是在那间古色古香的大厅里举行的。当陈伊玲镇静地站在考试委员会里几位有名的声乐专家面前,唱完了冼星海的那支有名的"二月里来",门外窗外挤挤挨挨的都站满了人,甚至连不带任何表情①的教授们也不免暗暗递了个眼色。按照规定,应试者还要唱一支外国歌曲,她演唱了意大利歌剧"蝴蝶夫人"②中的咏叹调"有一个良辰佳日"③,以她灿烂的音色和深沉的理解惊动四座,一向以要求严格闻名的苏林教授也不由颔首表示赞许,在他严峻的眼光下,隐藏着一丝微笑。大家都默无一言地注视陈伊玲：嫩绿色的绒线上衣，一条贴身的咖啡色西裤，宛如春天早晨一株亭亭玉立的小树。众目睽睽下，这个本来笑容自若的姑娘也不禁微微困惑了。

复试是在一星期后举行的。录取与否都取决于此。这时将决定一个人终生的事业。经过初试这一关，剩下的人现在已是寥寥无几；而复试将是各方面更其严格的要求下进行的。本市有名的音乐界人士都到了。这些考试委员和旁听者在评选时几乎都带着苛刻的挑剔神气。但是全体对陈伊玲都留下这样一个印象：如果合乎录取条件的只有一个人，那么这唯一的一个人无疑应该是陈伊玲。

谁知道事实却出乎意料之外。陈伊玲是参加复试的最后一个人，唱的还是那两支歌，可是声音发涩，毫无光彩，听起来前后判若两人。是因为怯场、心慌，还是由于身体不适，影响声音？人们甚至怀疑到她的生活作风上是否有不够慎重的地方④！在座的人面面相觑，大家带着询问和疑惑的眼光举目望她。虽然她掩饰不住自己脸上的困倦，一双聪颖的眼睛显得黯然无神，那顽皮的嘴角也流露出一种无可诉说的焦急，可是就整个看来，她通体是明朗的，坦率的，可以使人信任的；仅仅只因为一点意外的事故使她遭受挫折，而这正是人们感到不解之处。她抱歉地对大家笑笑，于是飘然走了。

苏林教授显然是大为生气了。他从来认为，要做一个真正为人民所爱戴的艺术家，首先要做一个各方面都能成为表率的人，一个高尚的人！歌唱家又何尝能例外！可是这样一个自暴自弃的女孩子，永远也不能成为一个有成就的歌唱家！他生气地侧过头去望向窗外。这个城市刚刚受到

356

一次今年最严重的台风的袭击,窗外断枝残叶狼藉满地,整排竹篱委身在满是积水的地上,一片惨淡的景象。

考试委员会对陈伊玲有两种意见:一种认为从两次考试可以看出陈伊玲的声音极不稳固,不扎实⑤,很难造就;另一种则认为给她机会,让她再试一次。苏林教授有他自己的看法,他觉得重要的是为什么造成她先后两次声音悬殊的根本原因,如果问题在于她对事业和生活的态度,尽管声音的禀赋再好,也不能录取她!这是一切条件中的首要条件!

可是究竟是什么原因呢?

苏林教授从秘书那里取去了陈伊玲的报名单,在填着地址的那一栏上,他用红铅笔划了一条粗线。表格上的那张报名照片是一张叫人喜欢的脸,小而好看的嘴,明快单纯的眼睛,笑起来鼻翼稍稍皱起的鼻子,这一切都像是在提醒那位有名的声乐专家,不能用任何简单的方式对待一个人——一个有生命有思想有感情的人。至少眼前这个姑娘的某些具体情况是这张简单的表格上所看不到的。如果这一次落选了,也许这个人终其一生就和音乐分手了。她的天才可能从此就被埋没。而作为一个以培养学生为责任的音乐教授,情况如果是这样,那他是绝对不能原谅自己的。

第二天,苏林教授乘早上第一班电车出发。根据报名单上的地址,好容易找到了在杨树浦⑥的那条僻静的马路,进了弄堂,蓦地不由吃了一惊。

那弄堂里有些墙垣都已倾塌,烧焦的栋梁呈现一片可怕的黑色,断瓦残垣中间时或露出枯黄的破布碎片,所有这些说明了这条弄堂不仅受到台风破坏,而且显然发生过火灾。就在这灾区的瓦砾场上,有些人大清早就在忙碌着张罗。

苏林教授手持纸条，不知从何处找起，忽然听见对屋的楼窗上，有一个孩子有事没事地⑦张口叫着：

"咪——咿——咿——咿——，吗——啊——啊——啊——"仿佛歌唱家在练声的样子。苏林教授不禁为之微笑，他猜对了，那孩子敢情就是陈伊玲的弟弟，正在若有其事地学着他姊姊练声的姿势呢。

从孩子口里知道：他的姊姊是个转业军人，从文工团回来的，到上海后就被分配到工厂里担任行政工作。她是个青年团员，——一个积极而热心的人，不管厂里也好，里弄也好，有事找陈伊玲准没有错！还是在二三天前，这里附近因为台风而造成电线走火，好多人家流离失所，陈伊玲就为了安置灾民，忙得整夜没有睡，终于影响了嗓子。第二天刚好是她去复试的日子，她说声"糟糕"，还是去参加考试了。

这就是全部经过。

"瞧，她还在那儿忙着哪！"孩子向窗外扬了扬手说，"我叫她！我去叫她！"

"不。只要告诉你姊姊：她的第二次考试已经录取了！她完全有条件成为一个优秀的歌唱家，不是吗？我几乎犯了一个错误！"

苏林教授从陈伊玲家里出来，走得很快。是的，这天早晨有什么使人感动的东西充溢在他胸口，他想赶紧回去把他发现的这个音乐学生和她的故事告诉每一个人。

The Second Test

He Wei

Professor Su Lin, a well-known expert on vocal music, found something very puzzling. Twenty-year-old girl Chen Yiling from the Chorus Training Class of more than 200 students had come out exceedingly well in the preliminary test, scoring high marks in vocal music, sightsinging, ear training and music theory. Her beautiful tone color and broad range, in particular, won high praise. But, to the great disappointment of everybody, she failed the second test. The professor, who had trained a large number of students, many of them now of international fame, had never seen a young girl with such a brilliant talent. And the above strange happening was something he had never known before.

The preliminary test took place in a spacious hall of antique style. Chen Yiling stood calmly before the eminent vocal music experts on the Test Committee. When she finished singing Xian Xinhai's famous *When February Comes*, throngs of listeners could be seen standing entranced outside the doors and windows, and even the professors, who usually wore an air of casual indifference, could not help exchanging knowing looks at one another. As it was required of each candidate to sing a foreign song as well, Chen sang the aria *Un bel di* from the Italian opera *Madama Butterfly*. The audience were amazed by her splendid tone color and deep comprehension. Even Professor Su, known for his strict demands. also nodded his approval, his stern eyes twinkling with delight. Chen, wearing a light green woollen sweater and close-fitting brown trousers, stood there like a graceful tree on a spring morning. However, under the silent stare of so many eyes, the smiling girl appeared somewhat ill at ease.

The second test came to pass a week later. The result of this test was to determine each candidate's fate — accepted or otherwise, and what his or her future career would be like. With most of the candidates already eliminated by the preliminary test, this second test was even more demanding in every respect. All celebrated local musicians were present. During the test almost all Test Committee members and visitors wore a harsh and nit-picking look. Nevertheless, they were all under the impression that of all the remaining candidates Chen would undoubtedly be the last one to fail the second test.

Unfortunately, the result was contrary to everybody's expectation. When Chen's turn came last, she sang the same two songs, but her voice was unpleasant and utterly lacklustre as if she were no longer her old self. Was it due to stage fright, nervousness or indisposition? People even suspected some sort of impropriety in her private life. They stared at each other in speechless despair and eyed her questioningly. Weariness was written all over her face. Her bright eyes now looked dejected and dull. And the corners of her otherwise playful mouth wore an expression of unspeakable anxiety. But, as a whole, she was bright, candid and trustworthy. People just could not understand what little accident, if any, had been the cause of her frustration. She smiled apologetically and disappeared out of the room.

Professor Su was obviously upset. He had always believed that to win people's genuine love and esteem, an artist must first of all be exemplary in every way, first of all a noble-minded person. A singer was of course no exception. But a girl like Chen, who had no urge for self-improvement, would never become a successful singer. He turned in anger to look out of the window. The town had just been hit by the worst typhoon of the year. The ground outside was strewn with broken twigs and dry leaves. Fallen bamboo fences on the sodden ground. What a pitiful sight!

The Test Committee were divided in their opinions

about Chen. Some held out little hope of her achieving success as a vocalist, saying that the two tests had shown her voice far from able to hold its own. Others wanted to give her an opportunity for another try. Professor Su, however, had a view of his own. He thought it important to find out the root cause of her failure in the second test. He maintained that if her failure was due to her questionable attitude towards her career and life, she should on no account be admitted no matter how highly gifted she was. That, he said, should be the first and foremost of all things to be considered.

Now what on earth was the cause of her failure?

Professor Su got Chen's application form for enrollment from his secretary and underlined in red pencil the address she had put down on it. The photo attached to the form showed a very cute face with a pretty little mouth, lucid guiless eyes and a nose which would pucker up a little bit whenever she smiled. All that seemed to warn the professor against treating a person in a simplistic way— a person alive with thought and emotion. There must be certain practical aspects of the young girl which the simple application form made no mention of. Her failure to pass the second test might mean her life-long divorce from music and hence a permanent stifling of her musical talent. Should that be the case, the professor, whose duty it was to foster young musical talents, would never forgive himself.

The next morning, Professor Su took the first tram of the day. Thanks to the address given on the application form, he finally managed to find the secluded street in Yangshupu. The moment he stepped into the lane, he was taken aback by what he saw.

There were broken walls, charred beams of a ghastly black and scorched rags here and there among debris — all telling of the destruction wrought by the recent typhoon and the ensuing fire. Since early in the morning, some people had already been busying themselves amongst the rubble.

Professor Su, with a slip of paper in hand, was wondering where to find the address when all of a sudden he heard a child crying out randomly from an upstairs window of the opposite building, like a singer practising his voice:

"Mi—yi—yi—yi—, ma—ah—ah—ah—" The professor could not help smiling. He guessed right that the kid was Chen's younger brother affectedly parroting his elder sister's voice.

The professor then learned from the child that his elder sister Chen, ex-member of a PLA art troupe, was now on the administrative staff of a factory after being transferred from the army to civilian work in Shanghai. As a Youth Leaguer, she was enthusiastic and earnest.

363

Whenever the factory or her neighborhood was in need of some help, she was always considered the right person to approach. Just a couple of days before, the neighborhood had caught fire as a result of electric wire sparking caused by the typhoon. Consequently, many families were left homeless. Chen spent a sleepless night caring for the disaster victims, which in turn affected her voice. The next day, when it occurred to her that it was the very day for the second test, she blurted out, "Oh, my!" Yet, she went to the test all the same.

That was the whole story.

"Look, she's still busy working over there!" exclaimed the child from the window, gesticulating with his raised hand. "Let me call her! I'll go and call her!"

"No, don't. But just tell your sister that she's been admitted after passing the second test! She has every qualification for being a superb singer, hasn't she? I've almost made a mistake!"

The professor walked away from Chen's house, and that very quickly. Yes, his bosom swelling with a thrill, he wanted to hurry back to let everybody know of the music student he had discovered and the whole story about her.

注　释

　　　　《第二次考试》是散文家何为
　　　　(1922—　　　)的前期代表作,1956 年 12
　　　　月 26 日在《人民日报》上发表后,立刻博
　　　　得好评。此文以情节取胜,构思精巧,寓
　　　　意深邃,乃一篇玲珑剔透的成功之作。

　　① "不带任何表情"意即"表情冷漠",现译为 wore
an air of casual indifference。

　　② "蝴蝶夫人"为意大利著名歌剧作曲家普契尼(Gia-
como Puccini)的作品,共三幕,于 1904 年 2 月 17 日在意大
利米兰首演。原名为 Madama Butterfly 或 Madame But-
terfly。

　　③ "有一个良辰佳日"为意大利歌剧《蝴蝶夫人》中的
著名女高音独唱曲。原名为 Un bel di 或 Un bel di ve-
dremo。另一中文译名为《晴朗的一天》。

　　④ "她的生活作风上是否有不够慎重的地方"指"她
在私生活方面恐有不够检点之处",故译为 some sort of
impropriety in her private life,其中 impropriety 意为"不
正当的行为"或"不合适的举止"。

⑤ "声音极不稳固,不扎实"译为 her voice far from able to hold its own,其中 to hold its own 是习语,意为"维持原有的状态"或"不衰退"。

⑥ "杨树浦"位于上海市东北部,濒临黄浦江,旧时为贫民区。

⑦ "有事没事地"意即"任意地"或"胡乱地",故译为 randomly。

下蛋·唱鸡及其它

谢　逸

笼里养着两只母鸡，一只爱唱，另一只喜静。主人根据母鸡下蛋之后报唱的现象，以为所有的蛋都是那只唱鸡产的①，因此很偏爱它②，捉得蟑螂也专是喂给它吃。但日子一久，秘密揭穿了：原来那只唱鸡下蛋很少，而不叫的那只却一天一个，且蛋刚落地就一声不响地离开鸡窝，由那只唱鸡站在蛋边大喊大叫③。

闲聊时和朋友谈及此事，他以为我是言外之意不在鸡，而是在论人。其实，古人早就以鸡喻人了，《尚书·牧誓》里就有"牝鸡无晨"④之句。说到人，在我们中确是有很多沉默寡言的人，他们牢牢蹲在自己的岗位上，夜以继日，埋头苦干，替国家创造了大量的物质财富，为人民作出一项又一项的优异成绩。他们像母鸡一样，吞的是粗糠老菜，产下的是蛋，而且往往一声不响⑤。但也有一种人，嘴尖舌长，能说会道，自我吹嘘，滔滔不绝，像那只爱唱的母鸡一样，占着个鸡窝不下蛋⑥。个别恶劣的还窃取别人的成果去报喜称功，一点不觉得惭愧。

本来，考核一个人的成绩，不是听他唱得好听不好听，而是看他"下蛋不下蛋"。但那善于炫耀和卖弄的人，生一个蛋就唱得像是生了十个似的，只做出三分成绩就吹成十分，碰上个凡事只用耳朵听不用眼睛看的糊涂长官，自然就博得了偏爱，于是一帆风顺，扶摇直上了⑦。而那些埋头"下蛋"的人，由于他们一声不响，默默无闻⑧，就很少为人所知，更不受重视。因此，他们既没有"蟑螂"可吃，甚至连个"下蛋的窝"也没有。

喜唱或是爱静，本来只是人的一种个性，由于是长期养成的习惯，要完全改过来也颇不容易，但是，在新长征的途程中，人的生命到底有限，而探索宇宙奥秘的道路却又那样的无限和悠长，结果一天到晚都用于高谈阔论，搞"假、大、空"，又哪有时间及精力去钻研和攻关呢？最重要的还是认真蹲在"窝"里⑨，多为九亿人民"下蛋"。

Egglaying, Cackling, Etc.

Xie Yi

There were two hens in a coop. One was fond of cackling while the other liked to keep quiet. As it is customary for a hen to cackle after laying an egg, the chicken raiser accordingly credited the cackler with all the eggs that had been laid. As a result, he became so partial to his favourite bird that he fed her with every cockroach he caught. With the passing of time, however, it became known that the cackler had in fact laid very few eggs while the non-cackler kept laying one egg a day. Every time, as soon as the latter laid an egg, she quit the coop quietly, leaving the former standing by the newly-laid egg shouting and yelling her head off.

Once, when I chatted with a friend about this, he thought what I had in mind was not the hen, but men in general. As a matter of fact, our forefathers long ago already drew an analogy between the hen and a human, as witness the Chinese idiom "No hen crows at dawn" (meaning "No woman is to usurp man's power") in *The*

Book of History: Mu Shi. It is true that there are among us many who stick to their posts and quietly immerse themselves in hard work day and night, creating enormous material wealth for the state and achieving one success after another for the people. Like the above-mentioned good layer, they eat simple food, but lay eggs, often without making a fanfare. There are among us, however, another kind of people who, armed with a glib tongue, indulge in incessant self-glorification and, like the above-mentioned cackler, hold on to the coop without laying any egg. Some few even go so far as to brazenly claim credit for work that was done by others.

The proper way to evaluate a person is of course by watching whether or not he "lays eggs", not by listening to him singing his own praises. When a braggart lays one egg, he will talk in such a way as if he had laid ten eggs. When he puts in a tiny bit of work, he will talk as if he had done ten times as much. He will naturally find favour with a muddleheaded boss who trusts his ears more than his eyes. The braggart will thus find himself quickly climbing up the social ladder. As to those engrossed in "laying eggs", because they are reserved and content to live in obscurity they gain little public attention, let alone recognition. They are given no "cockroaches" to eat. They do not even have a "shelter for egglaying".

It is in one's nature to be either noisy or quiet. As

370

something ingrained, it cannot be completely changed overnight. But life is short while the probe into the mysteries of the universe is long and unlimited. If we indulge in empty talk and trickery day and night, how can we have time and energy for serious study and tackling key problems confronting the country on its new Long March towards modernization? The most important thing is to stand fast to the "coop" and "lay" more "eggs" for this nation of 900,000,000 people.

注　释

谢逸(1917—　　　),广西人,为杂文
作家。此文写于 1980 年 8 月间,用比喻
的手法批评那些自我吹嘘、弄虚作假、骗
取名位的人,颂扬那些默默奉献,不争功
名的人。文章亦庄亦谐,饶有风趣,有很
强的现实针对性。

① "以为所有的蛋都是那只唱鸡产的"译为 credited
the cackler with all the eggs that had been laid,其中 cackler 即 the hen that was fond of cackling。又 to credit...with... 意即"把……归功于……"。

② "因此很偏爱它"译为 As a result, he became so
partial to his favorite bird,其中 his favorite bird 是 "它"
的意译。

③ "大喊大叫"译为 shouting and yelling her head
off,意同 shouting noisily 或 shouting at the top of her
voice,但稍较强调。

④ "'牝鸡无晨'"译为 "No hen crows at dawn"
(meaning "No woman is to usurp man's power"),其中括

号内的文字是译者增添的成分,起注释作用,有助于海外读者对原文成语的理解。

⑤ "往往一声不响"译为 often without making a fanfare。To make a fanfare 是成语,作"大吹大擂"解。

⑥ "占着个鸡窝不下蛋"译为 hold on to the coop without laying any egg,其中 to hold on to 是成语,作"抓住不放"解,和 to stick to 以及 to cling to 同义。

⑦ "一帆风顺,扶摇直上"译为 quickly climbing up the social ladder,其中 to climb up the ladder 是成语,作 to rise to power and position 解。

⑧ "一声不响,默默无闻"译为 are reserved and content to live in obscurity,其中 reserved 作"缄默寡言"解,content to live in obscurity 意即"甘于寂寞"。

⑨ "认真蹲在'窝'里"译为 to stand fast to the coop,其中 to stand to 是成语,和 to stick to 同义。

快乐的死亡

陆 文 夫

作家有三种死法。一曰自然的死,二曰痛苦的死,三曰快乐的死。

自然的死属于心脏停止跳动①,是一种普遍的死亡形式,没有特色,可以略而不议。快乐的死和痛苦的死不属于心脏停止跳动,是人还活着,作品已经、或几乎是没有了!

作家没有了作品,可以看作是个人艺术生命的死亡、职业的停顿。其中有些人是因为年事已高,力不从心②。这不是艺术的死亡,而是艺术的离休,他自己无可自责,社会也会尊重③他在艺术上曾经作出的贡献。

痛苦的死亡却不然,即当一个作家的体力和脑力④还能胜任创作的时候,作品已经没有了,其原因主要是由于各种苦难和折磨(包括自我折磨)所造成。折磨毁了他的才华,苦难消沉了意志,作为人来说他还活着,作为作家来说却正在或已死去。这种死亡他自己感到很痛苦,别人看了心里也很难受。

快乐的死亡却很快乐,不仅他自己感到快乐,别人看来也很快乐。昨天看见他大会上做报告,下面掌声如雷;今天又看见他参加宴会，为这为那地频频举杯⑤。昨天听见他在高朋中大发议论，语惊四座，今天又听见他在那些开不完的座谈会上重复昨天的意见。昨天看见他在北京的街头，今天又看见他飞到了广州……只是看不到或很少看到他的作品发表在哪里。

我不害怕自然的死，因为害怕也没用，人人不可避免。我也不太害怕痛苦的死，因为那时代已经过去⑥。我最害怕的就是那快乐的死，毫无痛苦，十分热闹，甚至还有点轰轰烈烈。自己很难控制，即很难控制在一定的范围之内。因为我觉得喝酒不一定完全是坏事，少喝一点可以舒筋活血，据说对心血管也是有帮助的。作家不能当隐士，适当的社会活动和文学活动可以开阔眼界，活跃思想，对创作也是有帮助的⑦。可是怎么才能不酗酒、不作酒鬼，这有益的定量究竟是多少呢？怕只怕三杯下肚，豪情大发，嘟嘟嘟，来个瓶底朝天，而且一顿喝不上便情绪不高，颇有怨言，甚至会到处去找酒喝。呜呼，快乐地死去！

Happy Death

Lu Wenfu

A writer can die three kinds of death: natural death, painful death, happy death.

Natural death, caused by the discontinuation of heartbeat, is a common form of death with no characterestics of its own, and therefore may as well be left out without any comment. In the case of happy death and painful death, which are not caused by the discontinuation of heartbeat, the writer, alive as he is, has stopped or almost stopped writing!

When a writer no longer produces any works, it is tantamount to the death of his artistic life or the end of his career. Some writers lay down their pens because they are too old to be equal to the task. We call it retirement from art rather than death of art. They have nothing to blame themselves for. And society at large will pay tribute to the contributions they have already made to art.

Painful death is quite another matter. It occurs when a writer abandons writing even though he is still sound in mind and body. It results mainly from various kinds of sufferings and torments (including self-inflicted torments). Torments ruin his talent while sufferings demoralize him. Though still alive as a man, he is dying or already dead as a writer. This kind of death causes not only much pain to the writer himself, but much sadness to other people as well.

Happy death is a joyful thing, bringing happiness to both the writer himself and other people. Yesterday we saw him addressing a big meeting amidst thunderous applause, and today we saw him attending a banquet, drinking nonstop to this and that. Yesterday we heard him talking volubly to a gathering of distinguished guests, capturing the attention of all present, and today we heard him repeating himself at one of those endless forums. Yesterday we met him on a Beijing street, and today we saw him flying to Guangzhou ... But never or very seldom do we find his new works seeing the light of day.

I do not fear natural death for nobody can avoid it, hence no use fearing. Nor do I fear painful death for it is something belonging to a bygone age. What I fear most is happy death, which is absolutely painless and full of bustle, excitement and even dramatic spectacle. It is difficult to exercise self-control, that is, difficult to keep within limits. Drinking is, to my mind, not always bad because a few spots may help blood circulation and is, as they say, good for the heart and blood vessels. Being no hermit, a writer stands to benefit in writing as long as he gets properly involved with social and literary activities to widen his field of vision and stimulate his thinking. But how can he avoid excessive drinking or becoming a drunkard? What is the safety limit in this respect? The trouble is after three cups of alcohol he will get wild and unrestrained and end in gulping down a whole bottle. One meal without liquor will upset him and set him complaining and searching around for drink. Alas, just to end up dying happily!

注　释

作者陆文夫（1927—　　）是小说家。此文写于1985年4月，是一篇有很强现实针对性的杂感，作者以辛辣的笔调调侃当前有些作家终日沉溺于社会活动、不务正业的现象。

① "心脏停止跳动"译为 the discontinuation of heart-beat，其中 discontinuation 也可译为 absence 或 stoppage 等。又 heartbeat 在此为不可数名词，故前面不用冠词。

② "年事已高，力不从心"译为 too old to be equal to the task，其中 to be equal to 的意思是 to have enough strength for。

③ "社会也会尊重"译为 society at large will pay tribute to，其中短语 at large 作 in general 解，用来强调 society，意即"整个社会"。

④ "体力和脑力"译为 in mind and body，也可译为 mentally and physically。

⑤ "为这为那地频频举杯"译为 drinking nonstop to this and that，也可译为 proposing repeated toasts to this

and that。其中 nonstop 意同 now and then 或 again and a-
gain 等,但略带讽刺味道。

⑥ "因为那时代已经过去" 译为 for it is something
belonging to a bygone age,其中 bygone age 指过去建国后
的一段极左时期,包括"文化大革命"时期。

⑦ "对创作也是有帮助的" 译为 stands to benefit in
writing,其中 stands 作"处于某种状态"(to be in a particular state)解。

耳闻不如一见？
——从焦尾琴谈起

顾均正

在郭老①新编的话剧"蔡文姬"里，提到了蔡文姬的父亲蔡邕(yōng)②所造的那张焦尾琴。最近我看了"蔡文姬"的演出，自然而然想起了焦尾琴，想起了关于焦尾琴的故事：

蔡邕因为不愿趋附权贵③，怕被人陷害，曾经亡命江南，往来于吴会之间(今江、浙一带)，计十二年。据说他在吴(今苏州)的时候，有一天听见邻家烧饭的柴火中发出一种爆裂的声音，他熟悉这种声音，知道这声音来自一种极好的桐木，这种桐木是造琴④的最好材料。他就跟邻家主人商量，把这段烧焦了的桐木要了来，造成一张琴。这张琴弹起来果然非常好听。因为它的一端⑤是烧焦的，所以大家都叫它焦尾琴。

当我想起这个故事的时候，使我对"耳闻不如目见"这句成语不能不有所怀疑。的确，我们认识这个物质世界，有时候不是用眼睛来看而是用耳朵来听的。蔡邕能够从木材燃烧时发出的爆裂声来辨别木材的好坏，充分说明了"耳闻"不一定"不如目见"。当然，"耳闻不如目见"这句话的原

381

意是指间接经验不如直接经验那样可靠，这是完全正确的。但是，如果对这句话只是从字面上来理解，认为耳朵听到的总不如眼睛看见的那样可靠，那对耳朵来说，却是极大的冤枉⑥。

我们应该承认，眼睛是直接经验的主要来源，可是我们同时也得承认，眼睛是最会骗人的。举一个极普通的例子来说，我们大家觉得早晨的太阳比中午的太阳大得多，可是如果你用照相机给太阳在早晨和中午各照一个相，你就会发现摄得的相片是一样大小的。谁会想到，在这个每天接触到的日常现象上，从古到今，无论是什么人，无论在什么地方，都一直在受着眼睛的骗？并且骗得我们好苦，不但古代的大学问家如孔子，没有能回答⑦为什么早晨的太阳看起来会大于中午的太阳，连现代的科学家，对这个问题也不曾有一个令人十分满意的解释。这个现象对迷信眼睛的人来说，是一个有力的讽刺。

当然，我们这样说，并不是要否定眼睛的作用。我们只是说明，眼睛虽然有非常广阔的活动范围，可是它是有缺点的。我们不能迷信眼睛，小看了耳朵的作用。

耳朵的活动范围虽然小，可是它的作用也不只是听听讲话，听听音乐。它还有其他的特殊功用。在某种场合，它不但无愧于⑧"以耳代目"这句话，而且比眼睛做得更好。

Is the Ear Less Reliable than the Eye?
——About the Story of *Jiao Wei Qin*

Gu Junzheng

In the play *Cai Wenji*, newly written by venerable Guo Moruo, reference is made to *jiao wei qin*, a zithern partly made of scorched wood by Cai Yong, father of Cai Wenji. Recently, after I saw the play on the stage, my mind naturally went to *jiao wei qin* and its story.

Cai Yong disliked playing up to bigwigs and, to avoid frame-ups, he went into exile in the South, wandering about for twelve years in Jiangsu and Zhejiang Provinces. It is said that one day during his stay in Suzhou when he heard the crackling of firewood from his next-door neighbour at cooking time, he knew the familiar sound came from paulownia, a kind of choice wood best for making zitherns. Now, talking it over with his neighbour, he was given the piece of scorched wood, which he subsequently made into a zithern. This musical instrument, when played, turned out to be extremely pleasant to the ear.

People called it *jiao wei qin* because the tail of its sound-board was made of scorched wood.

When I think of the story, I cannot help having doubts about the validity of the proverb, "Seeing is better than hearing." Fact is, to know the material world, we sometimes use not the eye, but the ear. That Cai Yong could tell the quality of wood by listening to its crackling sound while it was burning in the kitchen stove makes it crystal clear that "hearing" is not necessarily less reliable that "seeing". The above-mentioned proverb literally means that secondhand experience is less reliable than firsthand experience, which is perfectly true. But, if we should take this saying at its face value and regard the ear as invariably less reliable than the eye, we shall do the former a gross injustice.

While we agree that the eye is the main source of direct experience, we must admit that it is also most misleading. Take a most common example. We all agree that the sun is much bigger in the early morning than at noon. But if we take a photo of it in the early morning and at noon respectively, we shall find it of the same size in both cases. Who would have thought that, when it comes to this common phenomenon in our daily life, people the world over should have been fooled by their own eyes ever since time immemorial? The optical illusion has indeed landed us in indescribable trouble. Not only were great

384

ancient sages like Confucius stumped by the question why the sun was seemingly bigger in the early morning than at noon, even scientists of today have failed to give a wholly satisfactory explanation. This is a keen satire on those having blind faith in the eye.

Of course I do not mean to deny the role played by the eye. All I want to show is that although the eye has an extremely wide scope of activities, it is, nevertheless, far from being faultless. We should, therefore, never overtrust the eye and underestimate the usefulness of the ear.

Although the ear has a smaller scope of activities, its functions are not confined to listening to conversation or music only. It has other specific functions of its own. Under certain circumstances, it is not only worthy of the saying, "Let the ear do duty for the eye," it can even excel the eye.

注　释

顾均正(1902—1981)，浙江嘉兴人，
文学翻译家、杂文作家。《百闻不如一
见？》是他写的一篇富于知识性和趣味
性的科学小品。

① "郭老" 指郭沫若。"……老" 是我们对长者，尤其是
老年学者的常用亲密尊称，英语中无对应表达法，不能直
译。现把"郭老"译为 venerable Guo Moruo，英语 venerable 一字含有因高龄、经历等原因而令人敬重之意。

② "蔡邕"，译为 Cai Yong，是东汉著名文学家、书
法家。

③ "趋附权贵"译为 playing up to bigwigs 或 fawning
on those in power，其中 to play up to 是成语，作"奉承"、
"向……讨好"解。

④ "琴" 指我国古琴，即七弦琴，和欧洲古代弦乐器
zithern（齐特琴）相似，故译为 zithern。

⑤ "它的一端" 指琴的共鸣板的一端，故译为 the tail
of its soundboard。

⑥ "对耳朵来说，却是极大的冤枉" 译为 we shall do

the former a gross injustice，其中 to do somebody an injustice 是英语惯用搭配，作"冤屈某人"或"对某人不公平"解。

⑦ "不但古代的大学问家如孔子，没有能回答……"译为 Not only were great ancient sages like Confucius stumped by ...，其中 stumped 作"难住"、"难倒"解，意同 puzzled。

⑧ "无愧于……"在此作"配得上……"或"和……相称"解，故译 worthy of。

幼 年 鲁 迅

王 士 菁

　　在家里，领着幼年鲁迅的是保姆长妈妈。她是一个淳朴的农村妇女。最初大约是一个生活在农村里的年轻的孤孀，死掉了丈夫和丧失了土地之后，就从农村来到城里谋生。她的姓名，当时是没有人知道的，鲁迅的祖母叫她"阿长"，因此人们也就跟着叫她"阿长"，但孩子们却叫她"长妈妈"。她懂得许多莫名其妙的道理①，还有许多规矩，这一切都是孩子们所不理解的。譬如说，人死了，不说死掉，而说"老掉了"；死了人或生了孩子的屋里，是不应该走进去的；饭粒子落在地上，必须捡起来，最好是吃下去；晒裤子用的竹竿底下，是万不可钻过去的，等等。平时她不许孩子们乱走动②，拔一株草，翻一块石头，就说是顽皮，要去告诉母亲去。起初，孩子们并不怎么喜欢她。尤其是当她不留心踩死了鲁迅所心爱的隐鼠，这更使鲁迅十分生气。但是，有一件事，出乎意料之外，使鲁迅对她发生了敬意，因为，她对孩子们能够讲述一些"长毛"（关于太平天国）的故事；又一件事，更使鲁迅对她发生了很大的敬意，那就是，她不知从什么地方替鲁迅找到了③一部为他日夜所渴望的绘图《山海经》。

388

鲁迅对于绘图《山海经》的渴望已不止一天了。这事是由和他家同住在这个台门④里的远房叔祖⑤玉田老人惹起来的。他是一个胖胖的和蔼的老人，爱种一点珠兰、茉莉之类的花木。他在家里无人可以攀谈，所以就很喜欢和孩子们来往，有时简直称呼他们为"小友"。他的藏书很丰富，其中有一本叫《花镜》，上面印着许多好看的花草和树木，是一部孩子们最心爱的书。但老人却说还有一部更好看的哩，那是绘图的《山海经》。人面的兽，九头的蛇，三脚的鸟，生着翅膀的人，没有头的拿两乳当作眼睛的怪物，……这本书上都有。可惜，老人一时找不到，不知被放到哪里去了。孩子们怀着十分迫切的心情，都急于想看这本充满着奇异图画的书，但又不好意思逼着老人去寻找。问别人呢，很少有人知道。想买吧，不知到哪里去买，大街离得很远，只有正月间才能够去玩一趟，那时书铺的门却又是关着的。玩得热闹的时候倒也不觉得有什么，一到静下来，可就想起了那绘图的《山海经》。也许是鲁迅过于念念不忘这本书吧，连长妈妈也知道了⑥，来问是怎么一回事，鲁迅就把这事对她说了。

　　过了十多天，也许是一个月吧，长妈妈在她请假回家转来的时候，一见面，就将一包书递给了鲁迅。她高兴地说道："哥儿⑦，有画的《三哼经》，我给你找来了！"这是一个怎样出人意外的消息啊，它比逢年过节还使鲁迅兴奋。他赶紧接过来，打开纸包一看，是四本小小的书。啊！人面兽，九头蛇，……果然都在里面了。虽然这是一部纸张很黄，图像很坏，连动物的眼睛也都是长方形的，刻工印工都很粗糙的书，但它正是鲁迅所日夜盼望的书。后来，鲁迅把这一位贫农妇女和自己对她的深厚感情，写在一篇充满激情的散文里。

这确是四本小小的不平凡的书。鲁迅从长妈妈的手里，连带着她的那一份无比深厚的情意接受了过来。这是幼年的鲁迅第一次读到的比一切别的书更加使他感动的书。

　　在家庭里，祖母特别喜爱鲁迅。夏夜，鲁迅躺在一株大桂花树下的小板桌上乘凉，祖母摇着芭蕉扇坐在桌旁，一面摇着扇子，一面讲故事给他听，或是叫他猜谜语。祖母对于民间故事是很熟悉的。她会讲关于猫的故事，据说：猫是老虎的师父。老虎本来是什么也不会的，就投到猫的门下。猫教给它扑的方法，捉的方法，像自己捉老鼠一样。这一些学完了，老虎想：本领都学到了，谁也比不过自己了，只有做过它的老师的猫还比自己强，要是把猫杀掉，自己便是最强的脚色了。它打定了主意，便往猫身上扑过去。猫是早知道它的心思的⑧，一跳，便上了树。老虎却只能眼睁睁地在树下蹲着。猫没有将一切本领传授完，还没有教它上树哩。祖母还会讲"水满金山"的故事，——有个叫作许仙的，他救了两条蛇：一青一白，后来白蛇就化作女人来报恩，嫁给了许仙；青蛇化作丫环，也跟着。有个和尚叫作法海禅师，他看见许仙脸上有"妖气"⑨，于是就把许仙藏在金山寺的法座后面。白蛇娘娘前来寻夫，于是就"水满金山"。后来，白蛇娘娘中了法海禅师的计策，被骗装在一个小小的钵盂里了。这钵盂被埋在地下，上面造起一座塔来镇压她，这塔就是竖立在西湖边上的雷峰塔。幼年的鲁迅听了这个故事，心里很不舒服，他深为白蛇娘娘抱不平。当时，他的唯一的希望，就是这座镇压白蛇娘娘反抗的雷峰塔快些倒掉。后来，他把这个民间故事写在一篇反对黑暗反动统治的杂文里。

When Lu Xun Was a Child

Wang Shijing

As a child, Lu Xun was in the charge of a nurse called Mama Chang. She was an honest country woman. At first she must have been a young widow in the countryside, who went to town to seek a living for herself after her husband died and she lost her land. Nobody knew what her name was. As Lu Xun's grandmother called her "Achang", other people also called her by the same name. But the children usually called her "Mama Chang". She was so full of mysterious lore and had so many rules of behaviour that the children sometimes found her quite puzzling. For instance, if someone died, you should not say he was dead but "he has passed away". You should not enter a room where someone had died or a child had been born. If a grain of rice fell to the ground, you should pick it up, and the best thing was to eat it. On no account must you walk under the bamboo pole on which trousers or pants were hanging out to dry. She would not let the children get up to mischief. If they pulled up a weed or turned over a stone, she would say they were naughty and threaten to tell their mother. In the beginning, the children did not think much of her. Lu Xun was especially angry with her when she inadvertently stepped on and killed his favourite little mouse. However, one thing which unexpectedly made Lu Xun feel respect for her was that she often told the children stories of the "Long Hairs" (the Taiping Rebellion). Another thing which inspired Lu Xun with a still greater respect for her was that she was able to produce from nobody knew where an illustrated edition of the *Book of Hills and Seas*[1], which Lu Xun had been longing for day and night.

Lu Xun had been longing for an illustrated copy of the *Book of Hills and Seas* for sometime. The whole business started with a distant great-uncle named Yutian, who was living in the same compound. A fat and kindly old man, he liked to grow flowers such as chloranthus and jasmine. The old man was a lonely soul with no one to talk to, so he liked the children's company and often even called them his "young friends". He owned a big collection of books, one of which was called *The Mirror of Flowers*[2] with many beautiful illustrations of flowers and

---

[1] A book of geography which contains many legends, written in the 4th—2nd centuries B. C.

[2] A manual for gardeners by Chen Haozi of the 17th century.

trees. The children found this book most attractive. But the old man told them that the illustrated edition of the *Book of Hills and Seas* was even more attractive, with pictures of man-faced beasts, nine-headed snakes, three-footed birds, winged men and headless monsters who used their teats as eyes .... Unfortunately, he happened to have mislaid it. Eager as they were to look at the book with such strange pictures, the children did not like to press him to find it. None of the people the children asked knew where to get it, and the children had no idea where they could buy it themselves. The main street was a long way from their home, and the New Year holiday was the only time in the year when they were able to go there to look around, but during that period the bookshops were closed. As long as the children were playing, it was not so bad, but the moment they sat down they would think of the *Book of Hills and Seas*. Probably because Lu Xun harped on the subject so much, even Achang got wind of it and started asking what this *Book of Hills and Seas* was. Lu Xun then told her about it.

About a fortnight or a month later, Mama Chang came back after some leave at home and the moment she saw Lu Xun, she handed him a package. "Here, son!" she said cheerfully. "I've bought you that *Book of Holy Seas* with pictures." What an unexpected piece of news! To young Lu Xun it was even more thrilling than the New

Year holiday or a festival. He hastened to take the package and unwrap the paper. There were four small volumes and, sure enough, the man-faced beast, the nine-headed snake ... all of them were there. Although the paper was yellow and the drawings very poor — so much so that even the animals' eyes were oblong, and both the engraving and printing were very crude, nevertheless, it was Lu Xun's most treasured book. Later, in a highly impassioned essay Lu Xun paid tribute to this country woman of peasant origin and described his own deep affection for her.

The book was indeed something extraordinary. Lu Xun received it from Mama Chang's hands along with her incomparably deep affection for him. It touched the young Lu Xun more deeply than any other book he had read.

Of all the children at home, his grandmother loved Lu Xun most. On summer evenings when Lu Xun was lying on a small wooden table under an osmanthus tree to enjoy the evening cool, she would sit by the table with a palm-leaf fan in her hand. Waving the fan, she would tell him stories or ask him riddles. She was very familiar with folk tales. The cat, she said, was the tiger's teacher. Originally the tiger couldn't do any thing, so he turned to the cat for help. The cat taught him how to pounce and catch his prey the way that he caught rats. After these lessons the tiger said to himself, "Now that I've mastered all the skills no other creature is a match for me except my master the cat. If I kill the cat I shall be king of the beasts." He made up his mind to do this, and was about to pounce on the cat. But the cat knew what he was up to and he leaped up onto a tree. The tiger was left squatting below and glaring upwards. The cat had not taught all his skills: he had not taught the tiger to climb trees. His grandmother also told Lu Xun the story "Flooding Jinshan Monastery". A man named Xu Xian rescued two snakes, one white and one green. The white snake changed into a woman to repay Xu's kindness and married him, while the green snake changed into her maid and accompanied her. A Buddhist monk by the name of Fa Hai saw from Xu's face that he had been bewitched by an evil spirit, so he hid Xu behind the shrine in Jinshan Monastery, and when Lady White Snake came to look for her husband the whole place was flooded. In the end Fa Hai trapped Lady White Snake, and put her in a small alms-bowl. He buried this bowl in the ground, and built a pagoda over it to prevent her getting out. This was Leifeng Pagoda by West Lake. The story made young Lu Xun uncomfortable. He was deeply concerned at the injustice done to Lady White Snake, and his one wish at that time was for the pagoda imprisoning Lady White Snake underneath it soon to collapse. Later, Lu Xun used this folktale in an essay opposing the reactionary rule of the forces of darkness.

注　释

《幼年鲁迅》摘自王士菁著《鲁迅传》一书。

①"她懂得许多莫名其妙的道理"译为 She was so full of mysterious lore,其中 lore 的意思是"口头传说或信仰"。此句根据上下文也可译为 She was so full of superstitious beliefs。

②"她不许孩子们乱走动"意即"她不许孩子们调皮捣蛋",不宜按字面直译。现把它译为 She would not let the children get up to mischief,其中动词短语 to get up to 作"干(不好的事)解"。

③"她不知从什么地方替鲁迅找到了……"译为 she was able to produce from nobody knew where...,其中 nobody knew where 作名词用,是介词 from 的宾语。又 to produce 在此作"出示"、"拿出"解。

④"台门"即"院落",现译为 compound。

⑤"叔祖"可译为 great-uncle 或 granduncle。

⑥"连长妈妈也知道了"译为 even Achang got wind of it,其中 got wind of 是成语,作"听到……的消息"解。

⑦ "哥儿"译为 son,是英语中年长者对男孩或年轻男子的亲昵称呼。根据上下文,"哥儿"在此也可译为 young master。

⑧ "猫是早知道它的心思的"意即"猫早知道它要搞什么名堂",故译为 But the cat knew what he was up to,其中 up to 是成语,作"忙于(不好的事)"解。

⑨ "他看见许仙脸上有'妖气'"中的"妖气"不好直译,现按"被妖魔迷住"的意思把全句译为 Fa Hai saw from Xu's face that he had been bewitched by an evil spirit。此句也可译为 Fa Hai saw that Xu's face betrayed his obsession with an evil spirit 或 Fa Hai saw from Xu's face that he had been under the spell of a demon。

为奴隶的母亲

柔　石

　　她底丈夫是一个皮贩，就是收集乡间各猎户底兽皮和牛皮，贩到大埠上出卖的人。但有时也兼做点农作，芒种①的时节，便帮人家插秧，他能将每行插得非常直，假如有五人同在一个水田内，他们一定叫他站在第一个做标准。然而境况总是不佳，债是年年积起来了。他大约就因为境况的不佳，烟也吸了，酒也喝了，钱也赌起来了。这样，竟使他变做一个非常凶狠而暴躁的男子，但也就更贫穷下去，连小小的移借，别人也不敢答应了。

　　在穷底结果的病以后，全身便变成枯黄色，脸孔黄的和小铜鼓②一样，连眼白也黄了。别人说他是黄疸病，孩子们也就叫他"黄胖"了。有一天，他向他底妻说：

　　"再也没有办法了，这样下去，连小锅子也都卖去了。我想，还是从你底身上设法罢。你跟着我挨饿，有什么办法呢？"

　　"我底身上？……"

　　他底妻坐在灶后，怀里抱着她底刚满三周岁的男小孩。她讷讷地低声地问。

"你，是呀，"她底丈夫病后的无力的声音，"我已经将你出典了③……"

"什么呀？"他底妻几乎昏去似的。

屋内是稍稍静寂了一息。他气喘着说：

"三天前，王狼来坐讨了半天的债回去以后，我也跟着他去，走到了九亩潭边；我很不想要做人了。但是坐在那株爬上去一纵身就可落在潭里的树下，想来想去，终没有力气跳了。猫头鹰在耳朵边不住地哮，我底心被它叫寒起来，我只得回转身，但在路上，遇见了沈家婆，她问我，晚也晚了，在外做什么。我就告诉她，请她代我借一笔款，或向什么人家的小姐借些衣服或首饰去暂时当一当，免得王狼底狼一般的绿眼睛天天在家里闪烁④。可是沈家婆向我笑道：

"'你还将妻养在家里做什么呢，你自己黄也黄到这个地步了？'

"我低着头站在她面前没有答，她又说：

"'儿子呢，你只有一个了，舍不得。但妻——'

"我当时想：'莫非叫我卖去妻子么？'

"而她继续道：

"'但妻——虽然是结发的，穷了，也没有法，还养在家里做什么呢？'

"这样，她就直说出：'有一个秀才，因为没有儿子，年纪已五十岁了，想买一个妾；又因他底大妻不允许，只准他典一个，典三年或五年，叫我物色相当的女人：年纪约三十岁左右，养过两三个儿子的，人要沉默老实，又肯做事，还要对他底大妻肯低眉下首。这次是秀才娘子向我说的，假如条件合，肯出八十元或一百元的身价。我代她寻了好几天，终没有相当的女人。'她说：现在碰到我，想起了你来，样样都对的。当时问我底意见怎样，我一边掉了几滴泪，一边却被她催的答应她了。"

说到这里，他垂下头，声音很低弱，停止了。他底妻简直痴似的，话一句没有。又静寂了一息，他继续说：

"昨天，沈家婆到过秀才底家里，她说秀才很高兴，秀才娘子也喜欢，钱是一百元，年数呢，假如三年养不出儿子，是五年。沈家婆并将日子也拣定了——本月十八，五天后。今天，她写典契去了。"

这时，他底妻简直连腑脏都颤抖，吞吐着问：

"你为什么早不对我说？"

"昨天在你底面前旋了三个圈子，可是对你说不出。不过我仔细想，除出将你底身子设法外，再也没有办法了。"

"决定了么？"妇人战着牙齿问。

"只待典契写好。"

"倒霉的事情呀，我——一点也没有别的方法了么？"

"倒霉，我也想到过，可是穷了，我们又不肯死，有什么办法？今年，我怕连插秧也不能插了。"

"你也想到过春宝么？春宝还只有五岁，没有娘，他怎么好呢？"

"我领他便了。本来是断了奶的孩子。"

他似乎渐渐发怒了。也就走出门外去了。她，却呜呜咽咽地哭起来。

这时，在她过去的回忆里，却想起恰恰一年前的事：那时她生下了一个女儿，她简直如死去一般地卧在床上。死还是整个的，她却肢体分作四碎与五裂：刚落地的女婴，在地上的干草堆上叫:"呱呀,呱呀,"声音很重的,手脚揪缩。脐带绕在她底身上,胎盘落在一边,她很想挣扎起来给她洗好,可是她底头昂起来,身子凝滞在床上。这样,她看见她底丈夫,这个凶狠的男子,绯红着脸,提了一桶沸水到女婴的旁边。她简直用了她一生底最后的力向他喊:"慢!慢……"但这个病前极凶狠的男子,没有一分钟商量的余地,也不答半句话,就将"呱呀,呱呀,"声音很重地在叫着的女儿,刚出世的新生命,用他底粗暴的两手捧起来,如屠户捧将杀的小羊一般,扑通,投下在沸水里了!除出沸水的溅声和皮肉吸收沸水的嘶声以外,女孩一声也不喊。她当时剜去了心一般地昏去了。

　　想到这里,似乎泪竟干涸了。"唉!苦命呀!"她低低地叹息了一声。这时春宝向他底母亲的脸上看,一边叫:

　　"妈妈!妈妈!"

　　在她将离别底前一晚,她拣了房子底最黑暗处坐着。一盏油灯点在灶前,萤火那么的光亮。她,手里抱着春宝,将她底头贴在他底头发上。她底思想似乎浮漂在极远,可是她自己捉摸不定远在哪里。于是慢慢地跑回来,跑到眼前,跑到她底孩子底身上。她向她底孩子低声叫:

　　"春宝,宝宝!"

　　"妈妈,"孩子回答。

　　"妈妈明天要去了……"

　　"唔,"孩子似不十分懂得,本能地将头钻进他母亲底胸膛。

　　"妈妈不回来了,三年内不能回来了!"

402

她擦一擦眼睛，孩子放松口子问：

"妈妈哪里去呢？庙里么？"

"不是，三十里路外，一家姓李的。"

"我也去。"

"宝宝去不得的。"

"呃！"孩子反抗地。

"你跟爸爸在家里，爸爸会照料宝宝的：同宝宝睡，也带宝宝玩，你听爸爸底话好了。过三年……"

她没有说完，孩子要哭似地说：

"爸爸要打我的！"

"爸爸不再打你了，"同时用她底左手抚摸着孩子底右额，在这上，有他父亲在杀死他刚生下的妹妹后第三天，用锄柄敲他，肿起而又平复了的伤痕。

她似要还想对孩子说话；她底丈夫踏进门了。他走到她底面前，一只手放在袋里，掏取着什么，一边说：

"钱已经拿来七十元了。还有三十元要等你到了后十天付。"

停了一息说："也答应轿子来接。"

又停了一息："也答应轿夫一早吃好早饭来。"

这样，他离开了她，又向门外走出去了。

这一晚，她和她底丈夫都没有吃晚饭⑤。

第二天，春雨竟滴滴淅淅地落着。

轿是一早就到了。可是这妇人，她却一夜不曾睡。她先将春宝底几件破衣服都修补好；春将完了，夏将到了，可是她，连孩子冬天用的破烂棉袄都拿出来，移交给他底父

403

亲——实在,他已经在床上睡去了。以后,她坐在他底旁边,想对他说几句话,可是长夜是迟延着过去,她底话一句也说不出。而且,她大着胆向他叫了几声,发了几个听不清楚的音,声音在他底耳外,她也就睡下不说了。

等她朦朦胧胧地刚离开思索将要睡去,春宝又醒了。他就推叫他底母亲,要起来。以后当她给他穿衣服的时候,向他说:

"宝宝好好地在家里,不要哭,免得你爸爸打你。以后妈妈常买糖果来,买给宝宝吃,宝宝不要哭。"

而小孩子竟不知道悲哀是什么一回事,张大口子"唉,唉,"地唱起来了。她在他底唇边吻了一吻,又说:

"不要唱,你爸爸被你唱醒了。"

轿夫坐在门首的板凳上,抽着旱烟,说着他们自己要听的话。一息,邻村的沈家婆也赶到了。一个老妇人,熟悉世故的媒婆,一进门,就拍拍她身上的雨点,向他们说:

"下雨了,下雨了,这是你们家里此后会有滋长的预兆。"

老妇人忙碌似地在屋内旋了几个圈,对孩子底父亲说了几句话,意思是讨酬报。因为这件契约之能订的如此顺利而合算,实在是她底力量。

"说实在话,春宝底爸呀,再加五十元,那老头子可以买一房妾了。"她说。

于是又变向催促她——妇人却抱着春宝,这时坐着不动。老妇人声音很高地:

"轿夫要赶到他们家里吃中饭的,你快些预备走呀!"

可是妇人向她瞧了一瞧,似乎说:

"我实在不愿离开呢！让我饿死在这里罢！"

声音是在她底喉下，可是媒婆懂得了，走近到她前面，迷迷地向她笑说：

"你真是一个不懂事的丫头，黄胖还有什么东西给你呢？那边真是一份有吃有剩的人家，两百多亩田，经济很宽裕，房子是自己底，也雇着长工养着牛。大娘底性子是极好的，对人非常客气，每次看见人总给人一些吃的东西。那老头子——实在并不老，脸是很白白的，也没有留胡子，因为读了书，背有些偻偻的，斯文的模样。可是也不必多说，你一走下轿就看见的，我是一个从不说谎的媒婆。"

妇人拭一拭泪，极轻地：

"春宝……我怎么能抛开他呢！"

"不用想到春宝了，"老妇人一手放在她底肩上，脸凑近她和春宝。"有五岁了，古人说：'三周四岁离娘身'⑥，可以离开你了。只要你底肚子争气些，到那边，也养下一二个来，万事都好了。"

轿夫也在门首催起身了，他们噜哝着说：

"又不是新娘子，啼啼哭哭的。"

这样，老妇人将春宝从她底怀里拉去，一边说：

"春宝让我带去罢。"

小小的孩子也哭了，手脚乱舞的，可是老妇人终于给他拉到小门外去。当妇人走进轿门的时候，向他们说：

"带进屋里来罢，外边有雨呢。"

她底丈夫用手支着头坐着，一动没有动，而且也没有话。

两村的相隔有三十里路，可是轿夫的第二次将轿子放下肩,就到了。春天的细雨,从轿子底布篷里飘进,吹湿了她底衣衫。一个脸孔肥肥的,两眼很有心计的约摸五十四五岁的老妇人来迎她,她想:这当然是大娘了。可是只向她满面羞涩地看一看,并没有叫。她很亲昵似地将她牵上沿阶,一个长长的瘦瘦的而面孔圆细的男子就从房里走出来。他向新来的少妇,仔细地瞧了瞧,堆出满脸的笑容来,向她问:

"这么早就到了么?可是打湿你底衣裳了。"

而那位老妇人,却简直没有顾到他底说话,也向她问:

"还有什么在轿里么?"

"没有什么了,"少妇答。

几位邻舍的妇人站在大门外,探头张望的;可是她们走进屋里面了。

她自己也不知道这究竟为什么,她底心老是挂念着她底旧的家,掉不下她的春宝。这是真实而明显的,她应庆祝这将开始的三年的生活——这个家庭,和她所典给他的丈夫,都比曾经过去的要好,秀才确是一个温良和善的人,讲话是那么地低声,连大娘,实在也是一个出乎意料之外的妇人,她底态度之殷勤,和滔滔的一席话:说她和她丈夫底过去的生活之经过,从美满而漂亮的结婚生活起,一直到现在,中间的三十年。她曾做过一次的产,十五六年以前了,养下一个男孩子,据她说,是一个极美丽又极聪明的婴儿,可是不到十个月,竟患了天花死去了。这样,以后就没有再养过第二个。在她底意思中,似乎——似乎——早就叫她底丈夫娶一房妾,可是他,不知是爱她呢,还是没有相当的人——这一层她并没有说清楚;于是,就一直到现在。这样,竟说得这个具着朴素的心地的她,一时酸,一会苦,一时

406

甜上心头,一时又咸的压下去了。最后,这个老妇人并将她底希望也向她说出来了。她底脸是娇红的,可是老妇人说:

"你是养过三四个孩子的女人了,当然,你是知道什么的,你一定知道的还比我多。"

这样,她说着走开了。

当晚,秀才也将家里底种种情形告诉她,实际,不过是向她夸耀或求媚罢了。她坐在一张橱子的旁边,这样的红的木橱,是她旧的家所没有的,她眼睛白晃晃地瞧着它。秀才也就坐到橱子底面前来,问她:

"你叫什么名字呢?"

她没有答,也并不笑,站起来,走到床底前面,秀才也跟到床底旁边,更笑地问她:

"怕羞么?哈,你想你底丈夫么?哈,哈,现在我是你底丈夫了。"声音是轻轻的,又用手去牵着她底袖子。"不要愁罢!你也想你底孩子的,是不是?不过——"

他没有说完,却又哈的笑了一声,他自己脱去他外面的长衫了。

她可以听见房外的大娘底声音在高声地骂着什么人,她一时听不出在骂谁,骂烧饭的女仆,又好像骂她自己,可是因为她底怨恨,仿佛又是为她而发的。秀才在床上叫道:

"睡罢,她常是这么噜噜哝哝的。她以前很爱那个长工,因为长工要和烧饭的黄妈⑦多说话,她却常要骂黄妈的。"

日子是一天天地过去了。旧的家,渐渐地在她底脑子里疏远了,而眼前,却一步步地亲近她使她熟悉。虽则,春宝底哭声有时竟在她底耳朵边响,梦中,她也几次地遇到过

407

他了。可是梦是一个比一个缥缈，眼前的事务是一天比一天繁多。她知道这个老妇人是猜忌多心的，外表虽则对她还算大方，可是她底嫉妒的心是和侦探一样，监视着秀才对她的一举一动。有时，秀才从外面回来，先遇见了她而同她说话，老妇人就疑心有什么特别的东西买给她了，非在当晚，将秀才叫到她自己底房内去，狠狠地训斥一番不可。"你给狐狸迷着了么？""你应该称一称你自己底老骨头是多少重！"⑧像这样的话，她耳闻到不止一次了。这样以后，她望见秀才从外面回来而旁边没有她坐着的时候，就非得急忙避开不可。即使她在旁边，有时也该让开一些，但这种动作，她要做的非常自然，而且不能让旁人看出，否则，她又要向她发怒，说是她有意要在旁人的前面暴露她大娘底丑恶。而且以后，竟将家里的许多杂务都堆积在她底身上，同一个女仆那么样。有时老妇人底换下来的衣服放着，她也给她拿去洗了，虽然她说：

"我底衣服怎么要你洗呢？就是你自己底衣服，也可叫黄妈洗的。"可是接着说：

"妹妹呀，你最好到猪栏里去看一看，那两只猪为什么这样呃呃叫的，或者因为没有吃饱罢，黄妈总是不肯给它吃饱的。"

八个月了，那年冬天，她底胃却起了变化：老是不想吃饭，想吃新鲜的⑨面，番薯等。但番薯或面吃了两餐，又不想吃，又想吃馄饨，多吃又要呕。而且还想吃南瓜和梅子——这是六月里的东西，真稀奇，向哪里去找呢？秀才是知道在这个变化中所带来的预告了。他镇日地笑微微，能找到的东西，总忙着给她找来。他亲身给她到街上去买橘子，又托便人买了金柑来,他在廊沿下走来走去,口里念念有词的,不知说什么。他看她和黄妈磨过年的粉,但还没有磨了三升,就向她叫:"歇一歇罢,长工也好磨的,年糕是人人要吃的。"

有时在夜里,人家谈着话,他却独自拿了一盏灯,在灯下,读起《诗经》来了:

> 关关雎鸠,
> 在河之洲,
> 窈窕淑女,
> 君子好逑——

这时长工向他问:

"先生,你又不去考举人,还读它做什么呢?"

他却摸一摸没有胡子的口边,怡悦地说道:

"是呀,你也知道人生底快乐么?所谓:'洞房花烛夜,金榜挂名时。'你也知道这两句话底意思么?这是人生底最快乐的两件事呀!可是我对于这两件事都过去了,我却还有比这两件更快乐的事呢!"

这样,除出他底两个妻以外,其余的人们都大笑了。

这些事,在老妇人眼睛里是看得非常气恼了。她起初闻到她底受孕也欢喜,以后看见秀才的这样奉承她,她却怨恨她自己肚子底不会还债了。有一次,次年三月了,这妇人因为身体感觉不舒服,头有些痛,睡了三天。秀才呢,也愿她歇息歇息,更不时地问她要什么,而老妇人却着实地发怒了。她说她装娇,噜噜哳哳地也说了三天。她先是恶意地讥嘲她:说是一到秀才底家里就高贵起来了,什么腰酸呀,头痛呀,姨太太的架子也都摆出来了;以前在她自己底家里,她不相信她有这样的娇养,恐怕竟和街头的母狗一样,肚子里有着一肚皮的小狗,临产了,还要到处地奔求着食物。现在呢,因为"老东西"——这是秀才的妻叫秀才的名字——趋奉了她,就装着娇滴滴的样子了。

"儿子,"她有一次在厨房里对黄妈说,"谁没有养过呀?我也曾怀过十个月的孕,不相信有这么的难受。而且,此刻的儿子,还在'阎罗王的簿里',谁保的定生出来不是一只癞虾蟆呢?也等到真的'鸟儿',从洞里钻出来看见了,才可在我底面前显威风,摆架子,此刻,不过是一块血的猫头鹰,就这么的装腔,也显得太早一点!"

当晚这妇人没有吃晚饭,这时她已经睡了,听了这一番婉转的冷嘲与热骂,她呜呜咽咽地低声哭泣了。秀才也带衣服坐在床上,听到浑身透着冷汗,发起抖来。他很想扣好衣服,重新走起来,去打她一顿,抓住她底头发狠狠地打她一顿,泄泄他一肚皮的气。但不知怎样,似乎没有力量,连指也颤动,臂也酸软了,一边轻轻地叹息着说:

"唉,一向实在太对她好了。结婚了三十年,没有打过她一掌,简直连指甲都没有弹到她底皮肤上过,所以今日,竟和娘娘一般地难惹了。"

同时,他爬过到床底那端,她底身边,向她耳语说:

"不要哭罢,不要哭罢,随她吠去好了!⑩她是阉过的母鸡⑪,看见别人的孵卵是难受的。假如你这一次真能养出一个男孩子来,我当送你两样宝贝——我有一只青玉的戒指,一只白玉的……"

他没有说完,可是他忍不住听下门外的他底大妻底喋

喋的讥笑的声音,他急忙地脱去了衣服,将头钻进被窝里去,凑向她底胸膛,一边说:

"我有白玉的……"

肚子一天天地膨胀的如斗那么大,老妇人终究也将产婆雇定了,而且在别人的面前,竟拿起花布来做婴儿用的衣服。

酷热的暑天到了尽头,旧历的六月,他们在希望的眼中过去了。秋开始,凉风也拂拂地在乡镇上吹送。于是有一天,这全家的人们都到了希望底最高潮,屋里底空气完全地骚动起来。秀才底心更是异常地紧张,他在天井上不断地徘徊,手里捧着一本历书,好似要读它背诵那么地念去——"戊辰","甲戌","壬寅之年",老是反复地轻轻地说着。有时他底焦急的眼光向一间关了窗的房子望去——在这间房子内是有产母底低声呻吟的声音;有时他向天上望一望被云笼罩着的太阳,于是又走向房门口,向站在房门内的黄妈问:

"此刻如何?"

黄妈不住地点着头不做声响,一息,答:

"快下来了,快下来了。"

于是他又捧了那本历书,在廊下徘徊起来。

这样的情形,一直继续到黄昏底青烟在地面起来,灯火一盏盏的如春天的野花般在屋内开起,婴儿才落地了,是一个男的。婴儿底声音是很重地在屋内叫,秀才却坐在屋角里,几乎快乐到流出眼泪来了。全家的人都没有心思吃晚饭。

一个月以后，婴儿底白嫩的小脸孔，已在秋天的阳光里照耀了。这个少妇给他哺着奶，邻舍的妇人围着他们瞧[12]，有的称赞婴儿底鼻子好，有的称赞婴儿底口子好，有的称赞婴儿底两耳好；更有的称赞婴儿底母亲，也比以前好，白而且壮了。老妇人却正和老祖母那么地吩咐着，保护着，这时开始说：

　　"够了，不要弄他哭了。"

　　关于孩子底名字，秀才是煞费苦心地想着，但总想不出一个相当的字来。据老妇人底意见，还是从"长命富贵"或"福禄寿喜"里拣一个字，最好还是"寿"字或与"寿"同意义的字，如"其颐"，"彭祖"等，但秀才不同意，以为太通俗，人云亦云的名字。于是翻开了《易经》，《书经》，向这里面找，但找了半月，一月，还没有恰贴的字。在他底意思：以为在这个名字内，一边要祝福孩子，一边要包含他底老而得子底蕴义，所以竟不容易找。这一天，他一边抱着三个月的婴儿，一边又向书里找名字，戴着一副眼镜，将书递到灯底旁边去。婴儿底母亲呆呆地坐在房内底一边，不知思想着什么，却忽然开口说道：

　　"我想，还是叫他'秋宝'罢。"屋内的人们底几对眼睛都转向她，注意地静听着："他不是生在秋天吗？秋天的宝贝——还是叫他'秋宝'罢。"

　　秀才立刻接着说道：

　　"是呀，我真极费心思了。我年过半百，实在到了人生的秋期，孩子也正养在秋天；'秋'是万物成熟的季节，秋宝，实在是一个很好的名字呀！而且《书经》里没有么？'乃亦有秋，'我真乃亦有'秋'了！"

412

接着，又称赞了一通婴儿底母亲：说是呆读书实在无用，聪明是天生的。这些话，说的这妇人连坐着都觉得局促不安，垂下头，苦笑地又含泪地想：

"我不过因春宝想到罢了。"

秋宝是天天成长的非常可爱地离不开他底母亲了。他有出奇的大的眼睛，对陌生人是不倦地注视地瞧着，但对他底母亲，却远远地一眼就知道了。他整天地抓住了他底母亲，虽则秀才是比她还爱他，但不喜欢父亲；秀才底大妻呢，表面也爱他，似爱她自己亲生的儿子一样，但在婴儿底大眼睛里，却看她似陌生人，也用奇怪的不倦的视法。可是他的执住他底母亲愈紧，而他底母亲的离开这家的日子也愈近了。春天底口子咬住了冬天底尾巴；而夏天底脚又常是紧随着在春天底身后的；这样，谁都将孩子底母亲底三年快到的问题横放在心头上。

秀才呢，因为爱子的关系，首先向他底大妻提出来了：他愿意再拿出一百元钱，将她永远买下来。可是他底大妻底回答是：

"你要买她，那先给我药死罢！"

秀才听到这句话，气的只向鼻孔放出气，许久没有说；以后，他反而做着笑脸地：

"你想想孩子没有娘……"

老妇人也尖利地冷笑地说：

"我不好算是他底娘么？"

在孩子底母亲的心呢，却正矛盾着这两种的冲突了：一边，她底脑里老是有"三年"这两个字，三年是容易过去的，

413

于是她底生活便变做在秀才底家里底佣人似的了。而且想象中的春宝，也同眼前的秋宝一样活泼可爱，她既舍不得秋宝，怎么就能舍得掉春宝呢？可是另一边，她实在愿意永远在这新的家里住下去，她想，春宝的爸爸不是一个长寿的人，他底病一定是在三五年之内要将他带走到不可知的异国里去的，于是，她便要求她底第二个丈夫，将春宝也领过来，这样，春宝也在她底眼前。

有时，她倦坐在房外的沿廊下，初夏的阳光，异常地能令人昏朦地起幻想，秋宝睡在她底怀里，含着她底乳，可是她觉得仿佛春宝同时也站在她底旁边，她伸出手去也想将春宝抱近来，她还要对他们兄弟两人说几句话，可是身边是空空的。

在身边的较远的门口，却站着这位脸孔慈善而眼睛凶毒的老妇人，目光注视着她。这样，她也恍恍惚惚地敏悟："还是早些脱离罢，她简直探子一样地监视着我了。"

以后，秀才又将计划修改了一些，他想叫沈家婆来，叫她向秋宝底母亲底前夫去说，他愿否再拿进三十元——最多是五十元，将妻续典三年给秀才。秀才对他底大妻说：

"要是秋宝到五岁，是可以离开娘了。"

他底大妻正是手里捻着念佛珠，一边在念着"南无阿弥陀佛"，一边答：

"她家里也还有前儿在，你也应放她和她底结发夫妇团聚一下罢。"

秀才低着头，断断续续地仍然这样说：

"你想想秋宝两岁就没有娘……"

可是老妇人放下念佛珠说：

"我会养的，我会管理他的，你怕我谋害了他么？"

秀才一听到末一句话，就拔步走开了。老妇人仍在后面说：

"这个儿子是帮我生的，秋宝是我底；绝种虽然是绝了你家底种，可是我却仍然吃着你家底餐饭。你真被迷了，老昏了，一点也不会想了。你还有几年好活，却要拼命拉她在身边？双连牌位，我是不愿意坐的！"

老妇人似乎还有许多刻毒的锐利的话，可是秀才走远开听不见了。

在夏天，婴儿底头上生了一个疮，有时身体稍稍发些热，于是这位老妇人就到处地问菩萨，求佛药，给婴儿敷在疮上，或灌下肚里，婴儿底母亲觉得并不十分要紧，反而使这样小小的生命哭成一身的汗珠，她不愿意，或将吃了几口的药暗地里拿去倒掉了。于是这位老妇人就高声叹息，向秀才说：

"你看，她竟一点也不介意他底病，还说孩子是并不怎样瘦下去。爱在心里的是深的；专疼表面是假的。"

这样，妇人只有暗自挥泪，秀才也不说什么话了。

秋宝一周纪念的时候，这家热闹地排了一天的酒筵，客人也到了三四十，有的送衣服，有的送面，有的送银制的狮狂，给婴儿挂在胸前的，有的送镀金的寿星老头儿，给孩子钉在帽上的。他们祝福着婴儿的飞黄腾达，赞颂着婴儿的长寿永生；主人底脸孔，竟是荣光照耀着，有如落日的云霞反映着在他底颊上似的。

可是在这天，正当他们筵席将举行的黄昏时，来了一个客，从朦胧的暮光中向他们底天井走进，人们都注意他：一个憔悴异常的乡人，衣服补衲的，头发很长，在他底腋下，挟着一个纸包。主人骇异地迎上前去，问他是哪里人，他口吃似地答了，主人一时糊涂的，但立刻明白了，就是那个皮贩。主人更轻轻地说：

"你为什么也送东西来呢？你真不必的呀！"

来客胆怯地向四周看看，一边答说：

"要，要的……我来祝祝这个宝贝长寿千……"

他似没有说完，一边将腋下的纸包打开来了，手指颤动地打开了两三重的纸，于是拿出四只铜制镀银的字，一方寸那么大，是"寿比南山"四字。

秀才底大娘走来了，向他仔细一看，似乎不大高兴。秀才却将他招待到席上，客人们互相私语着。

两点钟的酒与肉，将人们弄得胡乱与狂热了：他们高声猜着拳，用大碗盛着酒互相比赛，闹得似乎房子都被震动了。只有那个皮贩，他虽然也喝了两杯酒，可是仍然坐着不动，客人们也不招呼他。等到兴尽了，于是各人草草地吃了一碗饭，互祝着好话，从两两三三的灯笼光影中，走散了。

而皮贩，却吃到最后，佣人来收拾羹碗了，他才离开了桌，走到廊下的黑暗处。在那里，他遇见了他底被典的妻。

"你也来做什么呢？"妇人问，语气是非常凄惨的。

"我哪里又愿意来，因为没有法子。"

"那末你为什么来的这样晚？"

"我哪里来买礼物的钱呀？！奔跑了一上午，哀求了一上午，又到城里买礼物，走得乏了，饿了，也迟了。"

妇人接着问：

"春宝呢？"

男子沉吟了一息答：

"所以，我是为春宝来的。……"

"为春宝来的？"妇人惊异地回音似地问。

男人慢慢地说：

"从夏天来，春宝是瘦的异样了。到秋天，竟病起来了。我又哪里有钱给他请医生吃药，所以现在病是更厉害了！再不想法救救他，眼见得要死了！"静寂了一刻，继续说："现在，我是向你来借钱的……"

这时妇人底胸膛内，简直似有四五只猫在抓她，咬她，咀嚼着她底心脏一样。她恨不得哭出来，但在人们个个向秋宝祝颂的日子，她又怎么好跟在人们底声音后面叫哭呢？她吞下她底眼泪，向她底丈夫说：

"我又哪里有钱呢？我在这里，每月只给我两角钱的零用，我自己又哪里要用什么，悉数补在孩子底身上了。现在，怎么好呢？"

他们一时没有话，以后，妇人又问：

"此刻有什么人照顾着春宝呢？"

"托了一个邻舍。今晚，我仍旧想回家，我就要走了。"

他一边说着，一边揩着泪。女的同时哽咽着说：

"你等一下罢，我向他去借借看。"

她就走开了。

三天以后的一天晚上，秀才忽然向这妇人道：

"我给你的那只青玉戒指呢？"

"在那天夜里，给了他了。给了他拿去当了。"

"没有借你五块钱么？"秀才愤怒地。

妇人低着头停了一息答：

"五块钱怎么够呢！"

秀才接着叹息说：

"总是前夫和前儿好，无论我对你怎么样！本来我很想再留你两年的，现在，你还是到明春就走罢！"

女人简直连泪也没有地呆着了。

几天后，他还向她那么地说：

"那只戒指是宝贝，我给你是要你传给秋宝的，谁知你一下就拿去当了！幸得她不知道，要是知道了，有三个月好闹了！"

妇人是一天天地黄瘦了。没有精彩的光芒在她底眼睛里起来，而讥笑与冷骂的声音又充塞在她底耳内了。她是时常记念着她底春宝的病的，探听着有没有从她底本乡来的朋友，也探听着有没有向她底本乡去的便客，她很想得到一个关于"春宝的身体已复原"的消息，可是消息总没有；她也想借两元钱或买些糖果去，方便的客人又没有，她不时地抱着秋宝在门首过去一些的大路边，眼睛望着来和去的路。这种情形却很使秀才底大妻不舒服了，她时常对秀才说：

"她哪里愿意在这里呢，她是极想早些飞回去的。"

有几夜，她抱着秋宝在睡梦中突然喊起来，秋宝也被吓醒，哭起来了。秀才就追逼地问：

"你为什么？你为什么？"

可是女人拍着秋宝，口子哼哼的没有答。秀才继续说：

"梦着你底前儿死了么，那么地喊？连我都被你叫醒了。"

女人急忙地一边答：

"不，不，……好像我底前面有一圹坟呢！"

秀才没有再讲话,而悲哀的幻象更在女人底前面展现开来,她要走向这坟去。

冬末了,催离别的小鸟,已经到她底窗前不住地叫了。先是孩子断了奶,又叫道士们来给孩子度了一个关,于是孩子和他亲生的母亲的别离——永远的别离的命运就被决定了。

这一天,黄妈先悄悄地向秀才底大妻说:

"叫一顶轿子送她去么?"

秀才底大妻还是手里捻着念佛珠说:

"走走好罢,到那边轿钱是那边付的,她又哪里有钱呢,听说她底亲夫连饭也没得吃,她不必摆阔了。路也不算远,我也是曾经走过三四十里路的人,她底脚比我大,半天可以到了。"

这天早晨当她给秋宝穿衣服的时候,她底泪如溪水那么地流下,孩子向她叫:"婶婶,婶婶,"——因为老妇人要他叫她自己是"妈妈",只准叫她是"婶婶"——她向他咽咽地答应。她很想对他说几句话,意思是:

"别了,我底亲爱的儿子呀!你底妈妈待你是好的,你将来也好好地待还她罢,永远不要再记念我了!"

可是她无论怎样也说不出。她也知道一周半的孩子是不会了解的。

秀才悄悄地走向她,从她背后的腋下伸进手来,在他底手内是十枚双毫角子,一边轻轻说:

"拿去罢,这两块钱。"

妇人扣好孩子底钮扣,就将角子塞在怀内的衣袋里。

老妇人又进来了,注意着秀才走出去的背后,又向妇人说:

"秋宝给我抱去罢，免得你走时他哭。"

妇人不做声响，可是秋宝总不愿意，用手不住地拍在老妇人底脸上。于是老妇人生气地又说：

"那末你同他去吃早饭去罢，吃了早饭交给我。"

黄妈拼命地劝她多吃饭，一边说：

"半月来你就这样了，你真比来的时候还瘦了。你没有去照照镜子。今天，吃一碗下去罢，你还要走三十里路呢。"

她只不关紧要地说了一句：

"你对我真好！"

但是太阳是升的非常高了，一个很好的天气，秋宝还是不肯离开他底母亲，老妇人便狠狠地将他从她底怀里夺去，秋宝用小小的脚踢在老妇人底肚子上，用小小的拳头搔住她底头发，高声呼喊她。妇人在后面说：

"让我吃了中饭去罢。"

老妇人却转过头，汹汹地答⑬：

"赶快打起你底包袱去罢，早晚总有一次的！"

孩子底哭声便在她底耳内渐渐远去了。

打包裹的时候，耳内是听着孩子底哭声。黄妈在旁边，一边劝慰着她，一边却看她打进什么去。终于，她挟着一只旧的包裹走了。

她离开他底大门时，听见她底秋宝的哭声；可是慢慢地远远地走了三里路了，还听见她底秋宝的哭声。

暖和的太阳所照耀的路，在她底面前竟和天一样无穷止地长。当她走到一条河边的时候，她很想停止她底那么无力的脚步，向明澈可以照见她自己底身子的水底跳下去了。但在水边坐了一会之后，她还得依前去的方向，移动她自己底影子。

　　太阳已经过午了，一个村里的一个年老的乡人告诉她，路还有十五里；于是她向那个老人说：

　　"伯伯，请你代我就近叫一顶轿子罢，我是走不回去了！"

　　"你是有病的么？"老人问。

　　"是的。"

　　她那时坐在村口的凉亭里面。

　　"你从哪里来？"

　　妇人静默了一时答：

　　"我是向那里去的；早晨我以为自己会走的。"

　　老人怜悯地也没有多说话，就给她找了两位轿夫，一顶没篷的轿。因为那是下秧的时节。

　　下午三四时的样子，一条狭窄而污秽的乡村小街上，抬过了一顶没篷的轿子，轿里躺着一个脸色枯萎如同一张干瘪的黄菜叶那么的中年妇人，两眼朦胧地颓唐地闭着。嘴里的呼吸只有微弱地吐出。街上的人们个个睁着惊异的目光，怜悯地凝视着过去。一群孩子们，争噪地跟在轿后，好像一件奇异的事情落到这沉寂的小村镇里来了。

　　春宝也是跟在轿后的孩子们中底一个，他还在似赶猪那么地哗着轿走，可是当轿子一转一个弯，却是向他底家里去的路，他却伸直了两手而奇怪了，等到轿子到了他家里的门口，他简直呆似地远远地站在前面，背靠在一株柱子上，面向着轿，其余的孩子们胆怯地围在轿的两边⑭。妇人走出来了，她昏迷的眼睛还认不清站在前面的，穿着褴褛的衣服，头发蓬乱的，身子和三年前一样的短小，那个八岁的孩子是她底春宝。突然，她哭出来地高叫了：

421

"春宝呀！"

一群孩子们，个个无意地吃了一惊，而春宝简直吓的躲进屋里他父亲那里去了。

妇人在灰暗的屋内坐了许久许久，她和她底丈夫都没有一句话。夜色降落了，他下垂的头昂起来，向她说：

"烧饭吃罢！"

妇人就不得已地站起来，向屋角上旋转了一周，一点也没有气力地对她丈夫说：

"米缸内是空空的……"

男人冷笑了一声，答说：

"你真在大人家底家里生活过了！米，盛在那只香烟盒子内。"

当天晚上，男子向他底儿子说：

"春宝，跟你底娘去睡！"

而春宝却靠在灶边哭起来了。他底母亲走近他，一边叫：

"春宝，宝宝！"

可是当她底手去抚摸他底时候，他又躲闪开了。男子加上说：

"会生疏得那么快，一顿打呢！"

她眼睁睁地睡在一张龌龊的狭板床上，春宝陌生似地睡在她底身边。在她底已经麻木的脑内，仿佛秋宝肥白可爱地在她身边挣动着，她伸出两手想去抱，可是身边是春宝。这时，春宝睡着了，转了一个身，他底母亲紧紧地将他抱住，而孩子却从微弱的鼾声中，脸伏在她底胸膛上。

沉静而寒冷的死一般的长夜，似无限地拖延着，拖延着……

422

A Slave Mother

Rou Shi

He was a dealer in animal skins which he bought
from hunters in the countryside and sold in town. Sometimes he also worked in the fields; early each summer he
turned farm-hand, transplanting rice for other people. As
he had learned to transplant the seedlings in wonderfully
straight rows, the peasants always asked him to help
them. But he never made enough money to support his
family and his debts mounted with each passing year. The
wretchedness of his life and the hopeless situation he was
in caused him to take to smoking, drinking and gambling,
and he became vicious and bad-tempered. As he grew
poorer and poorer, people stopped lending him money,
even in small sums.

With poverty came sickness. He grew sallow; his
face took on the sickly colour of a brass drum and even
the whites of his eyes became yellow. People said that he
had jaundice and urchins nicknamed him "Yellow Fellow".
One day, he said to his wife,

"There's no way out of it. It looks as if we'll even have to sell our cooking pot. I'm afraid we have to part. It's no use both of us going hungry together."

"We have to part?..." muttered his wife, who was sitting behind the stove with their three-year-old boy in her arms.

"Yes, we have to part," he answered feebly. "There's somebody willing to hire you as a temporary wife. ..."

"What?" she almost lost her senses.

There followed a brief silence. Then the husband continued, falteringly,

"Three days ago, Wang Lang came here and spent a long time pressing me to pay my debt to him. After he had left, I went out. I sat under a tree on the shore of Chiumou Lake and thought of committing suicide. I wanted to climb the tree and dive into the water and drown myself, but, after thinking about it, I lost courage. The hooting of an owl frightened me and I walked away. On my way home, I came across Mrs. Shen, the matchmaker, who asked me why I was out at night. I told her what had happened and asked her if she could borrow some money for me, or some lady's dresses and ornaments that I could pawn to pay Wang Lang so that he'd no longer be prowling after me like a wolf. But Mrs. Shen only smiled and said,

"'What do you keep your wife at home for? And you're so sick and yellow!'

"I hung my head and said nothing. She continued,

"'Since you've got only one son, you might find it hard to part with him. But as for your wife . . . .'

"I thought she meant that I should sell you, but she added,

"'Of course she is your lawful wife, but you're poor and you can't do anything about it. What do you keep her at home for? Starve her to death?'

"Then she said straight out, 'There's a fifty-year-old scholar who wants a concubine to bear him a son since his wife is barren. But his wife objects and will only allow him to hire somebody else's wife for a few years. I've been asked to find them a woman. She has to be about thirty years old and the mother of two or three children. She must be honest and hard-working, and obey the scholar's wife. The scholar's wife has told me that they are willing to pay from eighty to a hundred dollars for the right sort of woman. I've looked around for one for several days, but without any luck. But your wife is just the woman I've been looking for.'

"She asked me what I thought about it. It made me cry to think of it, but she comforted me and convinced me that it was all for the best."

At this point, his voice trailed off, he hung his head

and stopped. His wife looked dazed and remained speechless. There was another moment of silence before he continued.

"Yesterday, Mrs. Shen went to see the scholar again. She came back and told me that both the scholar and his wife were very happy about the idea of having you and had promised to pay me a hundred dollars. If you bear them a child they will keep you for three years, if not — for five. Mrs. Shen has fixed the date for you to go — the eighteenth of this month, that is, five days from now. She is going to have the contract drawn up today."

Trembling all over, the wife faltered,

"Why didn't you tell me this earlier?"

"Yesterday I went up to you three times, but each time I was afraid to begin. But after thinking it over I've come to realize that there's really nothing to be done but hire you out."

"Has it all been decided?" asked the wife, her teeth clattering.

"There's just the contract to be signed."

"Oh, what a poor wretch I am! Can't we really do anything else?"

"It's terrible, I know. But we're poor and we don't want to die. What else can we do? I'm afraid this year I won't even be asked to do any transplanting."

"Have you thought about Chun Bao? He's only three.

What will become of him without me?"

"I'll take care of him. You're not nursing him any longer, you know."

He became more and more angry with himself and went out. She broke into uncontrolled sobs.

Then, looking back upon the past, she remembered what had just happened one year before: She was lying on her bed more dead than alive after giving birth to a baby girl. The newborn infant was lying on a heap of straw on the ground, crying at the top of her lungs and twitching her little limbs. The umbilical cord was wound round her body and the placenta left by her side. The poor young woman was anxious to get up to wash her baby. But she could only manage to lift her head while her whole body seemed to remain glued to the bed. All of a sudden she saw her husband, fierce and flushed, come up to the baby with a bucket of boiling water. "Stop, stop! ..., " she threw what little strength she had into yelling at him. The vicious husband, nevertheless, was uncompromising. Without saying a word, he held up in both hands the baby with her cry of new life and, like a butcher slaughtering a small lamb, splashed her into the boiling water. The baby immediately stopped crying. All was silent except for the sizzling of her flesh in the boiling water. The young woman fainted away at the heart-rending scene.

At the painful recollection, she had no more tears to

shed, but sighed faintly, "Oh, what a miserable life!" Chun Bao stared at her, whimpering, "Mummy, mummy!"

On the eve of her departure, she was sitting in the darkest corner of the house. In front of the stove stood an oil lamp, its light flickering like that of a fire-fly. Holding Chun Bao close to her bosom, she pressed her head against his hair. Lost in deep thought, she seemed absolutely dead to the reality surrounding her. Later, she gradually came to, and found herself face to face with the present and her child. Softly she called him,

"Chun Bao, Chun Bao!"

"Yes, mummy!" the child replied.

"I'm going to leave you tomorrow. ..."

"What?" the child did not quite understand what she meant and instinctively cuddled closer to her.

"I'm not coming back, not for three years!"

She wiped away her tears. The little boy became inquisitive,

"Mummy, where are you going? To the temple?"

"No. I'm going to live with the Li family, about thirty *li* away."

"I want to go with you."

"No, you can't, darling!"

"Why?" he countered.

"You'll stay home with daddy, he'll take good care of you. He'll sleep with you and play with you. You just listen to daddy. In three years . . . . ."

Before she had finished talking the child sadly interrupted her,

"Daddy will beat me!"

"Daddy will never beat you again." Her left hand was stroking the scar on the right side of the boy's forehead — a reminder of the blow dealt by her husband with the handle of a hoe three days after he killed the baby girl.

She was about to speak to the boy again when her husband came in. He walked up to her, and fumbling in his pocket, he said,

"I've got seventy dollars from them. They'll give me the other thirty dollars ten days after you get there."

After a short pause, he added, "They've promised to take you there in a sedan-chair."

After another short pause, he continued, "The chair carriers will come to take you early in the morning as soon as they've had breakfast."

With this he walked out again.

That evening, neither he nor she felt like having supper.

The next day there was a spring drizzle.

The chair carriers arrived at the crack of dawn. The young woman had not slept a wink during the night. She had spent the time mending Chun Bao's tattered clothes. Although it was late spring and summer was near, she took out the boy's shabby cotton-padded winter jacket and wanted to give it to her husband, but he was fast asleep. Then she sat down beside her husband, wishing to have a chat with him. But he slept on and she sat there silently, waiting for the night to pass. She plucked up enough courage to mutter a few words into his ear, but even this failed to wake him up. So she lay down too.

As she was about to doze off, Chun Bao woke up. He wanted to get up and pushed his mother. Dressing the child, she said,

"Darling, you mustn't cry while I'm away or daddy will beat you. I'll buy sweets for you to eat. But you mustn't cry any more, darling."

The boy was too young to know what sorrow was, so in a minute he began to sing. She kissed his cheek and said,

"Stop singing now, you'll wake up daddy."

The chair carriers were sitting on the benches in front of the gate, smoking their pipes and chatting. Soon afterwards, Mrs. Shen arrived from the nearby village where she was living. She was an old and experienced matchmaker. As soon as she crossed the threshold, she

430

brushed the raindrops off her clothes, saying to the husband and wife,

"It's raining, it's raining. That's a good omen, it means you will thrive from now on."

The matchmaker bustled about the house and whispered and hinted to the husband that she should be rewarded for having so successfully brought about the deal.

"To tell you the truth, for another fifty dollars, the old man could have bought himself a concubine," she said.

Then Mrs. Shen turned to the young woman who was sitting still with the child in her arms, and said loudly,

"The chair carriers have to get there in time for lunch, so you'd better hurry up and get ready to go."

The young woman glanced at her and her look seemed to say, "I don't want to leave! I'd rather starve here!"

The matchmaker understood and, walking up to her, said smiling,

"You're just a silly girl. What can the 'Yellow Fellow' give you? But over there, the scholar has plenty of everything. He has more than two hundred *mou* of land, his own houses and cattle. His wife is good-tempered and she's very kind. She never turns anybody from her door without giving him something to eat. And the scholar is not really old. He has a white face and no beard. He stoops a little as well-educated men generally do, and he is quite gentlemanly. There's no need for me to tell you more about him. You'll see him with your own eyes as soon as you get out of the sedan-chair. You know, as a matchmaker, I've never told a lie. "

The young woman wiped away her tears and said softly,

"Chun Bao ... How can I part from him?"

"Chun Bao will be all right," said the matchmaker, patting the young woman on the shoulder and bending over her and the child. "He is already three. There's a saying, 'A child of three can move about free.' So he can be left alone. It all depends on you. If you can have one or two children over there, everything will be quite all right. "

The chair bearers outside the gate now started urging the young woman to set out, murmuring.

"You are really not a bride, why should you cry?"[1]

The matchmaker snatched away Chun Bao from his mother's arms, saying,

"Let me take care of Chun Bao!"

The little boy began to scream and kick. The matchmaker took him outside. When the young woman was in

---

[1] In old China, a bride usually cried before leaving her family.

the sedan-chair, she said,

"You'd better take the boy in, it's raining outside. "

Inside the house, resting his head on the palm of his hand, sat the little boy's father, motionless and wordless.

The two villages were thirty *li* apart, but the chair carriers reached their destination without making a single stop on the way. The young woman's clothes were wet from the spring raindrops which had been blown in through the sedan-chair screens. An elderly woman, of about fifty-five, with a plump face and shrewd eyes came out to greet her. Realizing immediately that this was the scholar's wife, the young woman looked at her bashfully and remained silent. As the scholar's wife was amiably helping the young woman to the door, there came out from the house a tall and thin elderly man with a round, smooth face. Measuring the young woman from head to foot, he smiled and said,

"You have come early. Did you get wet in the rain?"

His wife, completely ignoring what he was saying, asked the young woman,

"Have you left anything in the sedan-chair?"

"No, nothing," answered the young woman.

Soon they were inside the house. Outside the gate, a number of women from the neighbourhood had gathered and were peeping in to see what was happening.

Somehow or other, the young woman could not help thinking about her old home and Chun Bao. As a matter of fact, she might have congratulated herself on the prospects of spending the next three years here, since both her new home and her temporary husband seemed pleasant. The scholar was really kind and soft-spoken. His wife appeared hospitable and talkative. She talked about her thirty years of happy married life with the scholar. She had given birth to a boy some fifteen years before — a really handsome and lively child, she said — but he died of smallpox less than ten months after his birth. Since then, she had never had another child. The elderly woman hinted she had long been urging her husband to get a concubine but he had always put it off — either because he was too much in love with his wedded wife or because he couldn't find a suitable woman for a concubine. This chatter made the young woman feel sad, delighted and depressed by turns. Finally, the young woman was told what was expected of her. She blushed when the scholar's wife said,

"You've had three or four children. Of course you know what to do. You know much more than I do."

After this, the elderly woman went away.

That evening, the scholar told the young woman a great many things about his family in an effort to show off and ingratiate himself with her. She was sitting beside a red-lacquered wooden wardrobe — something she had never had in her old home. Her dull eyes were focused upon it when the scholar came over and sat in front of it, asking,

"What's your name?"

She remained silent and did not smile. Then, rising to her feet, she went towards the bed. He followed her, his face beaming.

"Don't be shy. Still thinking about your husband? Ha, ha, I'm your husband now!" he said softly, touching her arm. "Don't worry! You're thinking about your child, aren't you? Well ... "

He burst out laughing and took off his long gown.

The young, woman then heard the scholar's wife scolding somebody outside the room. Though she could not make out just who was being scolded, it seemed to be either the kitchen-maid or herself. In her sorrow, the young woman began to suspect that it must be herself, but the scholar, now lying in bed, said loudly,

"Don't bother. She always grumbles like that. She likes our farm-hand very much, and often scolds the kitchen-maid for chatting with him too much. "

Time passed quickly. The young woman's thoughts of her old home gradually faded as she became better and better acquainted with what went on in her new one. Sometimes it seemed to her she heard Chun Bao's muffled cries, and she dreamed of him several times. But these dreams became more and more blurred as she became occupied with her new life. Outwardly, the scholar's wife was kind to her, but she felt that ,deep inside, the elderly woman was jealous and suspicious and that, like a detective, she was always spying to see what was going on between the scholar and her. Sometimes, if the wife caught her husband talking to the young woman on his return home, she would suspect that he had bought her something special. She would call him to her bedroom at night to give him a good scolding. "So you've been seduced by the witch!" she would cry. "You should take good care of your old carcase." These abusive remarks the young woman overheard time and again. After that, whenever she saw the scholar return home, she always tried to avoid him if his wife was not present. But even in the presence of his wife, the young woman considered it necessary to keep herself in the background. She had to do all this naturally so that it would not be noticed by outsiders, for otherwise the wife would get angry and blame her for purposely discrediting her in public. As time went on, the scholar's wife even made the young woman do the work of a maidservant. Once the young woman decided to wash the elderly woman's clothes.

"You're not supposed to wash my clothes," the scholar's wife said. "In fact you can have the kitchen-maid wash your own laundry." Yet the next moment she said,

"Sister dear, you'd better go to the pigsty and have a look at the two pigs which have been grunting all the time. They're probably hungry because the kitchen-maid never gives them enough to eat."

Eight months had passed and winter came. The young woman became fussy about her food. She had little appetite for regular meals and always felt like eating something different — noodles, potatoes and so on. But she soon got tired of noodles and potatoes, and asked for meat dumplings. When she ate a little too much she got sick. Then she felt a desire for pumpkins and plums — things that could only be had in summer. The scholar knew what all this meant. He kept smiling all day and gave her whatever was available. He went to town himself to get her tangerines and asked someone to buy her some oranges. He often paced up and down the veranda, muttering to himself. One day, he saw the young woman and the kitchen-maid grinding rice for the New Year festival. They had hardly started grinding when he said to the young woman, "You'd better have a rest now. We can let the farm-hand do it, since everybody is going to eat the cakes."

Sometimes in the evening, when the rest of the household were chatting, he would sit alone near an oil lamp, reading the *Book of Songs*:

> "Fair, fair," cry the ospreys
> On the island in the river.
> Lovely is the good lady,
> Fit bride for our lord.
>
> . . . .

The farm-hand once asked him,

"Please, sir, what are you reading this book for? You're not going to sit for a higher civil service examination, are you?"

The scholar stroked his beardless chin and said in a gay tone,

"Well, you know the joys of life, don't you? There's a saying that the greatest joy of life is either to spend the first night in the nuptial chamber or to pass a civil service examination. As for me, I've already experienced both. But now there's a still greater blessing in store for me."

His remark set the whole household laughing — except for his wife and the young woman.

To the scholar's wife all this was very annoying. When she first heard of the young woman's pregnancy, she was pleased. Later, when she saw her husband lav-

438

ishing attentions on the young woman, she began to blame herself for being barren. Once, the following spring, it happened that the young woman fell ill and was laid up for three days with a headache. The scholar was anxious that she take a rest and frequently asked what she needed. This made his wife angry. She grumbled for three whole days and said that the young woman was malingering.

"She has been spoiled here and become stuck-up like a real concubine," she said, sneering maliciously, "always complaining about headaches or backaches. She must have been quite different before — like a bitch that has to go searching for food even when she is going to bear a litter of puppies! Now, with the old man fawning on her , she puts on airs!"

"Why so much fuss about having a baby?" said the scholar's wife one night to the kitchen-maid. "I myself was once with child for ten months, I just can't believe she's really feeling so bad. Who knows what she's going to have? It may be just a little toad! She'd better not try to bluff me, throwing her weight around before the little thing is born. It's still nothing but a clot of blood! It's really a bit too early for her to make such a fuss!"

The young woman who had gone to bed without supper was awakened by this torrent of malicious abuse and burst into convulsive sobs. The scholar was also shocked

439

by what he heard — so much so that he broke into a cold sweat and shook with anger. He wanted to go to his wife's room, grab her by the hair and give her a good beating so as to work off his feelings. But, somehow or other, he felt powerless to do so; his fingers trembled and his arms ached with weariness. Sighing deeply, he said softly, "I've been too good to her. In thirty years of married life, I've never slapped her face or given her a scratch. That's why she is so cocky."

Then, crawling across the bed, he whispered to the young woman beside him,

"Now, stop crying, stop crying, let her cackle! A barren hen is always jealous! If you manage to have a baby boy this time, I'll give you two precious gifts — a blue jade ring and a white jade...." Leaving the last sentence unfinished, he turned to listen to his wife's jeering voice outside the room. He hastily took off his clothes, and, covering his head with the quilt and nestling closer to the young woman, he said,

"I've a white jade. ..."

The young woman grew bigger and bigger around the waist. The scholar's wife made arrangements with a midwife, and, when other people were around, she would busy herself making baby's clothes out of floral prints.

The hot summer had ended and the cool autumn

breeze was blowing over the village. The day finally came when the expectations of the whole household reached their climax and everybody was agog. His heart beating faster than ever, the scholar was pacing the courtyard, reading about horoscopes from an almanac in his hand as intently as if he wanted to commit the whole book to memory. One moment he would look anxiously at the room with its windows closely shut whence came the muffled groans of the expectant mother. The next, he would look at the cloudy sky, and walk up to the kitchen-maid at the door to ask,

"How is everything now?"

Nodding, the maid would reply after a moment's pause,

"It won't be long now, it won't be long now."

He would resume pacing the courtyard and reading the almanac.

The suspense lasted until sunset. Then, when wisps of kitchen smoke were curling up from the roofs and lamps were gleaming in the country houses like so many wild flowers in spring, a baby boy was born. The new-born baby cried at the top of his voice while the scholar sat in a corner of the house, with tears of joy in his eyes. The household was so excited that no one cared about supper.

A month later, the bright and tender-faced baby made his debut in the open. While the young woman was breast-feeding him, womenfolk from the neighbourhood gathered around to feast their eyes upon the boy. Some liked his nose; others, his mouth; still others, his ears. Some praised his mother, saying that she had become whiter and healthier. The scholar's wife, now acting like a granny, said,

"That's enough! You'll make the baby cry!"

As to the baby's name, the scholar racked his brains, but just could not hit upon a suitable one. His wife suggested that the Chinese character *shou*, meaning longevity, or one of its synonyms, should be included in his name. But the scholar did not like it — it was too commonplace. He spent several weeks looking through Chinese classics like the *Book of Changes* and the *Book of History* in search of suitable characters to be used as the baby's name. But all his efforts proved fruitless. It was a difficult problem to solve because he wanted a name which should be auspicious for the baby and would imply at the same time that he was born to him in old age. One evening, while holding the three-month-old baby in his arms, the scholar, with spectacles on, sat down near a lamp and again looked into some book in an effort to find a name for the boy. The baby's mother, sitting quietly in a corner of the room, appeared to be musing. Suddenly she said.

"I suppose you could call him 'Qiu Bao'." Those in the room turned to look at the young woman and listened intently as she continued, "*Qiu* means autumn and *Bao* means treasure. So since he was born in autumn, you'd better call him 'Qiu Bao'."

The scholar was silent for a brief moment and then exclaimed,

"A wonderful idea! I've wasted a lot of time looking for a name for the baby! As a man of over fifty, I've reached the *autumn* of my life. The boy too was born in *autumn*. Besides, *autumn* is the time when everything is ripe and the time for harvesting, as the *Book of History* says. 'Qiu Bao' is really a good name for the child."

Then he began to praise the young woman, saying that she was born clever and that it was quite useless to be a bookworm like himself. His remarks made the young woman feel ill at ease. Lowering her head and forcing a smile, she said to herself with tears in her eyes,

"I suggested 'Qiu Bao' simply because I was thinking of my elder son Chun Bao."[1]

Qiu Bao daily grew handsomer and more attached to his mother. His unusually big eyes which stared tirelessly

---

[1] Meaning "Spring Treasure".

at strangers would light up joyfully when he saw his mother, even when she was a long distance away. He always clung to her. Although the scholar loved him even more than his mother did, Qiu Bao did not take to him. As to the scholar's wife, although outwardly she showed as much affection for Qiu Bao as if he were her own baby, he would stare at her with the same indefatigable curiosity as he did at strangers. But the more the child grew attached to his mother, the closer drew the time for their separation. Once more it was summer. To everybody in the house, the advent of this season was a reminder of the coming end of the young woman's three-year stay.

The scholar, out of his love for Qiu Bao, suggested to his wife one day that he was willing to offer another hundred dollars to buy the young woman so that she could stay with them permanently. The wife, however, replied curtly,

"No, you'll have to poison me before you do that!"

This made the scholar angry. He remained silent for quite a while. Then, forcing himself to smile, he said,

"It's a pity that our child will be motherless ... ."

His wife smiled wryly and said in an icy and cutting tone,

"Don't you think that I might be a mother to him?"

As to the young woman, there were two conflicting ideas in her mind. On the one hand, she always remembered that she would have to leave after the three years were up. Three years seemed a short time and she had become more of a servant than a temporary wife. Besides, in her mind her elder son Chun Bao had become as sweet and lovely a child as Qiu Bao. She could not bear to remain away from either Qiu Bao or Chun Bao. On the other hand, she was willing to stay on permanently in the scholar's house because she thought her own husband would not live long and might even die in four or five years. So she longed to have the scholar bring Chun Bao into his home so that she could also live with her elder son.

One day, as she was sitting wearily on the veranda with Qiu Bao sleeping at her breast, the hypnotic rays of the early summer sun sent her into a daydream and she thought she saw Chun Bao standing beside her; but when she stretched out her hand to him and was about to speak to her two sons, she saw that her elder boy was not there.

At the door at the other end of the veranda the scholar's wife, with her seemingly kind face but fierce eyes, stood staring at the young woman. The latter came to and said to herself,

"I'd better leave here as soon as I can. She's always spying on me!"

Later, the scholar changed his plan a little; he decided he would send Mrs. Shen on another mission: to find out whether the young woman's husband was willing to take another thirty dollars — or fifty dollars at most — to let him keep the young woman for another three years. He said to his wife,

"I suppose Qiu Bao's mother could stay on until he is five."

Chanting "Buddha preserve me" with a rosary in her hand, the scholar's wife replied,

"She has got her elder son at home. Besides, you ought to let her go back to her lawful husband."

The scholar hung his head and said brokenly,

"Just imagine, Qiu Bao will be motherless at two . . . ."

Putting away the rosary, his wife snapped,

"I can take care of him, I can manage him. Are you afraid I'm going to murder him?"

Upon hearing the last sentence, the scholar walked away hurriedly. His wife went on grumbling,

"The child has been born for me. Qiu Bao is mine. If the male line of your family came to an end, it would affect me too. You've been bewitched by her. You're old and pigheaded. You don't know what's what. Just think how many more years you may live, and yet you're trying to do everything to keep her with you. I certainly don't want another woman's tablet put side by side with mine in the family shrine!"

446

It seemed as if she would never stop pouring out the stream of venomous and biting words, but the scholar was too far away to hear them.

Every time Qiu Bao had a pimple on his head or a slight fever, the scholar's wife would go around praying to Buddha and bring back Buddha's medicine in the form of incense ash which she applied to the baby's pimple or dissolved in water for him to drink. He would cry and perspire profusely. The young woman did not like the idea of the scholar's wife making so much fuss when the baby fell slightly ill, and always threw the ash away when she was not there. Sighing deeply, the scholar's wife once said to her husband,

"You see, she really doesn't care a bit about our baby and says that he's not getting thinner. Real love needs no flourishes; she is only pretending that she loves our baby. "

The young woman wept when alone, and the scholar kept silent.

On Qiu Bao's first birthday, the celebration lasted the whole day. About forty guests attended the party. The birthday presents they brought included baby clothes, noodles, a silver pendant in the shape of a lion's head to be worn on the baby's chest and a gold-plated image of the God of Longevity to be sewn to the baby's bonnet. The guests wished the baby good luck and a long life. The host's face flushed with joy as if reflecting the reddening glow of the setting sun.

Late in the afternoon, just before the banquet, there came into the courtyard from the deepening twilight outside an uninvited guest, who attracted the attention of all the others. He was an emaciated-looking peasant, dressed in patched clothes and with unkempt hair, carrying under his arm a paper-parcel. Greatly astonished and puzzled, the host went up to inquire where he hailed from. While the newcomer was stammering, it suddenly occurred to the host that this was none other than the skin dealer — the young woman's husband. Thereupon, the host said in a low voice,

"Why do you bring a gift? You really shouldn't have done this!"

The newcomer looked timidly about, saying,

"I ... I had to come ... I've come to wish the baby a long life. ... "

Before he had finished speaking, he began to open the package he had brought. Tearing off three paper wrappings with his quivering fingers, he took out four bronze-cast and silver-plated Chinese characters, each about one square inch in size, which said that the baby would live as long as the South Mountain.

The scholar's wife appeared on the scene, and looked

448

displeased when she saw the skin dealer. The scholar, however, invited the skin dealer to the table, where the guests sat whispering about him.

The guests wined and dined for two hours and everybody was feeling happy and excited. They indulged in noisy drinking games and plied one another with big bowls of wine. The deafening uproar rocked the house. Nobody paid any attention to the skin dealer who sat silently after drinking two cups of wine. Having enjoyed their wine, the guests each hurriedly took a bowl of rice; and, bidding one another farewell, they dispersed in twos and threes, carrying lighted lanterns in their hands.

The skin dealer sat there eating until the servants came to clear the table. Then he walked to a dark corner of the veranda where he found his wife.

"What did you come for?" asked the young woman with an extremely sad note in her voice.

"I didn't want to come, but I just couldn't help it."

"Then why did you come so late?"

"I couldn't get any money to buy a birthday gift. I spent the whole morning begging for a loan and then I had to go to town to buy the gift. I was tired and hungry. That's why I came late."

The young woman asked, "How's Chun Bao?"

Her husband reflected for a moment and then answered,

"It's for Chun Bao's sake that I've come. ..."

"For Chun Bao's sake!" she echoed in surprise. He went on slowly,

"Since this summer Chun Bao has grown very skinny. In the autumn, he fell sick. I haven't been able to do anything for him because I haven't had any money. So his illness is getting more serious. I'm afraid he won't live unless we try to save him!" He continued after a short pause, "I've come to borrow some money from you. ..."

Deep inside her, the young woman had the feeling that wild cats were scratching and biting her, gnawing at her very heart. She was on the verge of bursting into tears, but on such an occasion when everybody was celebrating Qiu Bao's birthday she knew she had to keep her emotions under control. She made a brave effort to keep back her tears and said to her husband,

"How can I get hold of any money? They give me twenty cents a month as pocket money here, but I spend every cent of it on my baby. What can we do now?"

Both were speechless for a while, then the young woman asked again,

"Who is taking care of Chun Bao while you're here?"

"One of the neighbours. I've got to go back home tonight. In fact I ought to be going now," he answered, wiping away his tears.

"Wait a moment," she told him tearfully, "let me go

and try to borrow some money from him. "

And with this she left him.

Three days later, in the evening, the scholar suddenly asked the young woman,

"Where's the blue jade ring I gave you?"

"I gave it to him the other night. He pawned it. "

"Didn't I lend you five dollars?" countered the scholar irritably.

The young woman, hanging her head, answered after a moment's pause,

"Five dollars wasn't enough!"

The scholar sighed deeply at this and said, "No matter how good I try to be to you, you still love your husband and your elder son more. I wanted to keep you for another couple of years, but now I think you'd better leave here next spring!"

The young woman stood there silent and tearless.

Several days later, the scholar again reproached her, "That blue jade ring is a treasure. I gave it to you because I wanted Qiu Bao to inherit it from you. I didn't think you would have it pawned! It's lucky my wife doesn't know about it, otherwise she would make scenes for another three months. "

After this the young woman became thinner and paler. Her eyes lost their lustre; she was often subjected to sneers and curses. She was forever worrying about Chun Bao's illness. She was always on the lookout for some acquaintance from her home village or some traveller going there. She hoped she could hear about Chun Bao's recovery, but there was no news. She wished she could borrow a couple of dollars or buy sweets for some traveller to take to Chun Bao, but she could find no one going to her home village. She would often walk outside the gate with Qiu Bao in her arms, and there, standing by the roadside, she would gaze with melancholy eyes at the country paths. This greatly annoyed the scholar's wife who said to her husband,

"She really doesn't want to stay here any longer. She's anxious to get back home as soon as she can."

Sometimes at night, sleeping with Qiu Bao at her bosom, she would suddenly wake up from her dreams and scream until the child too would awake and start crying. Once, the scholar asked her,

"What's happened? What's happened?"

She patted the child without answering. The scholar continued,

"Did you dream your elder son had died? How you screamed! You woke me up!"

She hurriedly answered, "No, no ... I thought I saw a new grave in front of me!"

He said nothing, but the morbid hallucination contin-

452

ued to loom before her — she saw herself approaching the grave.

Winter was drawing to a close and the birds began twittering at her window, as if urging her to leave quickly. The child was weaned, and her separation from her son — permanent separation — was already a foregone conclusion.

On the day of her departure, the kitchen-maid quietly asked the scholar's wife,

"Shall we hire a sedan-chair to take her home?"

Fingering the rosary in her hand, the scholar's wife said, "Better let her walk. Otherwise she will have to pay the fare herself. And where will she get the money? I understand her husband can't even afford to have three meals a day. She shouldn't try to be showy. It's not very far from here, and I myself have walked some forty *li* a day. She's more used to walking than I am, so she ought to be able to get there in half a day."

In the morning, as the young woman was dressing Qiu Bao, tears kept streaming down her cheeks. The child called, "Auntie, auntie" (the scholar's wife had made him call herself "mummy", and his real mother, "auntie"). The young woman could not answer for weeping. She wanted so much to say to the child,

"Good-bye, darling! Your 'mummy' has been good to you, so you should be good to her in the future. Forget

453

about me forever!" But these words she never uttered. The child was only one and a half years old, and she knew that he would never understand what she wanted to say.

The scholar walked up quietly behind her, and put ten twenty-cent silver coins into her palm, saying softly,

"Here are two dollars for you."

Buttoning up the child's clothes, she put the ten silver coins into her pocket.

The scholar's wife also came in, and, staring hard at the back of the retreating scholar, she turned to the young woman, saying,

"Give me Qiu Bao, so that he won't cry when you leave."

The young woman remained silent, but the child was unwilling to leave his mother and kept striking the scholar's wife's face with his little hands. The scholar's wife was piqued and said,

"You can keep him with you until you've had breakfast."

The kitchen-maid urged the young woman to eat as much as possible, saying,

"You've been eating very little for a fortnight. You are thinner than when you first came here. Have you looked at yourself in the mirror? You have to walk thirty *li* today, so finish this bowl of rice!"

The young woman said listlessly, "You're really kind

to me!"

It was a fine day and the sun was high in the sky. Qiu Bao continued to cling to his mother. When the scholar's wife angrily snatched him away from her, he yelled at the top of his voice, kicking the elderly woman in the belly and pulling at her hair. The young woman, standing behind, pleaded,

"Let me stay here until after lunch."

The scholar's wife replied fiercely over her shoulder,

"Hurry up with your packing. You've got to leave sooner or later!"

From then on, Qiu Bao's cries gradually receded from the young woman's hearing.

While she was packing, she kept listening to his crying. The kitchen-maid stood beside her, comforting her and watching what she was putting into her parcel. The young woman then left with the same old parcel she had brought with her when she first came.

She heard Qiu Bao crying as she walked out of the gate, and his cries rang in her ears even after she had plodded a distance of three *li*.

Stretching before her lay the sun-bathed country road which seemed to be as long as the sky was boundless. As she was walking along the bank of a river, whose clear water reflected her like a mirror, she thought of stopping there and putting an end to her life by drowning herself.

But, after sitting for a while on the bank, she resumed her journey.

It was already afternoon, and an elderly villager told her that she still had fifteen *li* to go before she would reach her own village. She said to him,

"Grandpa, please hire a litter for me. I'm too tired to walk."

"Are you sick?" asked the old man.

"Yes, I am." She was sitting in a pavilion outside a village.

"Where have you walked from?"

She answered after a moment's hesitation,

"I'm on my way home; this morning I thought I would be able to walk the whole way."

The elder lapsed into sympathetic silence and finally hired a litter for her.

It was about four o'clock in the afternoon when the litter carriers entered a narrow and filthy village street. The young woman, her pale face shrunken and yellowed like an old vegetable leaf, lay with her eyes closed. She was breathing weakly. The villagers eyed her with astonishment and compassion. A group of village urchins noisily followed the litter, the appearance of which stirred the quiet village.

One of the children chasing after the litter was Chun Bao. The children were shouting and squealing like little

456

pigs when the litter carriers suddenly turned into the lane leading to Chun Bao's home. Chun Bao stopped in surprise. As the litter stopped in front of his home, he leaned dazed against a post and looked at it from a distance. The other children gathered around and craned their necks timidly. When the young woman descended from the litter, she felt giddy and at first did not realize that the shabbily dressed child with dishevelled hair standing before her was Chun Bao. He was hardly any taller than when she had left three years before and just as skinny. Then, she blurted out in tears,

"Chun Bao!"

Startled, the children dispersed. Chun Bao, also frightened, ran inside the house to look for his father.

Inside the dingy room, the young woman sat for a long, long while. Both she and her husband were speechless. As night fell, he raised his head and said,

"You'd better prepare supper!"

She rose reluctantly, and, after searching around the house, said in a weak voice,

"There's no rice left in the big jar. . . . "

Her husband looked at her with a sickly smile,

"You've got used to living in a rich man's house all right. We keep our rice in a cardboard box."

That night, the skin dealer said to his son,

"Chun Bao, you go to bed with your mother!"

Chun Bao, standing beside the stove, started crying. His mother walked up to him and called,

"Chun Bao, Chun Bao!" But when she tried to caress him, the boy shunned her. His father hissed,

"You've forgotten your own mother. You ought to get a good beating for that!"

The young woman lay awake on the narrow, dirty plank-bed with Chun Bao lying, like a stranger, beside her. Her mind in a daze, she seemed to see her younger son Qiu Bao — plump, white and lovely — curled up beside her, but as she stretched out her arms to embrace him, she saw it was Chun Bao, who had just fallen asleep. The boy was breathing faintly, his face pressed against his mother's breast. She hugged him tightly.

The still and chilly night seemed to drag on endlessly. ...

注　释

作家柔石,浙江宁海人,中共党员,1931 年在上海惨遭国民党杀害,年仅30。《为奴隶的母亲》是他于 1930 年写成的最优秀的短篇小说。作品揭露当时浙东一带农村典妻制度的野蛮和残酷,对农村劳动妇女的苦难表示了极大的同情。

①"芒种"为中国 24 节气之一,约在每年 6 月上、中旬,该时农村多忙于夏收夏种。如英译为 Mangzhong 或 wheat in the ear,势必借助脚注,详加说明,否则外国读者无法理解。现结合上下文干脆把它译为 early each summer。

②"小铜鼓"译为 a brass drum。注意 brass 和 bronze、copper 在颜色上的区别。三者之中,仅 brass 是浅黄色。

③"我已经将你出典了……"如逐字直译为 I've pawned you 或 I've hired you out,均欠达意。现以增词释义的办法译为 There's somebody willing to hire you as a temporary wife,可较清楚地交代原意。

④ "免得王狼底狼一般的绿眼睛天天在家里闪烁"译为 so that he'd no longer be prowling after me like a wolf，用 prowling after（潜行觅食）代替原文中有关比喻，同样传神。

⑤ "这一晚，她和她底丈夫都没有吃晚饭。"意即夫妇两人都不想吃饭，故译为 That evening，neither he nor she felt like having supper。如按字面直译为 That evening，both husband and wife did not eat supper，就未能表达原句含义。

⑥ "三周四岁离娘身"译为 A child of three can move about free，有节奏，有韵律，易于上口。

⑦ "烧饭的黄妈"即在厨房干活的女仆，可简译为 the kitchen-maid。

⑧ "你应该称一称你自己底老骨头是多少重"意即"你应该珍惜自己的身子"，故译为 You should take good care of your old carcase，其中 carcase 本作"死尸"解，指活人的"身躯"时，是带有轻蔑或嘲笑口气的用语。

⑨ "想吃新鲜的面，番薯等"意即"想换别的东西吃，如面、番薯等"，故全句译为 always felt like eating something different — noodles，potatoes and so on。

⑩ "随她吠去好了"译为 let her cackle，其中 cackle 本指母鸡下蛋后的略咯声，现在的意思是"胡说八道"。此句如直译为 let her bark 也可，但因和文中母鸡的比喻连用，就不如前者合适。

⑪ "阉过的母鸡"实为"不产蛋的母鸡"，故译为 a · barren hen。不能把它译为 a capon，因那是阉过的公鸡。

⑫ "邻舍的妇人围着他们瞧"译为 womenfolk from the neighbourhood gathered around to feast their eyes upon the boy，其中 to feast their eyes upon 是成语，作"尽情地欣赏"解。

⑬ "老妇人却转过头，汹汹地答"译为 The scholar's wife replied fiercely over her shoulder，其中 over her shoulder 是习语，作"回头"解。

⑭ "其余的孩子胆怯地围在轿的两边"译为 The other children gathered and craned their necks timidly，其中 craned their necks（伸长脖子张望）是添加成份，原文虽无其词而有其意。

致蒋经国信

廖承志

经国吾弟：

咫尺之隔，竟成海天之遥①。南京匆匆一晤，瞬逾三十六载。幼时同袍，苏京把晤，往事历历在目②。惟长年未通音问，此诚憾事。近闻政躬违和，深为悬念③。人过七旬，多有病痛，至盼善自珍摄。

三年以来，我党一再倡议贵我两党举行谈判④，同捐前嫌，共竟祖国统一大业⑤。惟弟一再声言"不接触，不谈判，不妥协"，余期期以为不可。世交深情，于公于私，理当进言⑥，敬希诠察。

祖国和平统一，乃千秋功业⑦。台湾终必回归祖国，早日解决对各方有利。台湾同胞可安居乐业，两岸各族人民可解骨肉分离之痛，在台诸前辈及大陆去台人员亦可各得其所，且有利于亚太地区局势稳定和世界和平。吾弟尝以"计利当计天下利，求名应求万世名⑧"自勉，倘能于吾弟手中成此伟业⑨，必为举国尊敬，世人推崇，功在国家，名留青史⑩。所谓"罪人"之说，实相悖谬。局促东隅，终非久计。明若吾弟，自当了然⑪。如迁延不决，或委之异日⑫，不仅徒生困扰,吾弟亦将难辞其咎⑬。再者,和平统一纯属内政。外人巧言令色,意在图我台湾,此世人所共知者。当断不断,必受其乱⑭。愿弟慎思。

孙先生手创之中国国民党,历尽艰辛,无数先烈前仆后继,终于推翻帝制,建立民国⑮。光辉业迹,已成定论。国共两度合作,均对国家民族作出巨大贡献。首次合作,孙先生领导,吾辈虽幼,亦知一二。再次合作,老先生主其事,吾辈身在其中,应知梗概。事虽经纬万端,但纵观全局,合则对国家有利,分则必伤民族元气⑯。今日吾弟在台主政,三次合作,大责难谢。双方领导,同窗挚友,彼此相知,谈之更易⑰。所谓"投降"、"屈事"、"吃亏"、"上当"之说,实难苟同。评价历史,展望未来,应天下为公,以国家民族利益为最高准则⑱,何发党私之论!至于"以三民主义统一中国"云云,识者皆以为太不现实,未免自欺欺人⑲。三民主义之真谛,吾辈深知,毋须争辩。所谓台湾"经济繁荣,社会民主,民生乐利"等等,在台诸公,心中有数,亦毋庸赘言。试为贵党计,如能依时顺势,负起历史责任,毅然和谈,达成国家统一,则两党长期共存,互相监督,共图振兴中华之大业。否则,偏安之局⑳,焉能自保。有识之士,虑已及此㉑。事关国民党兴亡绝续㉒,望弟再思。

近读大作,有"切望父灵能回到家园与先人同在"㉓之语,不胜感慨系之。今老先生仍厝于慈湖,统一之后,即当迁安故土,或奉化,或南京,或庐山,以了吾弟孝心。吾弟近曾有言:"要把孝顺的心,扩大为民族感情,去敬爱民族,奉献于国家。"旨哉斯言,盍不实践于统一大业!就国家民族而论,蒋氏两代对历史有所交代㉔;就吾弟个人而言,可谓忠孝两全。否则，吾弟身后事何以自了。尚望三思。

　　吾弟一生坎坷，决非命运安排，一切操之在己㉕。千秋功罪，系于一念之间。当今国际风云变幻莫测，台湾上下众议纷纭。岁月不居，来日苦短，夜长梦多㉖，时不我与。盼弟善为抉择㉗，未雨绸缪。"寥廓海天，不归何待？"

　　人到高年，愈加怀旧，如弟方便，余当束装就道，前往台北探望，并面聆诸长辈教益。"度尽劫波兄弟在，相逢一笑泯恩仇"。遥望南天，不禁神驰㉘，书不尽言，诸希珍重，伫候复音㉙。

　　老夫人前请代为问安。方良、纬国及诸侄不一。

　　　　顺祝
近祺！

　　　　　　　　　　　　　　　　廖承志
　　　　　　　　　　　　一九八二年七月二十四日

A Letter to Chiang Ching-Kuo

Liao Chengzhi

July 24, 1982

Dear brother Ching-Kuo,

Who would have expected that the short distance between us should be keeping us poles apart! It is now more
than 36 years since our brief encounter in Nanjing. The
days we spent together in childhood as well as later in the
Soviet capital, however, are still as fresh as ever in my
memory. But it's a pity indeed that we haven't heard from
each other for so many years. Recently it filled me with
much concern to learn of your indisposition. Men aged
over seventy are liable to illness. I hope you will take
good care of yourself.

For three years, we have repeatedly proposed bilateral talks between the two parties to let bygones be bygones
and strive together for the great cause of national reunification. But you have time and again insisted upon having
"no contact, no talks and no compromise", which I truly
think inadvisable. In view of the public and personal con-

cerns as well as the long-standing deep friendship between our two families, I feel duty-bound to offer you a word of advice for careful consideration.

The peaceful reunification of the motherland will be a great achievement to go down in history. Taiwan is bound to be reunited eventually with the motherland. An early settlement of the problem will be in the interests of all. The compatriots in Taiwan will be able to live in peace and happiness, the people of all nationalities on both sides of the Taiwan straits will be relieved of the pains of separation from their own flesh and blood, and our senior folks in Taiwan and those formerly migrated there from the mainland will all be properly placed and provided for. And, moreover, it will contribute to the stability of Asia and the Pacific region as well as to world peace. You used to seek self-encouragement from the motto, "The interests to be considered should be the interests of all; the fame to be sought should be an everlasting fame." If you should be instrumental in bringing about the great cause of national reunification, you will certainly win esteem and praise nationwide and your meritorious service to the country will earn you a niche in the temple of fame. It is sheer absurdity to think yourself "guilty" for rendering such a service. After all, dragging out your existence in that tight eastern corner is by no means a permanent solution. This should be crystal clear to a man of your wis-

466

dom. Procrastination, hesitation or sleeping over the problem will only lead to adversity and you, my brother, will hardly be able to escape censure. Moreover, peaceful reunification is entirely an internal affair of China. As is known to all, outsiders who are talking glibly against it have designs on our Taiwan. To be irresolute when a prompt decision should be taken would only spell disaster. I, therefore, would like you to think this over carefully.

After going through untold hardships during which countless revolutionaries unflinchingly laid down their lives, the Kuomintang founded by Dr. Sun Yat-sen finally overthrew the monarchy and established the republic. This has been universally recognized as a glorious achievement. The Kuomintang and the Communist Party twice cooperated and on both occasions they made tremendous contributions to the country and the nation. We know something about the first cooperation, led by Dr. Sun Yat-sen, though we were still young at that time. The second cooperation was presided over by your father and, as participants in it, we should know what it was all about. Complicated as the matter was, an overall view of the situation will show that united, the country and the nation benefit; divided, they suffer. Now, as head of the Taiwan administration, you have unshirkable responsibility for bringing about the third cooperation. Leaders from

467

both sides will find it easier to talk the matter over since they know each other well, having formerly been schoolmates and close friends. I find it really hard for me to subscribe to those views which describe cooperation as "surrender", "humiliating", "suffering losses" or "being duped". In reviewing history or looking ahead to the future, one should be public-minded and put the interests of the country and the nation above all. Why harp on the narrow interests of a party? Such remarks as "unifying China with the Three People's Principles" are regarded by all thinking people as unrealistic, deceptive and ostrich-like. People of our generation know the true meaning of the Three People's Principles quite well and there is no need to argue about it. Neither is there any need to dwell on such assertions as Taiwan's "economic prosperity, democracy and easy livelihood", the truth of which all gentlemen in Taiwan must be quite aware of. To my mind, if you, for the sake of your party, shoulder the historic task and, going with the stream, take part in peace talks for our national reunification, the two parties will be able to co-exist for a long time to come, supervising each other and making a common effort to revitalize China. Otherwise, content as you are with your present rule over the tight eastern corner, how can such a situation be expected to last for long? This is a question already on the minds of thinking people. It is a matter of survival or extinction for the Kuomintang and I hope you will think it over again.

Recently I was profoundly moved when I read one of your writings in which you expressed the "longing for my father's soul to return to the homeland and be among the forefathers". The remains of your father, now still temporarily placed at Cihu, shall, upon national reunification, be immediately moved to the final resting place in Fenghua, Nanjing or Lushan in fulfilment of your filial wishes. You recently said, "Filial devotion should be expanded into national devotion, which means love of the nation and dedication to the country." Well said! Why don't you apply it to the great cause of national reunification? As far as the country and the nation are concerned, you will have fulfilled the task imposed on you and your father by history; as far as you yourself are concerned, this will be an expression of both loyalty and filial piety. Otherwise how could you account for yourself after your passing away? I hope you will think more about it.

Dear brother, the frustrations marking your lifetime are by no means predestined. You yourself alone are master of your own fate. Merits and demerits to be recorded in history hinge on the decision made in a moment. The present international situation is capricious. Throughout Taiwan people of all strata are talking about their future. Time does not stay and brief is the day. A long night invites bad dreams; time and tide wait for no man. I hope you, my brother, will make a wise choice and repair the house before it rains. "Vast is the expanse of sky and water. What are you waiting for, staying away from home?"

The longing for old friends grows with age. If it suits your convenience, I will pack and go on a visit to Taibei to consult our elders. "For all the disasters the brotherhood has remained; a smile at meeting and enmity is banished. " When I look south towards the distant horizon, my heart cannot help going out to my compatriots there. No word is enough to express what I wish to say. It is hoped that you will take good care of yourself. I am looking forward to a reply from you.

Please convey my regards to your mother as well as to Fang-Liang, Wei-Kuo and the children.

Best wishes to you.

Liao Chengzhi

注　释

廖承志 1982 年 7 月 24 日致台湾蒋
经国信曾由我国新华社译成英文电讯
稿。现参阅该电讯稿加以重译，并附原
译于书后。

① "咫尺之隔，竟成海天之遥" 的原译为 No one ever
expected that a strip of water should have become so vast
a distance，未充分表达原文的感叹口气以及 "海天之遥"
与当前两岸的关系。现改译为 Who would have expected
that the short distance between us should be keeping us
poles apart，其中 poles apart 作 widely separated 解。此句
形式上为疑问句，实为感叹句，故句尾接感叹号。

② "幼时同袍，苏京把晤，往事历历在目" 的原译为
From our childhood friendship to our chats in the Soviet
capital，everything in the past is still alive in my memory，
基本上逐字直译，流畅不足。现改译为 The days we spent
together in childhood as well as later in the Soviet capital，
however，are still as fresh as ever in my memory，其中 are
still as fresh as ever 比 still remain fresh 强调。

③ "近闻政躬违和,深为悬念" 的原译为 Recently I was told that you are somewhat indisposed and this has caused me much concern, 采用复合句逐字直译,欠简练。现用简单句改译为 Recently it filled me with much concern to learn of your indisposition。

④ "我党一再倡议贵我两党举行谈判,同捐前嫌" 的原译为 our party has repeatedly proposed talks with your party to bury the hatchet。为了避免 party 一词的重复出现,现改译为 we have repeatedly proposed bilateral talks between the two parties to let bygones be bygones。

⑤ "共竟祖国统一大业" 的原译为 work jointly to accomplish the great cause of national reunification。为突出 "共同力求" 的内涵,现将此句改译为 strive together for the great cause of national reunifieation。

⑥ "世交深情,于公于私,理当进言" 的原译为 Considering both the public interests and our close friendship which has lasted for generations, I regard it as my duty to offer some advice which I hope you will consider carefully, 其中有三处欠妥:1."于公于私"译为 the public interests,未交代"于私";2."世交深情"中的"世交"实际上只从双方父辈(廖仲恺和蒋介石)开始,原译却把它扩大到"祖祖辈辈"(for generations);3.句子欠紧凑。现改译为 In view of the public and personal concerns as well as the long-standing deep friendship between our two families, I feel duty-bound to offer you a word of advice for careful consideration。

⑦ "乃千秋功业"译为 a great achievement to go down in history,其中 to go down 是成语,作"被载入"解,也可译为 to be recorded in history。

⑧ "计利当计天下利,求名应求万世名"译为 The interests to be considered should be the interests of all；the fame to be sought should be an everlasting fame,前后都是简单句,形成排比。原译为 The interests to be considered should be the interests of all；the fame to be sought should be a fame that would last forever,前后稍欠匀称。

⑨ "倘能于吾弟手中成此伟业"译为 If you should be instrumental in bringing about the great cause of national reunification,其中 instrumental 作"有助于"(helpful)解。原译为 If the great cause of national reunification would be accomplished through your work,语言欠地道。又 would 一词用得欠规范,应改为 should。

⑩ "功在国家,名留青史"译为 your meritorious service to the country will earn you a niche in the temple of fame,其中 a niche in the temple of fame 是成语,作"留芳百世"解,与 a lasting fame 同义。

⑪ "明若吾弟,自当了然"译为 This should be crystal clear to a man of your wisdom。原译为 This is of course quite clear for a man as intelligent as you。注意 wisdom 着重"判断是非的能力",intelligent 着重"理解力"。

⑫ "委之异日"译为 sleeping over the problem,其中 sleep over 或 sleep on 是成语,作"暂缓对……作出决定"(to postpone a decision about...)解。原译是 leaving the problem to other days.

⑬ "难辞其咎"译为 hardly be able to escape censure，其中 censure 和 the blame 同义，但前者比较有力。

⑭ "当断不断，必受其乱"译为 To be irresolute when a prompt decision should be taken would only spell disaster，其 spell 作"招致"、"带来"解。

⑮ "孙先生手创之中国国民党，历尽艰辛，无数先烈前仆后继，终于推翻帝制，建立民国"的原译为 The Kuomintang founded by Dr. Sun Yat-sen endured countless hardships and finally overthrew the monarchy and established the republic；numerous revolutionaries advanced wave after wave and laid down their lives for the cause，其中把"无数先烈前仆后继"单独译成一句，使全文缺乏连贯性，层次不清。现改译为 After going through untold hardships during which countless revolutionaries unflinchingly laid down their lives，the Kuomintang founded by Dr. Sun Yat-sen finally overthrew the monarchy and established the republic。

⑯ "事虽经纬万端，但纵观全局，合则对国家有利，分则必伤民族元气"的原译为 Though the matter was as complicated as could be，an all-round view of the situation would show that cooperation is beneficial to the country and the nation while division is detrimental to them，其中未能用简练的手法表达原文后半部的排比结构；同时 would 一词也用得欠规范。现改译为 Complicated as the matter was，an overall view of the situation will show that united, the country and the nation benefit; divided, they suffer。

⑰ "双方领导,同窗挚友,彼此相知,谈之更易" 的原译为 It would be easier to talk the matter over when leaders on both sides used to be schoolmates and close friends who know one another well, 其中后半部分缺乏逻辑性。现改译为 Leaders from both sides will find it easier to talk the matter over since they know each other well, having formerly been schoolmates and close friends。

⑱ "应天下为公,以国家民族利益为最高准则" 意即 "应一心为公,以国家民族利益高于一切",故英译为 should be public-minded and put the interests of the country and the nation above all。原译为 should bear in mind the public interests of the country and the nation, and use this as the supreme criterion, 与原文意思有出入,原因是对原文的理解仅限于某些字面。

⑲ "识者皆以为太不现实,未免自欺欺人" 译为 are regarded by all thinking people as unrealistic, deceptive and ostrichlike, 其中 thinking people 意即 "有见解的人"; ostrichlike 本来的意思是 "鸵鸟般的" 或 "藏头露尾的",现作 "自欺的" 解。

⑳ "偏安之局" 的意思为 "偏据一方以自安",故译为 content as you are with your present rule over the tight eastern corner。

㉑ "有识之士,虑已及此" 意即 "有头脑的人都已经为此担忧"。原译为 This is a question those who are sensible are already turning over in their minds。现改译为 This is a question already on the minds of thinking people。原译中的 turning over in their minds 作"反复思考"解；on the minds 才作"担忧"解。

㉒ "事关国民党兴亡绝续"的原译为 It involves the survival and development of the Kuomintang，其中把"兴亡绝续"译为 survival and development，与原意有出入。现将原句改译为 It ia a matter of survival or extinction for the Kuomintang。

㉓ "与先人同在"的原译为 be reunited with the fore-fathers，稍欠自然。现改译为 be among the forefathers。

㉔ "蒋氏两代对历史有所交代"的原译为 this would be an answer of the two generations of the Chiangs to history，由于逐字直译，未能达意。现改译为 you will have fulfilled the task imposed on you and your father by history。

㉕ "一切操之在己"的上一句为"决非命运安排"，故英译时按"由自己掌握命运"的意思译为 You yourself alone are master of your own fate。原译为 Everything depends on yourself。

㉖ "夜长梦多"中的"梦"为"恶梦"，比喻"不好的事"或"节外生枝"，故译全句为 A long night invites bad dreams。原译为 A long night is fraught with dreams。

㉗ "善为抉择"的意思应为"作出明智的选择"，故译为 will make a wise choice。

㉘ "不禁神驰"译为 my heart cannot help going out

476

to...，其中 to go out to 是成语，作"在感情上被……所吸
引"（be emotionally drawn to）解。

㉙ "伫候复音"的原译为 I am waiting impatiently for
a reply。现改译为 I am looking forward to a reply from
you。

Dear brother Ching-Kuo,

No one ever expected that a strip of water should have become so vast a distance. It is now 36 years since our brief rendezvous in Nanjing. From our childhood friendship to our chats in the Soviet capital, everything in the past is still alive in my memory. But it's unfortunate that we haven't heard from each other for so many years. Recently I was told that you are somewhat indisposed and this has caused me much concern. Men in their seventies are often afflicted with illness. I sincerely hope that you will take good care of yourself.

Over the past three years, our party has repeatedly proposed talks with your party to bury the hatchet and work jointly to accomplish the great cause of national re-unification. But you have time and again announced that there should be "no contact, no talks and no compromise", which I think is inadvisable. Considering both the public interests and our close friendship which has lasted for generations, I regard it as my duty to offer some advice which I hope you will consider carefully.

The peaceful reunification of the motherland would be a great achievement to be recorded in history. Taiwan is bound to return to the embrace of the motherland eventually. An early settlement would be in the interests of all. The compatriots in Taiwan would be able to live in peace and happiness, the people of all nationalities on both sides of the Taiwan straits would no longer have to endure the pains of separation from their kith and kin, and the elders in Taiwan and those who have moved there from the mainland would all be properly placed and provided for. And this would contribute to the stability of Asia and the Pacific region as well as to world peace. You used to spur yourself on with the axiom: "The interests to be considered should be the interests of all; the fame to be sought should be a fame that would last forever. " If the great cause of reunification would be accomplished through your work, you will certainly win the esteem of the nation and the praise of all. You would be doing a meritorious service to the country and your name would be inscribed in the temple of fame. It is preposterous to regard such a service as a "guilt". After all, putting up in that tight eastern corner is not a long-term solution. This is of course quite clear for a man as intelligent as you. Hesitation, procrastination or leaving the problem to other days would only lead to difficulty and distress and you, my brother, would hardly be able to escape the blame. Moreover, peaceful reunification is entirely an internal affair of China. Those outsiders who talk glibly about it have designs on our Taiwan. This is common knowledge. When a decision needs to be made, irresolution is bound to bring trouble. I hope you will consider this carefully.

The Kuomintang founded by Dr. Sun Yat-sen endured countless hardships and finally overthrew the monarchy and established the republic; numerous revolutionaries advanced wave after wave and laid down their lives for the cause. History has recorded this as a glorious contribution. The Kuomintang and the Communist Party twice cooperated and on both occasions they made tremendous contributions to the country and the nation. We know something about the first cooperation, led by Dr. Sun Yat-sen, though we were still young at that time. The second cooperation proceeded with your father in the chair and, as participants in it, we should know what it was all about. Though the matter was as complicated as could be, an all-round view of the situation would show that cooperation is beneficial to the country and the nation while division is detrimental to them. Since you are presiding over the administration of Taiwan, you have unshirkable responsibility for the realization of cooperation for the third time. It would be easier to talk the matter over when leaders on both sides used to be schoolmates and close friends who know one another well. I find it really hard for me to subscribe to those views which describe cooperation as "surrender", "humiliating", "suffering losses" or "being duped". In reviewing history or looking forward to the future, one should bear in mind the public interests of the country and the nation, and use this as the supreme criterion, instead of basing oneself on a party's selfish interests. Such talks as "reunifying China with the Three People's Principles" are regarded by all sensible people as unrealistic, deceptive and self-deceiving. People of our generation know the true meaning of the Three People's Principles quite well and there is no need to argue about it. Neither is there any need to dwell on such assertions as Taiwan's "economic prosperity, democracy and easy livelihood", the truth of which the venerable gentlemen in Taiwan know clearly. For the sake of your party, I would think that if you would take up the historial responsibility and resolutely take part in peace talks to accomplish national reunification as required by time and tide, the two parties would be able to co-exist for a long time to come, supervising each other while joining in glorious effort to revitalize China. Otherwise how could the situation existing in that small corner to be maintained for long? This is a question those who are sensible are already turning over in their minds. It involves the survival and development of the Kuomintang

481

and I hope you will think it over again.

I recently read one of your writings in which you expressed "fervent hopes that my father's soul would be able to return to the homeland and be reunited with the forefathers". I was overwhelmed with emotion when I read this. The remains of your father are still placed temporarily at Cihu. After reunification, they should be moved back and buried in the native soil — in Fenghua, Nanjing or Lushan — in fulfilment of your filial wishes. You recently said, "Filial devotion should be expanded into national devotion, which means love of the nation and dedication to the country." This is an excellent statement. Why don't you apply it to the great cause of national reunification? As far as the country and the nation are concerned, this would be an answer of the two generations of the Chiangs to history; as far as you yourself are concerned, this would be an expression of both loyalty and filial piety. Otherwise how could you account for yourself after your passing away? It is hoped that you would think more about it.

Dear brother! Your life has been marked by frustrations, which should not be attributed to fate. Everything depends on yourself. The good and ill to be judged in the next thousand years hinges on the decision made in a moment. The present international situation is capricious. Throughout Taiwan people of all strata are talking about their future. Time does not stay and brief is the day. A long night is fraught with dreams; time does not wait for us. I hope you, my brother, would be good at making the choice and repair the house before it rains. "Vast is the expanse ·of sky and water. What are you waiting for, staying away from home?"

The longing for old friends grows with age. If it is convenient to you, I would pack and set out for a visit to Taibei to seek enlightenment from our elders. "For all the disasters the brotherhood has remained; a smile at meeting and enmity is banished. " When I look towards the distant southern sky, my heart is already there. No word is enough to express what I wish to say. It is hoped that you will take good care of yourself. I·am waiting impatiently for a reply.

Please convey my regards to your mother as well as to Fang-Liang, Wei-Kuo and the children.

Best wishes to you.

Liao Chengzhi
July 24, 1982